Feminine Sense in Southern Memoir

FEMININE SENSE
IN SOUTHERN
MEMOIR

*Smith, Glasgow, Welty, Hellman,
Porter, and Hurston*

WILL BRANTLEY

University Press of Mississippi
Jackson

Copyright © 1993 by the University Press of Mississippi
All rights reserved
Manufactured in the United States of America

98 97 96 95   4 3 2 1

First paperback edition, 1995

The paper in this book meets the guidelines for permanence and durability of the Committee on Production Guidelines for Book Longevity of the Council on Library Resources.

Library of Congress Cataloging-in-Publication Data

Brantley, Will.
    Feminine sense in Southern memoir : Smith, Glasgow, Welty,
Hellman, Porter, and Hurston / Will Brantley.
        p.   cm.
    Includes bibliographical references and index.
    ISBN 0-87805-614-9 (alk. paper)—ISBN 0-87805-802-8 (pbk.: alk. paper)
    1. Women authors, American—Southern States—Biography—History
and criticism.   2. American prose literature—Southern States—
History and criticism.   3. American prose literature—Women
authors—History and criticism.   4. American prose literature—20th
century—History and criticism.   5. Women and literature—Southern
States—History—20th century.   6. Women—Southern States—
Intellectual life.   7. Femininity (Psychology) in literature.
8. Southern States in literature.   9. Autobiography—Women authors.
I. Title.
PS261.B67   1993
810.9′9287—dc20   92-39650
                                                                 CIP

British Library Cataloging-in-Publication data available

For my parents,
Grace Josey Brantley and
William Oliver Brantley, Sr.

Contents

Introduction

In 1972 Eudora Welty was asked by the *Paris Review* if she "ever felt part of a literary community, along with people like Flannery O'Connor, Carson McCullers, Katherine Anne Porter or Caroline Gordon?" Welty's response was what might have been expected: "I'm not sure there's any dotted line connecting us up, though all of us knew about each other and all of us, I think, respected and read each other's work and understood it. And some of us are friends of long standing. I don't think there was any passing about of influences, but there's a lot of pleasure in thinking in whose lifetimes your own lifetime has happened to come along" (Prenshaw, *Conversations* 80–81). Welty is right: there is no one line of development, but, rather, many lines, many patterns, and many points of intersection. Borrowing Welty's metaphor, my overriding aim in this study is to connect some of the more significant "dots"—Welty herself, Ellen Glasgow, Lillian Hellman, Katherine Anne Porter, Lillian Smith, and Zora Neale Hurston—through an intertextual examination of selected nonfiction prose that acknowledges each writer's distinctiveness and changing perspectives over a lifetime.

Chapter 1 defines the sociohistorical role of the woman of letters in the twentieth-century South; it also explores the ways in which her work has been marginalized by recent intellectual histories.

Chapter 2 explains the significance of Lillian Smith and what I call her confessional tract, *Killers of the Dream* (1949; revised in 1961). Smith represents a sharp disruption of a conservative critical agenda that has dominated most appraisals of twentieth-century southern writing. Smith's ethics, her analyses of women and autobiography, racism and sexism, provide useful points of reference for examining the other writers in this study, each of whom speaks with her own voice of dissent regarding gender norms, problems of race, and patriarchal power structures.

The remaining chapters focus on connections between specific texts. Chapter 3 defines the achievement of Ellen Glasgow's *The Woman Within* (written primarily in the late 1930s but published in 1954) and Eudora Welty's *One Writer's Beginnings* (1984), two autobiographies that center on the woman writer's inner life and demonstrate the legitimacy of making this life the object of public attention. Chapter 4 explores the ethical and political positions outlined by Lillian Hellman in *Scoundrel Time* (1976) and Katherine Anne Porter in *The Never-Ending Wrong* (1977), two remarkably similar memoirs that define the individual in conflict with reactionary forces in modern American history. Chapter 5 considers the problematic intersections of region, nation, gender, and race in Zora Neale Hurston's controversial autobiography, *Dust Tracks on a Road* (1942; expanded with previously unpublished chapters in 1984). This chapter examines the tensions within a text that combines both conservative and liberal sentiments before explaining why this synthesis becomes even more pronounced in Hurston's subsequent essays.

Each chapter is exploratory in what I hope is the best sense of that term. I do not argue that these six writers can be seen as alike in every sense; nor do I push my comparisons beyond the logic of their boundaries. With these precautions in mind, I can identify a number of generally overlapping goals, one of which is primary: to situate these authors within a context of southern feminism and the more inclusive discourse of modern American liberalism. Concomitantly, I illustrate the importance of ethics—of ideals imagined and realized—in their self-portraits.

Throughout, I explore the relevance of autobiographical theory (and especially feminist autobiographical theory) to the self-writing of this group of authors. I attempt to explain the major ways in which an understanding of different self-writing genres can make more accessible a group of often misunderstood texts. With the exception of *One Writer's Beginnings*, all of the major works in this study were either critically panned or else received a set of highly mixed notices. With

Hellman's *Scoundrel Time* and Porter's *The Never-Ending Wrong*, many of the early reviewers apparently misunderstood how memoirs tend to inscribe the self and its development. Following their lead, subsequent critics have overlooked many of the most significant dimensions of Hellman's and Porter's self-revelations in these two late works.

Though I acknowledge that we are interested in the self-writing and nonfiction prose of southern women writers because they are who they are, I want to show how and why this body of writing can be seen as more than a mere foil to their "creative" work. Thus I intend this study to provide a new and broader context in which to read these authors. I offer it as another contribution to the current movement to deprovincialize the Southern Renaissance—to redefine it without abstract a priori conditions for what constitutes "southernness." Though the region does at times take center stage in their autobiographical prose, none of the writers in this study can be regarded as a regional enthusiast willing to perpetrate regional myths (this despite the fact that each retained a certain loyalty to her southern background). It is therefore necessary to explore each writer's awareness of the ways in which not only region but also other historical and material contingencies have given shape to her sense of identity.

In the end, what I underscore is a common independence and self-reflexivity—two hallmarks of the liberal tradition. Carson McCullers, another southern writer, has written that consciousness of self "is the first abstract problem that the human being solves" (*Mortgaged Heart* 259). It is actually a problem that one goes on solving, for, as Virginia Woolf makes clear in a well-known essay on Montaigne, "To tell the truth about oneself, to discover oneself near at hand, is not easy." The problem, as Woolf defines it—and as I explore here—is that "beyond the difficulty of communicating oneself, there is the supreme difficulty of being oneself. This soul, or life within us, by no means agrees with the life outside us" (*Common Reader* 59).

This study reflects the support and encouragement of many generous people, all of whom deserve more recognition than I can give them here.

Signe Hovde and Angelo Pitillo provided the emotional anchor that made it possible for me to sustain a project of this nature. Other friends did their share to keep me in good humor for the better part of four years. These include (by city): Valentina Argo, Connie Davis, Robert McBath, Mara McFadden, Margaret Parker, Stephen Stubbs, and Viola Witherspoon—all in Atlanta; Jerry and Lise Esch, Paula Harvey, and Franklin Cham in Madison, Wisconsin; Lawrence Thom, Russ Trent, and Jon Witherspoon in New York City; and Norinne Starna in Santa Barbara, California. I echo the sentiments of Zora Neale Hurston: "I am just sort of assembled up together out of friendship and put together by time."

I am grateful to Victor A. Kramer, Ted Spivey, Virginia Spencer Carr, and the late Kenneth England, the professors who—in their own unique ways—stimulated my early interest in southern writing. I must also express my gratitude to those colleagues—John O. Lyons, Thomas Schaub, Anne Goodwyn Jones, Henry Jenkins, Helen Tiegreen-Colcord, and Amanda C. Gable—who responded to various parts of the draft as it evolved. I am especially grateful to Linda Tate, who carefully read the entire manuscript at the time when I most needed her perspective.

Elizabeth Evans and Kenneth Knoespel at the Georgia Institute of Technology and Muriel Zimmerman at the University of California, Santa Barbara, provided encouragement in addition to accommodating teaching schedules. I wish finally to thank two women who have been a steady source of inspiration: Seetha A-Srinivasan, my editor at the University Press of Mississippi, and Annis Pratt, from whom I have learned much and to whom I owe much.

Feminine Sense in Southern Memoir

1.

SOUTHERN WOMEN OF LETTERS IN THE TWENTIETH CENTURY

In her Introduction to an anthology of short stories by and about women, Susan Cahill made the following observation in 1975: "A sense of the humanistic value of writing fiction emerges again and again from Katherine Mansfield's *Journal*, Katherine Anne Porter's *Notes on Writing*, Flannery O'Connor's essays, Carson McCullers's journalism, and Doris Lessing's interviews. Through them all runs a common theme, a vision of their art as a moral imperative, as an act of faith" (xiii). This comment is significant in that it calls attention to women's nonfiction prose as a body of writing that within itself is deserving of critical attention. That three of the five writers cited by Cahill are southern is also significant, for southern women writers, especially those of the thirties, forties, and fifties, have produced a large body of nonfiction prose in which they have defined themselves as twentieth-century writers while reflecting on their society, their politics, and the nature and characteristics of the work they have produced.

It is doubtful that Ellen Glasgow, Eudora Welty, Lillian Smith, Lillian Hellman, Katherine Anne Porter, or Zora Neale Hurston ever consciously appropriated the descriptive phrase "woman of letters." One of Glasgow's contemporaries, the New Orleans writer Grace King, did, however, use the phrase as part of the title for her 1932 autobiography, *Memories of a Southern Woman of Letters*. As Anne Goodwyn Jones observes in an article on women as chroniclers of southern life, the phrase suggests "the status [King] enjoyed as an upperclass white lady with a great deal of authority in New Orleans 'high' culture" ("Southern Literary Women" 75). King's "authority" was genuine but limited to a given locale; like other southern women writers of her generation, King wrote at a time when men were taking over the academy, defining the literary canon, and establishing themselves as the arbiters of culture. By 1952, the year Allen Tate published his seminal essay, "The Man of Letters in the Modern World," few would have contested Tate's assertion that the true duty of the modern man of letters is "to supervise the culture of language, to which the rest of culture is subordinate, and to warn us when our language is ceasing to forward the ends proper to man" (*Essays* 16). Tate saw himself as a guardian of language. His function was "more defensive than shaping," as Paul Lauter observes; like other New Critics, Tate wished to protect "the remnants of culture rapidly being ground under" (449). Few southern women writers before, during, or after Grace King's generation—the early 1900s—have envisioned such lofty goals for themselves. They are "women of letters" in a less restrictive sense.

In her early study of Tate and the Agrarian circle, Louise Cowan provides a more pragmatic definition of the man of letters when she claims that Tate, like his colleagues John Crowe Ransom and Donald Davidson, are genuine men of letters in a larger, more encompassing regard; they are writers who have pursued "their craft on many fronts at once" and who have allowed "their critical ideas to interact with their creative imaginations" (xix). Cowan's definition seems equally suited to the group of writers included in this study, all of whom have practiced their craft on many fronts—at times speculative, at times polemical, at times intimate and informal, at times experimental—and each of whom, in her nonfiction as well as her fiction or drama, has engaged problems of region, nation, and self; of race, sex, and class. Ellen Glasgow, who published her first novel in 1897, continuing to write until her death in 1945, is perhaps the consummate example of the twentieth-century southern woman of letters who has used her self-writing and occasional nonfiction prose as a repository of her intellectual interests. The author of nineteen novels, numerous short stories, poems, essays, and reviews, a distinguished book of self-criticism (the collected prefaces to her novels), a controversial autobiography, and hundreds of letters written with an obvious eye to publication, Glasgow, in the tradition of nineteenth-century belles lettres, used her nonfiction as a means of addressing issues that were important to her at the moment—issues ranging all the way from suffrage and feminism, to southern culture and politics (she was an early opponent of the one-party system), to progressive reform and skeptical philosophy.

Obviously, this study cannot encompass the entire body of nonfiction prose by twentieth-century southern women writers; the focus is much narrower. In part as a necessary structuring device, the study is concerned chiefly with book-length self-studies: Lillian Smith's *Killers of the Dream*, Glasgow's *The Woman Within*, Eudora Welty's *One Writer's Beginnings*, Lillian Hellman's *Scoundrel Time*, Katherine Anne Porter's *The Never-Ending Wrong*, and Zora Neale Hurston's *Dust Tracks on a Road*. Because they raise a different set of questions about audience, this work has not treated collections of letters, such as Flannery O'Connor's *The Habit of Being* (1979) or Caroline Gordon's *The Southern Mandarins* (1984). Even more important, the focus is that group of writers who in their self-writing—in addition to their more widely read fiction and drama—suggest a tradition of liberalism and dissent. In *Tomorrow Is Another Day*, (1981), her pioneering study of the southern woman writer between 1859 and 1936, Anne Goodwyn Jones observes the emergence of such a tradition in the work of a generation of southern women writers that includes Mary Johnston, Frances Newman, Grace King, and Kate Chopin:

> Figures are impossible here, of course, but one can suggest the outlines of a tradition of liberalism—often veiled rather than direct—in Southern women's writings. It is a tradition that grew in the soil of the South's historical endorsement of Southern women as writers and of the Southern woman's own rejection of the tradition of patriarchy. Its hallmarks include the critique, implicit or direct, of racial and sexual oppression, of the hierarchical caste and class structures that pervade cultural institutions, and of the evasive idealism that pushes reality aside. And it parallels the tradition of Southern women in radical social action that Jacquelyn Hall and Sara Evans discuss. (45)

With Glasgow, Hellman, Porter, Smith, and even with Welty and Hurston, the tradition that Jones defines becomes less veiled and less indirect. In addition to their rejection of patriarchy, or anything that would inhibit self-development and human wholeness, and in addition to their various critiques of provincialism, nationalism, racism, and sexism, none of these writers has ever fully embraced any form of religious orthodoxy; all were or are skeptics (most would qualify as agnostics), though each has expressed a deep respect and reverence for the mystery that constitutes human life. It is in fact their shared reverence for the ineffable—for that which cannot be explained—that has prevented them from accepting any one system of belief, such as Marxism or Agrarianism, that can be defined any more rigidly than, say, the general tenets of Jeffersonian idealism. All might agree that it is the elusive quality of art that makes it worth pursuing; and each would probably accept Sherwood Anderson's contention that the true grotesque is someone who has embraced only one truth.

In this respect, it might be argued that no southern woman writer is more concerned with the shape and force of mystery than Flannery O'Connor, but for both her and Caroline Gordon, the source of mystery is transcendental and rooted in their belief in Christ and what they see as the presence of his grace in life and art. Theirs is another chapter in the story of the woman of letters and the Southern Renaissance, which is not to say that there are not many interconnections (some of which will be highlighted) between their self-writing and that of the six women discussed at length.[1]

It should not be assumed that O'Connor is excluded from this study because her angle of vision is not that of a southern liberal. Ted Spivey, who knew O'Connor well, notes that in conversation she frequently expressed what can only be called liberal social views (278). Throughout *The Habit of Being*, O'Connor, though she expressed no patience with Yankee agitators, made it clear that desegregation was the only moral route for the South to take. Yet like many other white southerners who "officially" opposed segregation, O'Connor apparently could not find the nerve to violate the conventions of her region that made it so uncomfortable for her to entertain the African-American writer James Baldwin at her home in Milledgeville (*Habit* 329). If, as Morton Sosna maintains, the litmus test for the southern liberal is that he or she opposes the idealogy of white supremacy, then O'Connor passes the test (if perhaps with low marks). It is the larger agenda of liberalism that O'Connor tends to reject, as she makes clear in a letter to her friend Cecil Dawkins: "The liberal approach is that man has never fallen, never incurred guilt, and is ultimately perfectible by his own efforts. Therefore, evil in this light is a problem of better housing, sanitation, health, etc. and all mysteries will eventually be cleared up." O'Connor realizes that to an extent she is overgeneralizing; she acknowledges that "there are degrees of adherence" to the liberal philosophy as she defines it, but that liberalism is in general the route taken by "the modern" rather than the traditional (Catholic) southerner such as herself (302–3).[2]

In any context, liberalism, as a term used to embody a set of beliefs or attitudes, deserves careful attention. As Anne Jones uses the term, and as it will be appropriated in this study, liberalism is roughly synonymous with the progressivism that was adopted by the movement of that name in the first decade or so of the twentieth century. "Since the 1930's, when it was popularized by Franklin D. Roosevelt to define his New Deal program, liberalism in American politics," Dorothy Ross observes, "has generally denoted the whole spectrum of reform thought between conservatism on the right and socialism on the left" (750). Progressive liberals have embraced suffrage and economic equality; though not always successful, they have initiated collective bargaining, labor legislation, child protection laws, public education reform, better treatment of the mentally ill, and a wide assortment of other goals that are always accompanied by a body of writing that theoretically or philosophically justifies the proposed changes. At the heart of progressive or reform liberalism is a belief in human rationality and accountability, and if not a belief in human perfectability (as O'Connor would have it), at least a desire to make life better for the entire diversity of the nation's citizens.

To say that the liberal generally looks to the future while the conservative looks to the past is to make a distinction that too neatly accounts for all their differences but that nonetheless contains an element of truth, as does the distinction made by Forrest McDonald in his overview of American conservatism. McDonald quotes the American poet and historian Peter Viereck who called conservatism "the political secularization of the doctrine of original sin"; McDonald then cites Eric Voegelin, the conservative political scientist who claimed that liberalism, in opposition to conservatism, is "the political secularization of the heresy of gnosticism"—or, more simply, the belief that mankind's responsibility is to the here and now and not the hereafter (354). In contrast to the liberal, the conservative distrusts rationality and, above all else, abstract theory. Conservatives put their faith in various modes of traditionalism (in Christianity for instance), in social continuity, and in what they take to be prescribed moral rights and duties.

All of these characteristics have been used to describe perhaps the most influential circle of southern thinkers, the Fugitives/Agrarians, a group of men who looked to the past for meaning, who defended the South's customs, traditions, and folkways, and who attempted to salvage its declining, semifeudalistic Agrarian system that, at the time they produced their famous 1930 manifesto, was under threat by an industrial order that to them represented anything but progress and reform. These men, who put their beliefs into their nonfiction as well as their fiction and poetry, have defined and dominated much of the discourse of intellectual history in the twentieth-century South. In their devotion to a way of life rooted in myth, and in their refusal or seeming inability to confront the very real problems of racism—and sexism—in the South (a negligence on their part that seems at times reactionary), the Agrarians represent one of the most clearly articulated movements in American conservatism.

Yet even the Agrarians were not without a number of liberal impulses, and some eventually came to embrace New Deal measures; as Flannery O'Connor noted, there are "degrees of adherence." It is not impossible to retain a sense of original sin and still express liberal social sentiments, as is true of Katherine Anne Porter. Nor is it impossible to advance a liberal cause such as feminism and refuse to call oneself a feminist, as is true of Welty or, again, Porter, and as Zora Neale Hurston demonstrates, it is not impossible to denounce the worst excesses of American capitalism and still reject the liberal social welfare state that emerged as an attempt to combat those excesses. Liberalism is full of tensions that have evolved from the radical individualism that, as Dorothy Ross observes, "stands at the core of liberal theory, whether humanistic or capitalistic in origin" (760).

As a political and social movement, liberalism is of course rooted in John Locke's theories of libertarianism and individualism and in his sometimes contradictory ideas about Christian humanism (charity) and democratic capitalism (property). These opposing inclinations have led liberals to move in what Ross identifies as "conflicting directions": "The egalitarian assumptions that are at the root of liberalism and supported by its universalistic language have had an inherently expansive, democratic thrust. When historical conditions have allowed, those groups excluded from privilege have been able to justify their inclusion by liberal arguments" (751). Through such arguments, liberals such as Eleanor Roosevelt and Adlai E. Stevenson have advanced the cause of civil liberties and have appealed to an increasingly eclectic population, but at the same time, Ross reminds us, liberalism has been continually at odds with its "economic biases, which have tended to narrow individual rights to property rights . . . and to erode our understanding of the distinctive characteristics of society, polity, and personality that do not fit the mold of the capitalist market" (751).[3]

Southern liberalism is an especially vexing issue, for, as Lillian Smith would argue, many—perhaps most—southern male liberals have been conservatives at heart. One thing is for certain: liberalism, or at least reform liberalism, has tended to encourage self-scrutiny, and this is as true of southern liberals as it is of their counterparts in other regions. As the Swedish social scientist Gunnar Myrdal observed in his monumental *An American Dilemma* (1944)—still one of the best explorations of both conservatism and liberalism in their southern setting— it was two "nonscalawag liberals," Walter Hines Page, editor of the North Carolina *State Chronicle* (1883), and George Washington Cable, author of *The Silent South* (1885), who, more than any other figures, started the tradition of southern self-criticism, still a predominantly liberal tradition. Like Lillian Smith, their successor, Page and Cable were frequently denounced by their fellow southerners, but they were also the source of a certain regional pride and they wielded more influence than their small circle of followers might at first suggest.[4]

In the 1930s and 1940s, southern liberals focused much of their energies on exposing the shortcomings of a one-party system and a radical ideology that required white men and women to disfranchise themselves in order to retain white supremacy. During these decades, southern liberals were given tremendous support by Franklin Roosevelt's New Deal, which, as Myrdal observed, was sponsored by "the same party which locally meant Solid South, cultural traditionalism, and political reaction" (463). Lillian Hellman and Lillian Smith were long-time Roosevelt devotees, and Hurston, though she criticized Roosevelt for leading the country into what she believed to be a form of statism, nonetheless benefited from the liberal and state-sponsored cultural programs launched by the New Deal, as did Eudora Welty, who has credited her sense of Mississippi's cultural diversity to her experience as a publicist with the Works Progress Administration. As Myrdal and others have made clear, the New Deal, often in small ways, helped to undermine the status quo throughout the South. This was a process complemented by World War II, a war fought to preserve the American Creed with its set of loosely defined ideals that, in Myrdal's words, have meant different things to different people but could never be confused with southern traditionalism.

Who then are the great southern liberals? Myrdal does not provide a comprehensive list, but in addition to a few highly visible political figures such as Congressman Claude Pepper, a handful of well-known academicians like University of North Carolina President Frank P. Graham, and several newspaper editors, notably Virginius Dabney and Mark Ethridge, Myrdal does cite "such writers of fiction as Erskine Caldwell, Paul Green, William Faulkner, Ellen Glasgow, Julia Peterkin, DuBose Heywood, and Thomas S. Stribling" (468).[5] He might have included transplanted northerner Harry Golden and W. J. Cash or more of the writers in this study had their reputations been more firmly established in 1944. These men and women reached professional standards that, as Myrdal notes, exceeded the average of the region—they helped to lend a cultural facade to the South—but they were by no means the region's only intellectuals. For all their traditionalism, the Agrarians were also intellectuals of the first order. Like Agrarianism, southern liberalism has tended to be an academic enterprise, yet if southern liberals have failed to realize their goals, it is in part because they—unlike the Agrarians—have rarely united or organized themselves effectively. Myrdal's remark that southern liberals are fundamentally a "fraternity of individuals, with independent minds" (467) is by and large correct.

Yet for all his insight into the nature of southern liberalism—which he maintains "is not liberalism as it is found elsewhere in America or in the world" (466)—many of Myrdal's observations seem less suited to southern female liberals than to their male counterparts. Myrdal claims that southern liberalism lacks almost any trace of radical thought, that it is, in essence, a "mild liberalism" (469). Yet Ellen Glasgow, to cite one example, was unapologetic in her support of liberal causes (not only a defender of feminism, she was also an outspoken forerunner of the current movement against cruelty to animals), and Lillian Smith was altogether radical in her deconstruction of the ideology of white supremacy and in her call for an immediate end to racial discrimination in the South.

Though Smith was in fact reluctant to align herself too closely with any one political objective for achieving her goals (she believed that change must start from within), this was by no means true of other southern women radicals such as Myra Page, Grace Lumpkin, and Fielding Burke.[6] Very few southern women liberals—Smith, or social activists and journalists Virginia Durr and Anne Braden—have, in order not to alienate potential readers on the basis of race alone, felt the need to balance their regional patriotism against their reform efforts. In this regard they differ from a tendency that Myrdal observed in most of their male colleagues, in Howard W. Odum or Virginius Dabney, for example. Further, Myrdal's theory that southern African-American intellectuals are "at heart" liberals (469) may be true but still needs qualification. Zora Neale Hurston, though she supported a number of progressive causes, expressed grave reservations about the value of the term "liberal," especially when it becomes synonymous with the white southerner who favors racial integration; in this sense, Hurston rightly argued, the term actually excludes African-Americans. As noted earlier, Hurston was very distrustful of the liberalism she associated with Franklin Roosevelt's New Deal; and, because she felt that it implied that African-Americans could not learn unless they were in the presence of whites, she even objected to the 1954 Supreme Court move to desegregate the public schools. The strain of liberalism that runs throughout Hurston's self-writing is the radical individualistic strain rather than the reform impulse associated with a white liberal such as Lillian Smith.

Finally, while Myrdal has shown that southern liberals were (and often still are) provincial by nature, he also argues that they have been quite adept in seeing that "the future of their cause is virtually interwoven with political developments in the North and in the world" (472). This was especially true of southern liberals during the New Deal when federal legislation became the "strongest liberalizing force" throughout the region. It is for this very reason, however, that one might question Myrdal's conclusion that "the central concern of the southern liberal is always the South" (472). This assertion, though it may seem applicable to Hodding Carter or even to Ralph McGill, cannot be said to apply to any of the women in this study—not even to Lillian Smith, who, though she usually kept the South at the center of her work, understood quite clearly how fully interconnected the poor white and black southerner's plight is with that of oppressed minorities throughout the world, and whose attack on segregation encompassed barriers of race, class, and sex. The liberalism embodied by the writers in this study is in no way exclusively "regional." It is more rewarding to situate their self-writings within the larger discourse of American liberalism than to see them as mere southern liberals; they are southern liberals primarily to the extent that they are liberals from the South.

While a writer such as Smith or Hellman was known to the public because of her outspoken views, the same cannot be said, for instance, of Eudora Welty. In fact, at this point one can hear the voice of William F. Buckley saying "hold on a minute, just how are you so sure that Eudora Welty is a liberal?" Buckley, who in his review of *Scoundrel Time* called Lillian Hellman "the ugliest of them all," interviewed Welty and Walker Percy in 1972 with a series of questions designed to place these two writers squarely within the predominantly conservative southern tradition (Prenshaw, *Conversations* 92–114). At least as ardently as any other modern southern writer, Welty has disdained any one label that would neatly categorize her as this or that kind of writer. When pressured to explain how she could live in Mississippi during the turbulent sixties and not write protest fiction, Welty responded with a frequently quoted essay, "Must the Novelist Crusade?" (1965), in which she made a passionate and bold, if at times confusing, plea for the individual writer's privacy and right to produce the literature of his or her choice. Yet Welty is also the author of "Where Is the Voice Coming From" (1963) and "The Demonstrators" (1966), two of the most powerful southern stories written during the civil rights era.[7]

Like most of her fellow fiction writers of the South, Welty has not been active in political affairs—with one important exception. In the early 1950s, she actively supported the presidential candidacy of Adlai E. Stevenson. One of the most highly regarded liberals of a generally conservative decade, Stevenson is remembered now for having conducted major campaigns on an unusually high intellectual level. An outspoken foe of Senator Joseph McCarthy, whom he saw as a dangerous demagogue, Stevenson denounced Cold-War ideologies, defended peaceful coexistence with Russia, and, as United States ambassador to the United Nations, advanced the cause of internationalism that had been a prominent thrust of his presidential campaigns. Though Stevenson lost (on two occasions) to Dwight Eisenhower, he nonetheless articulated a coherent philosophy of liberalism that included a forceful critique of a nation that, to his way of thinking, was drifting ever further into self-satisfaction and complacency.

Each of these qualities endeared Stevenson to the nation's thinkers, some of whom, including Welty, accepted the invitation of the *New Republic* to send the defeated candidate a 1953 New Year's greeting. Welty told Stevenson that he had galvanized a number of "political ignoramuses" such as herself: "with your appearance on the national scene, we found out how deeply concerned we could be . . . and we are finding that the conception you gave us of politics prevails steadily over the news of the day, and stirs us still." For Welty, Stevenson's politics made room for "the voice of passionate intelligence"; his campaign "was to a good many people like something symbolic of what happened inside themselves at a crisis," at a point when the most important "inner convictions" took to the "huge fateful stage of the outside world—to politics—there to get whacked, too." Most evocative is Welty's conclusion: "We don't want to lose to even a short oblivion the candidate whose declared guiding concern it is to see man stand up in the dignity of reason. . . . With that we were shown the compassionate side of a coin that rings forever with the purity and fierceness of that desire whose other side was the anger of Swift" (8).

Beyond a shared preference for liberal ideals, one might still ask why isolate the work of these six women? A suitable response might cite Rozsika Parker and Griselda Pollock, who in *Old Mistresses* (1981) assert that "the existence and activity of women in art throughout history is of itself a sufficient justification for historical enquiry" (47). Yet Parker and Pollock understand the danger of any study that focuses exclusively on women; they note, for example, that the threat represented by eighteenth-century women artists "to existing stereotypes of male creativity was contained by consistently comparing women artists with each other rather than with other artists working in their field"

(32). Parker and Pollock also expose what may be a less immediately apparent danger; studies that focus solely on women often presuppose an essential femininity that does not hold up under careful scrutiny. These are indeed significant objections to isolating the work of women writers, but they must be weighed against other considerations, for as Parker and Pollock also maintain, to do nothing but compare women with men "loses sight of the particularity of women's participation in a given period in an attempt to make them more acceptable to current art [and, by extension, literary] history" (47).

That no one has dealt at length with the nonfiction prose of southern women writers as a body of writing that may constitute a tradition within itself is in no way astonishing; only in the past two decades have critics begun to explore the work of women writers for its own distinctive features, and—until the 1980s—the emphasis was generally awarded to fiction, poetry, and drama rather than to reflective essays and autobiographical writings. There is a real need, however, to look carefully at the intellectual and autobiographical prose of southern women writers, for as Lillian Smith noted in an interview, "there's a male and female South, which are two different entities. Then there's a black South and a white South, which are two more cleavages. That makes four Souths. 'The South' has usually meant the male, white South. It does not need to mean that any more, and, indeed, it doesn't" (Long 38).

Smith made this observation in 1965, the year before her death. From hindsight, Smith's remark seems almost prescient: sociologists, literary critics, and intellectual historians now question the status of "The South" as icon—as one definable reality with clear ideological parameters. Yet most recent studies of the South and the intellectual content of its twentieth-century literary renaissance indicate that the current revisionary impulse has produced a series of mixed results. While literary critics and intellectual historians continue to undermine the value of limited definitions and discrete boundaries, they still choose to focus overwhelmingly on the literature and intellectual life of southern white men. The southern woman of letters remains a marginal or shadowy presence in most attempts to understand, redefine, or theorize the Southern Renaissance.

By now it is generally conceded that Allen Tate, more than any other writer, set the agenda for discussion of both the origin and direction of the renascent movement in southern letters. Tate's thinking tended towards the binary. In a 1945 essay, "The New Provincialism," he pits provincialism against regionalism. Those who take the provincial view Tate labels "sociologists of fiction," though one might easily substitute the term "liberal" for "sociologist." These men (none of whom Tate identifies by name) see "in material welfare and legal justice the whole solution to the human problem"; in contrast are the traditionalists—writers such as Caroline Gordon and Robert Penn Warren—who take their values from "the classical-Christian world, based upon the regional consciousness, which held that honor, truth, imagination, human dignity, and limited acquisitiveness, could alone justify a social order however rich and efficient it may be" (*Essays* 544–45). Though this essay appeared fifteen years after *I'll Take My Stand*, Tate's agrarian values are still very much intact, values he would continue to parlay in his own act of canon formation, a 1947 anthology called, appropriately enough, *A Southern Vanguard*.

It is the concluding passage of "The New Provincialism" (where Tate reflects upon an essay he published ten years earlier, "The Profession of Letters in the South") that has over the past several decades dominated appraisals of the Southern Renaissance. It is a passage worth citing in full: "But if the provincial outlook, as I have glanced at it here, is to prevail, there is no reason to think that the South will remain immune to it. With the war of 1914–1918, the South re-entered the world—but gave a backward glance as it stepped over the border: that backward glance gave us the Southern renascence, a literature conscious of the past in the present." Tate then quotes from his earlier essay: "From the peculiarly historical consciousness of the Southern writer has come good work of a special order; but the focus of this consciousness is quite temporary. It has made possible the curious burst of intelligence that we get at the crossing of the ways" (*Essays* 545–46). This passage indicates that Tate was drawn not only to one particular theme—the past in the present—but that he had already put a seal on the Southern Renaissance as something that will have ended once this theme has been exhausted. There is little wonder that Tate favors Glasgow's *The Sheltered Life* (1932), a work in which Tate's central theme is more readily apparent than in, say, *Virginia* (1913) or some of Glasgow's lesser-known novels. It is also understandable that on the basis of the stories collected as *The Old Order* (1944), Tate would include

Katherine Anne Porter as one of the traditionalists. One wonders how he might categorize the international Porter of "Hacienda," "The Leaning Tower," or, most important, *Ship of Fools* (1962).

One need only look at the histories and critical works on the Southern Renaissance that appeared in the three decades following Tate's essays to see how fully entrenched his thesis became. Thomas Daniel Young's *The Past in the Present: A Thematic Study of Modern Southern Fiction* (1981) provides perhaps the fullest expression of Tate's thesis and also one of the clearest expressions of its limitations, for though Young's subtitle indicates that his focus is the fiction of the modern South, he includes the work of only seven writers and, on the whole, confines himself to only those novels that clearly manifest the past/present theme: Faulkner's *The Unvanquished* (1938), Tate's *The Fathers* (1938), Warren's *All the King's Men* (1946), Eudora Welty's *The Optimist's Daughter* (1972), Walker Percy's *The Moviegoer* (1961), and, surprisingly, John Barth's *The End of the Road* (1971). Young also includes O'Connor's *Complete Stories* (1971), even though O'Connor's fiction does not conform as neatly to the mold as do the other works. It is the religious dimension of O'Connor's work—another one of Tate's touchstones—that justifies her inclusion in Young's study.

Since 1945 Tate's successors have fleshed out the scope of his somewhat slender design. Cleanth Brooks, Walter Sullivan, M. E. Bradford, and Hugh Holman, to cite only four influential critics of southern literature, have all extended the argument presented by Tate.[8] Only one of these men, Holman, has expressed misgivings about his role in perpetuating Tate's original argument. In one of his last essays, "No More Monoliths, Please: Continuities in the Multi-Souths," Holman claims that "Despite the southerner's vaunted admiration for the concrete, we who study southern writing have not proved immune to the disease. We too seek easy or inclusive answers. . . . The result is usually a schema in which a sentimentalized version of Scott was used defensively in the antebellum period, an exploitative local collorism dominated the postbellum period, and a glorious, even sacramental, agrarianism illumines the twentieth century" (xiv).

To illustrate the tendency to schematize, Holman cites an except from "Ellen Glasgow and the Southern Literary Tradition," an essay of his that appeared in 1964—his "literary nonage." In his delineation of the predominant characteristics that define southern writing, Holman had isolated these features: "a sense of evil, a pessimism about man's potential, a tragic sense of life, a deep-rooted sense of the inter-play of past and present, a peculiar sensitivity to time as a complex element in narrative art, a sense of place as a dramatic dimension, and a thoroughgoing belief in the intrinsic value of art as an end in itself" (xiv). Even if Holman could not bring himself to disagree with Tate about what constitutes the best in southern writing, he realized that his definition—repeated in study after study—had become prescriptive, even proscriptive, and inadequate in its attempt to reckon with the complexity of a literary movement that included not only Faulkner but also, among others, T. S. Stribling, Erskine Caldwell, Grace Lumpkin, Majorie Kinnan Rawlings, Julia Peterkin, and James Lane Allen, as well as "excellent work on the southern experience done by historians and sociologists," even if "our customary definition of literature is too narrow to include much of it" (xix). In short, Holman urges readers and critics to see a "many-colored multitude of southern writers" that in its diversity offers fertile territory for the critical approaches that have grown out of structuralism and semiotics, feminism, and African-American studies. It is with Holman's exhortation—"let us say to our-selves and to those who will follow us, *No more monoliths, please!*" (xxiii)—that one can understand and evaluate the revisionary impulse in the work of recent critics and intellectual historians of the South and its literary renaissance.[9]

Richard Gray goes perhaps further than any of his colleagues in accepting Tate's central thesis—a fact that helps to account for Hol-man's complaint that this book displays the "simplistic fault of too lim-ited a view of what southern writing has been and is" (xv). Gray's main point, in *The Literature of Memory* (1977), is that whatever else the southern writer set out to accomplish, "his preoccupation with history and the 'source of available ideas' that it offered would be a constant, the polestar of his journey. And whatever he said, the plain farmer and fine planter would remain the men at the center of his message, the points around which the energies of his traditionalism seemed to gather" (935). While Gray's paradigm works reasonably well with the Agrarians and with parts of Faulkner, Warren, and even with certain novels by Ellen Glasgow, it becomes frustrating to watch Gray analyze writers like Elizabeth Madox Roberts and Katherine Anne Porter within the scheme of a constricting premise that is, at best, only marginal to their more deeply felt concerns as modern women writers. By the time he comes to Carson McCullers and Flannery O'Connor, later writers of the Southern Renaissance, neither of whom gave much attention to the theme of "the past in the present," Gray seems uncomfortable with his own paradigm, as is evident in his defense of McCullers, a "minor" writer, one of whose most compelling qualities is that "in some strange way she manages to make history function as an *absent presence* in her work" (273). Gray does not lose track of the South's unique history—its "areas of darkness" such as slavery, nostalgia, and intense guilt "not found elsewhere" (37)—and he knows that these areas must be seen in the context of a seemingly pervasive need on the part of southerners to mythologize the past. Yet *The Literature of Memory* suffers from a thesis that underplays the significance of gender in this process of mythologization—this despite the fact that Gray can be commended for including more women writers in this book than does any other single-authored study of the Southern Renaissance.

Richard King's *A Southern Renaissance: The Cultural Awakening of the American South, 1930–1955* (1980) has much in common with Gray's work, for King too is interested in the process of mythologization and particularly the mythic components of what he calls the southern family romance, the pivotal figures "of which were the father and grandfather and whose essential structure was the literal and symbolic family" (7). King observes that his book, though it gives near equal attention to fiction and nonfiction, is not "intended as a complete intellectual (or literary) history of the Southern Renaissance" (7). What interests King are the varieties of historical consciousness and self-consciousness that led some southern writers—W. J. Cash and Lillian Smith, for example—to, as King puts it, demystify and even reject "the tradition of the Southern family romance, white Southern racism, and the received truths about Southern political culture" (8). Such an examination was indeed welcomed in 1980, and while King never diminishes the influence or significance of the writers he analyzes, he is explicit about his own angle of vision. "I have little use," he writes in his Preface, "for Southern conservatism of the Agrarian or aristocratic or any other sort. Yet, as I suggest at the end of the book, the Southern liberalism voiced by intellectuals by the mid-1950s was . . . a worldview rather than a fighting creed. In a sense, my study falls in this tradition of Southern intellectual liberalism" (x).

At the heart of King's work is his awareness that the Southern Renaissance "was by no means the exclusive property of the conservative spirit and those who protested the appearance of the modern world" (6). From this perspective, it is not surprising that King would feature the work of writers like Cash and Smith and seriously question the theories of previous critics, among them C. Vann Woodward and Louis P. Simpson.[10] King convincingly argues, for example, that Woodward misrepresents the renaissance as just a literary movement. "It was certainly that," King counters, "but it also represented an outpouring of history, sociology, political analysis, autobiography, and innovative forms of journalism. W. J. Cash, James Agee, Lillian Smith, Howard Odum, and William Alexander Percy were as central to the Southern Renaissance as William Faulkner, Robert Penn Warren, Allen Tate, and John Crowe Ransom" (5). King further and justifiably rejects Simpson's contention—an extension of what he calls "the neo-Catholic tradition of the Tate wing of the Vanderbilt Agrarians" (6)—that the renaissance was primarily religious in its emphasis: "Surely history and memory, loss and absence, were central preoccupations in much Southern writing in the years after 1930 (as they were in much writing before those years). But Simpson's claim that Faulkner and his contemporaries were essentially religious writers is debatable, to put it mildly" (7).

It is because King was one of the first to seriously and effectively challenge previous conceptualizations that his own exclusions stand in sharp relief. King notes that he does not include Richard Wright and Ralph Ellison because they do not "take the south and its tradition as problematic"; nor does he include women writers like Eudora Welty, Carson McCullers, Flannery O'Connor, and Katherine Anne Porter: "my reading of them indicates that whatever the merits of their work— and they are considerable—they were not concerned primarily with the larger cultural, racial, and political themes that I take as my focus. For whatever reasons—and the one woman I do treat, Lillian Smith, urged women to address themselves to these larger themes—they did not place the region at the center of their imaginative visions" (8–9). This rationale of exclusion does not hold up well under close scrutiny. While women writers of the Southern Renaissance were not concerned primarily with King's "larger themes," they rarely failed to address the problematic nature of their region; and they rarely if ever ignored cultural, political, and racial issues. King constructs a number of paradigms that display his own androcentric bias. To cite only one instance, he asserts that "young Southerners [i.e., young male southerners] saw World War I as a chance to demonstrate the heroism which had been drummed into them as one of the transcendent virtues of the Southern tradition. . . . In this sense the Southern Renaissance, at least in its literary manifestations, drew less from the Depression experience than from the cultural impact of the war" (14). Whatever its applicability to a writer like Faulkner, it is unlikely that such a theory explains anything significant about the work of Welty, McCullers, or O'Connor, just three of the South's women writers whose writings are far more attuned to the depression experience than to the cultural impact made by the Great War.

Published two years before *A Southern Renaissance*, Michael O'Brien's *The Idea of the South* (1978) offers no encompassing definition of the Southern Renaissance itself. Yet, like King, O'Brien does observe that southerners have felt compelled "to work out a definition of Southern culture and fix their place in it" (xi). What King refers to as an "introspective revolution" of the 1930s and 1940s, O'Brien identifies as the result of modernism with its enlargement of "the existential obligation of self-definition" (xvii). The title of O'Brien's book contains the gist of his thesis; the South is not a solid or integrated social reality, but rather a matter of social perception—an idea, or, more accurately, many ideas. Hence, O'Brien focuses on those images of the South that a given writer appropriates; he concentrates most forcefully on what he calls "the borderline between the comfort of the nineteenth-century literal definitions of Southern identity and the faltering of such coherent images under the fragmenting influence of modernism" (xv). O'Brien's subjects in *The Idea of the South* are all male southerners "who hazarded themselves as students of Southern history and society" (xv); even Lillian Smith fails to figure in O'Brien's scheme. Her omission, as well as that of other women writers, is to be regretted. Smith certainly saw herself as a student of the South who, as a woman, took more hazards than her male colleagues. Smith's exclusion makes no sense in light of the concerns O'Brien places at the heart of his study— his focus, for example, on the dispute between the liberal sociology of Chapel Hill and the conservative aestheticism of the Nashville Agrarians and his understanding that "in their history can be found many of the themes and tensions that have characterized the modern problem of Southern identity" (xv). Essentially, O'Brien delineates a liberal-conservative continuum that is applicable to both southern male and female writers, but in *The Idea of the South*, he opts to include only one gender.

O'Brien's book anticipated Daniel Singal's longer study, *The War Within: From Victorian to Modernist Thought in the South, 1919–1945* (1982), clearly the most ambitious of the works on the intellectual underpinnings of the Southern Renaissance to appear thus far. Like O'Brien, Singal focuses on the cultural forces that shaped the South's intellectual life between the two wars; and like his predecessors, Singal begins by positioning himself in relation to Allen Tate, whose seminal analysis he rejects because "it does not accord well with the facts of southern history" (xii). Social change cannot within itself account for the Southern Renaissance. By the time the New Deal had made a real impact on southern agriculture (in the late thirties), or by the time the South became industrialized (in the years after World War II), the renaissance was already in full force. Singal argues persuasively that as a literary movement the renaissance sprang from a "deep dissatisfaction with traditional values and assumptions, not [from] social realities per se" (xiii). For Singal, the renaissance documents a crisis—a period of cultural transition—that he attempts to chronicle and explain in the service of illuminating the larger currents of modernism that he believes are nowhere more evident than in the South.

While critics have faulted Singal for a too-limited definition of modernism—he offers five distinguishing characteristics, most of which hinge on the willingness of twentieth-century writers to form less-idealized perspectives than those of their Victorian predecessors—Singal is correct in noting that Victorian values were especially pronounced in the South.[11] His is a thesis corroborated, in part, by sociologists who have explored the still lingering image and ideal of the Victorian lady in her southern setting (see Atkinson and Boles). Still, Singal's book, as challenging as it is, examines in depth no African-American authors and only one woman, Ellen Glasgow, a writer Singal sees as transitional, a "Southern Post-Victorian" like historian Ulrich B. Phillips and social scientist Broadus Mitchell, rather than a "Modernist by the Skin of Her Teeth," the second of Singal's three categories, which includes sociologist Howard W. Odum, Faulkner, and the Agrarians.

In the Coda to *The War Within*, Singal devotes two paragraphs to Lillian Smith, a southern writer "in the deepest Modernist sense" (374). By this point in his narrative, he has made it clear that race is a key component in modernist thought as well as an explosive problem in the South where "ever since the Civil War the Victorian dichotomy had supplied a principal bulwark for southern white supremacy, with blacks cast customarily as savages (or undisciplined children) and whites as the foremost paladins of civilization" (9). With Lillian Smith, Singal observes, "the assault against the Victorian ethos reached maturity. Her account of the psychic forces sustaining segregation identified the Victorian dichotomy, with its separation of mind and body, as the chief culprit" (374). Given this assessment, one wonders why Smith is accorded roughly one page in a lengthy book on modernism and the intellectual life of the South. In like manner, one might wonder why Robert Penn Warren, rather than Katherine Anne Porter or Zora Neale Hurston, is the single fiction writer included in Part Three of Singal's study, "The Modernist Generation Arrives."

Fred Hobson's *Tell About the South: The Southern Rage to Explain* (1983) appeared a year after *The War Within*. Hobson's subjects are "certain individual Southerners—some journalists, some teachers, some belletrists, some writers of no precise description—who have approached the South with a purpose that went beyond professional interest or intellectual curiosity, who have responded to it emotionally, even viscerally, and have written books, usually of a highly personal nature, in which they have set forth their feelings" (4). Hobson constructs a binary paradigm: the "apologists" compose a school of remembrance in opposition to the "critics" who comprise something resembling a school of shame and guilt. In the first group are writers like Thomas Nelson Page and Donald Davidson; in the second are, among others, George Washington Cable, W. J. Cash, and Lillian Smith, the one female author who figures prominently in Hobson's study. One generalization is central to Hobson's analysis; the apologists, who held sway until the turn of the century, "tended to be of a poetic nature . . . while the critics (to call them liberals is generally accurate) tended to rest their case on history, on observed fact, and draw their position, their attitude, from the documented Southern past" (7). This is a provocative generalization, if somewhat too neat; Lillian Smith, for example, displays a pronounced poetic temperament and, in the main, rests her case not so much on the southern past as on the psychology of racism itself. Nonetheless, Hobson's subjects are those southerners—he uses Quentin Compson as their model—who have borne an inordinate burden of consciousness and who together have produced something on the order of a major confessional literature.

Early on, Hobson declares that his target of inquiry is not the southern novelist—that is, not the male southern novelist—for "his story, at least in the most notable cases, has already been told"; nor is Hobson concerned with historians and scholars since they lack the kind of "passion" that characterizes the writers he does choose to discuss (4). Even though Hobson (like his male colleagues) makes clear his rationale for dealing primarily with a cast of white male characters,[12] his exclusion of any woman writer other than Smith should prompt readers to ask if his analysis is applicable to writers of both genders. Surely Flannery O'Connor—a writer whose nonfiction prose often focuses on the parallel between the biblical fall and that of the South, a southern writer with a sense of both tragedy and transcendence—might merit analysis in a work that underscores the importance of such issues to the South. Her absence from Hobson's study may be accounted for by the fact that O'Connor was a fiction writer, but, then, so was Lillian Smith. Does O'Connor lack Smith's passion? Does she and other women writers of the South share Smith's rage to explain? And if not, why? When Hobson writes, "The Southerner had a true rage to explain only when he had an enemy across the line issuing an indictment that had to be answered, or when he had an enemy within Southern society forcing him to repress his feelings until the internal pressure became so great he had to spew them out" (15), one wants to know if such an assertion accounts in any way for the self-reflexive writings of not only the major women writers of the Southern Renaissance but also of more recent southern women writers like Rosemary Daniell, whose confessional *Fatal Flowers: On Sin, Sex, and Suicide in the Deep South* (1980), is a book full of rage, but—significantly—one told from the perspective of Caddy rather than Quentin Compson.

In 1986 Richard Gray published *Writing the South: Ideas of an American Region*, a supplement of sorts to his earlier *The Literature of Memory*. Gray calls *Writing the South* "no more than a series of notes" offered "in the belief that the South is primarily a concept, a matter of knowing even more than being . . . an idea of order [in the Wallace

Stevens sense], a structuring principle" (xii). Aligning himself with O'Brien, Gray's new approach stems from his desire to show that, for as long as southern literature has existed, southerners have "been engaged not so much in writing about the South as in writing the South" (xii). Gray's method is to focus on individual writers and periods of crisis, to identify a given writer's mode of argument and discourse. Yet it is because he is willing to move beyond conventional assumptions—beyond concepts of the South as something that can be clearly defined or fully known—that Gray's book is in one respect a major disappointment. A quick scan of his table of contents reveals that Gray has chosen to discuss at length only one woman writer, Eudora Welty. This decision is particularly disappointing in light of his previous book, *The Literature of Memory*, which, one recalls, included not only Glasgow and Welty but also Caroline Gordon, Katherine Anne Porter, Carson McCullers, Flannery O'Connor, and even Elizabeth Madox Roberts, a writer often excluded from books about southern writing. Gray's acknowledgement that his "map" fails to chart "many places in the Southern argument" (xiii) does not make his decision to focus almost exclusively on one gender and one race any less disappointing.

At least four concerns unite the work of the southern intellectual historians. One is a new emphasis upon the nature of discourse and the structures a writer appropriates in the service of "writing the South." Another emphasis is the relation of the South and its artists to the larger currents of modernism, an emphasis embedded in the need to see southern literature in a context that accommodates, but is not exclusive to, regionalism. A third concern is that critics no longer confine themselves solely to literary figures or traditional literary genres, that our perceptions have broadened about what constitutes a culture's literature. It might also be noted that even though each of these men has his own thematic focus, each tends to favor a biographical approach to his subjects; each attempts, in Singal's words, to root his discussion of the South and its culture within a writer's "individual sensibility" (xiii); or, in the words of O'Brien, to assess "the idea of the South held by that person, its coming, changing, and going" (xvi).

In short, these works have significantly challenged previous theories and have drawn attention to writers once thought incidental or at best marginal to the history of southern writing. Yet collectively these same works have done much to diminish the significance of work by women writers (as well as that of African-Americans) and the role the southern woman of letters has played in producing a diverse, wide-spread, and engendered body of literature that includes not only fiction, poetry, and drama but many forms of self-writing as well.

Addressing the Organization of American Historians in 1984, Anne Goodwyn Jones made essentially the same observation; though her remarks were aimed at King's *A Southern Renaissance* and Singal's *The War Within*, they are pertinent to the work of Gray, O'Brien, and Hobson as well: "at the same time that we are watching these men expand the definition of the Renaissance, we are also watching a process of constriction, an exclusion of some names that have, since it took place, conventionally been thought of as major figures in the Southern Renaissance" (2). Excluded are African-American writers such as James Weldon Johnson, Jean Toomer, and Richard Wright, and women authors such as Katherine Anne Porter, Caroline Gordon, and Carson McCullers, none of whom is represented in the more recent intellectual histories. Jones understands that a table of contents is within itself an act of canon formation that has consequences for the future; further, she explains that while writers like King and Singal display a set of attitudes that are "if not explicitly feminist, compatible with feminist thinking" (10), they have nonetheless presented a view of the Southern Renaissance that must be questioned. "The great cultural story, the story we continue to receive as canonical for the South, the story Singal and King analyze and enact in their texts, is," Jones asserts, "the southern man's mind writ large" (16).

Jones's insistence on revisionism in her comments to the Organization of American Historians predates and bears useful comparison to an argument advanced by Michael Kreyling in his 1988 review-essay, "Southern Literature: Consensus and Dissensus." Published as "The Extra," one in a series of polemical articles in *American Literature*, Kreyling's argument is that southern literary study has been swathed in a consensus that "grants 'South' the privilege of icon: sacred rather than historical" (85). Such consensus is nowhere more apparent for Kreyling than in the recent *History of Southern Literature* (1985), a work that surveys the whole of southern writing, a long-awaited volume edited by the men who until the mid-eighties established the topics for southern literary study—Louis D. Rubin, Lewis P. Simpson, Thomas Daniel Young, and others.[13] By explaining how the renascent critics have undervalued politics and ideology, how they have failed to examine not only their own interests but also the flaws in their own definitions, Kreyling delivers a hard-hitting exposé. He shows, for example, how James Mellard's essay, "The Fiction of Social Commitment," which deals with novels by writers like Stribling and Caldwell, also excludes writers such as Allen Tate and Stark Young and thus seems "designed to persuade us that all political or social statement is necessarily 'liberal' and modern dissent from the truth as the agrarian critics had revealed it." As Kreyling correctly observes, "Dissensus would be helpful here if only to prod us to acknowledge that Tate's novel [*The Fathers*] is as political as Stribling's works" (91). The renascent critics are lingering apostles of the New Criticism with its formalist and conservative platform.[14] Kreyling is not off the mark when he writes that their "fixation with technique" obscures both ideology and history (93) and that, if one does not want to see southern literature become the exclusive domain of "the southernists," one must accept "the challenges of dissensus" (95), challenges that are rooted in ideological questions about race, class, gender and history and that will of necessity challenge the previously safe and conservative discourse of southern literary criticism.

As of this writing, the most recent study to address the nature of the Southern Renaissance, its beginnings and ideological dimensions, is Michael O'Brien's *Rethinking the South: Essays in Intellectual History* (1988). Although O'Brien's new book focuses primarily on the link between the South's intellectual culture and Romanticism, it devotes an important chapter to the renascent period, tellingly titled "A Heterodox Note on the Southern Renaissance." (If Kreyling sounded the alarm on orthodoxy, O'Brien, apparently eager to move beyond the more restricted scope of his earlier study, responds with his own arsenal.) O'Brien offers what is to date the most compelling attack on the limitations of Tate's thesis and its adoption by his successors. He cites Edmund Wilson's rejection of Tate's New Critical bias that explicitly ideological works of literature are in effect propaganda; he doubts the validity of Tate's claim that "the South's presence in the modern world was drastically altered by the First World War, that the region was any more in and of that world in 1920 than it had been in 1910" (162); he argues that Tate's generation was not the first to thematize the past in the present; and he strongly rejects the "half-baked" myth that the southern mind is in any way "concrete" (165). In brief, O'Brien explains why Tate's Edenic community never existed: "By no stretch of anything but a phenomenological imagination can so huge and diverse an area as the South be designated a community" (166).

Like Richard King, O'Brien understands that Tate was a "partisan" and that "by defining the characteristics of the Renaissance, he was delimiting a canon, of those who exemplified his definition" (166). Further, O'Brien underscores the religious nature of Tate's renaissance: it "was a Christian eschatological drama, after the fashion of T. S. Eliot, embodying, to use Frank Kermode's phrase, 'the sense of an ending' " (167). Tate and his followers stand in opposition to critics like King and O'Brien who have led the way for an examination of the renaissance as less of an ending than a beginning. Critics and historians are beginning to study the renaissance, O'Brien notes, in order "to explain the origins of the sea change of the 1950s and 1960s, to make intelligible Selma, black enfranchisement, civil rights. . . . If the culture of the South awoke, Selma is what it awoke to do" (167).

Such an awakening has understandably broadened the focus of southern literary study. O'Brien points to the differences between the recent intellectual histories and two standard and influential collections of essays edited by Louis Rubin and Robert Jacobs, *Southern Renascence: The Literature of the Modern South* (1953) and *South: Modern Southern Literature and Its Cultural Setting* (1961). Of the twenty some writers included in these anthologies, O'Brien notes that sixteen are linked in one way or another to the Fugitives and Agrarians: "It is a coherent canon, tightly conforming to Tate's standards, themselves duly elaborated in thematic essays" (167). A glance at the contents of the more recent studies, including Morton Sosna's *In Search of the Silent South: Southern Liberals and the Race Issue* (1977), reveals a reassessment, a new set of concerns, a canon in flux. What the presence of figures such as Howard Odum, Rupert Vance, C. Vann Woodward, Lillian Smith, W. J. Cash, and William Alexander Percy reveals is not only the inclusion of more liberal writers but also a heightened if not altogether new interest in questions of race and ideology that, in turn, have fostered a revised perception of genre so that "sociology, historical narrative, political analysis, these become legitimate, coequal with the lyric or the novel" (168).

If O'Brien overlooks the fact that disturbs Jones and other feminists—that, while the canon has expanded in terms of ideology and genre, it has also been constricted in terms of gender—he does provide the most expansive definition of the renaissance to date. In *A Southern Renaissance*, Richard King remarked (in a footnote) that a complete history of the renaissance would have to take into account its music, art, and politics. O'Brien pushes this observation to its farthest limit: "The major contribution of Southern culture to the world in this century is, beyond doubt, music. . . . It would be a shame to be without *Understanding Poetry*, but there would still be I. A. Richards. But take away W. C. Handy, Louis Armstrong, King Oliver, Duke Ellington, Dizzy Gillespie, and you deprive the world of something that only the American South could give" (169). O'Brien's is a radical view (and a radical departure from his earlier work). His definition is not likely to please a great many literary scholars; in fact, in a review of O'Brien's book, Richard King complains that O'Brien seems not to think there was anything remarkable about the Southern Renaissance at all ("The South and Cultural Criticism" 711). Clearly O'Brien's goal is demystification, but most important to this consideration of six very different southern women of letters, each with her own focus and agenda—her own modes of discourse—is O'Brien's insistence that "there is no single renaissance, but several, because there are many individuals and groups of differing persuasions. . . . The Agrarian themes of 1930 are dead and moribund, but a lively culture goes on" (171).

In his important essay "No More Monoliths, Please," Hugh Holman urged critics to avoid canonizing their "personal tastes and individual values by making them the cards of admission and the frames for analysis of southern writers either of the past or the present" (xxii). Yet critics have not always heeded Holman's sensible advice. Even when their intent has been to expand the canon as well as the means of inquiry and previous conceptual schemes, even when their goals seem above suspicion, critics have devised paradigms that, taken as a whole, have helped to write women and African-American writers out of the intellectual history of the Southern Renaissance. This silencing by omission has been accomplished, paradoxically, as their works simultaneously demonstrate that Tate and his successors were constricted by a too narrow view of both theme and genre. Whatever his biases, Tate, to his credit, did not confine his paradigms to the work of one gender; Tate saw Faulkner as the undisputed genius of the renaissance, but

Faulkner's presence did not preclude the importance of the work produced by Elizabeth Madox Roberts, Ellen Glasgow, Katherine Anne Porter, or that of his wife, Caroline Gordon.

Inarguably, southern women writers sometimes benefited from the support and recognition they received from male writers, especially the southern New Critics, though at times the amount of support has been exaggerated. For instance, A. S. Knowles claims that Carson Mc-Cullers—"primarily a writer of the Forties, a period dominated by Southern writers and Southern critics," a period characterized by both genius and cultishness—was valued chiefly because she produced the kind of books that, in theory at least, suited the critical temperament of "the symbol-oriented proponents of the New Criticism" who were "concentrated in the South." Thus, Knowles claims, "in dealing with Carson McCullers we are dealing with a writer who was favored by a self-supporting coterie that held sway over American letters for a decade" (98). The problem with this assertion is that a survey of early criticism of McCullers reveals that if they did admire her work, the New Critics never gave it any sustained attention in print.

The extent to which the careers of women writers of the Southern Renaissance were boosted or—in the long term—hurt by their male colleagues is perhaps the subject of another study; suffice it here to acknowledge that with the single exception of Caroline Gordon, southern women were not part of the institutionalization of criticism that received its leading impetus from southern male writers during the midpart of this century—this despite the fact that their fiction often appeared in journals and publications edited by the southern New Critics. Though Flannery O'Connor produced no major critical pieces on individual authors, Ted Spivey has shown that if one looks carefully at her remarks about the kind of critic she wanted to review her books, one would see that she could not have meant the New Critic with his almost exclusive emphasis on the text itself (273–75).[15] Throughout *The Eye of the Story* (1978), Welty expresses apprehension about critics who need to tear a work apart in order to show that they understand how it might have been put together. As Michael Kreyling states, the need to dismantle a work is at odds with Welty's own critical method: "The critic who goes at literature as if it were a riddle or a specimen too often saps the very living thing he is supposed to nurture with what Welty calls imagination" ("Words into Criticism" 227–28). The evidence would appear to suggest that in general southern women writers have not shared the worldview that gave credence to the New Criticism; their preference is not for difficult forms like metaphysical poetry; indeed, words like "tension" and "structure" are rarely part of their critical vocabularies.[16] Even in reflections on their own work, southern women writers have avoided explicit formal analysis. One need only compare McCullers's "The Flowering Dream: Notes on Writing" (*The Mortgaged Heart*) to Allen Tate's "Narcissus as Narcissus" (*Essays of Four Decades*) to detect the fundamental difference.

Though Carson McCullers's natural sympathies are clearly with the liberals of her native region, she is not included in the body of this work primarily because she did not publish a book-length self-study.[17] McCullers toyed with the idea of writing an autobiography and did in fact produce a number of autobiographical essays, including "Notes on Writing: The Flowering Dream." Her biographer, Virginia Spencer Carr, points out that McCullers in fact wrote several versions of this piece, destroying those she felt were "too personal" (469); and her sister, Margarita Smith, observes that McCullers was still at work on a final version of the piece at the time of her death in 1967. It is tempting to assume that McCullers—a writer who, like Thomas Wolfe, often blurred the line between fictional autobiography and autobiographical fiction—feared the intensely personal only because she knew that male critics and historians have too often assumed that women write about the personal—their own lives—no matter what forms they attempt, and, consequently, she wanted to vex their efforts to show that she was in fact Mick Kelly or F. Jasmine Addams.[18] Whatever the source of her reticence, McCullers is altogether typical of other southern women writers of her generation who turned to autobiography, either the book-length work or the shorter autobiographical sketch. Rarely do these women emphasize the mundane details of their daily lives (O'Connor once remarked that not much could be said of a life lived between the house and the chicken coop). Rather, as McCullers's "Notes on Writing: The Flowering Dream," Glasgow's collected Prefaces in *A Certain Measure* (1943), Porter's " 'Noon Wine': The Sources," or Welty's "Writing and Analyzing a Story" all demonstrate, the woman writer of the Southern Renaissance has given the most significant attention to the (re)sources of her own creativity—to her position as an artist with what Susan Cahill would call a "moral imperative."

There is at the moment no critical consensus on the nature of southern autobiography. William Howarth claims that "Southern writers" have frequently turned to autobiography as "a genre in which personal and regional fortunes persistently intertwine. Writing a life story, whether it be fictional or factual, delivers to the writer a particularly sharp sense of place and of the voice needed to love/hate it" (7). It is apparent, however, that by "Southern writers," Howarth really means southern male writers, for later in his essay, "Writing Upside Down: Voice and Place in Southern Autobiography," he claims that "until recently, few Southern women writers—O'Connor, Carson McCullers, Katherine Anne Porter—turned to autobiography, perhaps in deference to the Southern tradition that privileges women only through fictive masks" (15–16). George Core contradicts Howarth's assessment but presents an argument that, were it true, would be cause for even greater alarm. "When we survey Southern literature from its beginnings until the past decade or so," Core asserts, "we find precious little in the way of autobiography, which is to say little that falls under the heading of even reminiscence or memoir; and there is nothing to speak of so far as diaries and journals are concerned. Colonel William Byrd is an exception, of course . . . And even Byrd's principal works are a good distance from autobiography" (52). So much for Mary Boykin Chesnut's massive diary of the Civil War, or Harriet Jacobs's *Incidents in the Life of a Slave Girl* (1861), or Katharine Du Pre Lumpkin's *The Making of a Southerner* (1947), or—to bring the matter closer to our immediate attention—Ellen Glasgow's *The Woman Within*, Zora Neale Hurston's *Dust Tracks on a Road*, and Eudora Welty's *One Writer's Beginnings*.

James Olney and Elizabeth Fox-Genovese take less exclusive approaches to the nature of autobiography by southern writers. In "Autobiographical Traditions Black and White," Olney shows that "autobiography, straight and fictional, has been the heart and soul of Afro-American literature from the beginning to the present time" but that "no similar claim could be made about the literature of the white South" (74). Olney provides a sustained comparison of Eudora Welty's *One Writer's Beginnings* and Richard Wright's *Black Boy* (1945); born one year apart, both writers grew up in Jackson, Mississippi. Welty's book, Olney observes, "tells of *one* writer's beginnings, *this* writer's beginnings; it is not the generic tale of a white girl growing up in the

South as, one might say, Wright's book is the generic tale of a black boy growing up in the South" (72). According to Olney, the African-American's autobiographical testimony "is not something done individually but is the revelation of a whole group experience; or perhaps we should say that in the individual experience is to be read the entire group experience" (76).

While this remark does most assuredly typify Wright's autobiography (or the *Narrative of the Life of Frederick Douglass*, 1845, or even *The Autobiography of Miss Jane Pittman*, 1971), it contradicts the experience that Zora Neale Hurston re-creates in *Dust Tracks on a Road*. In her desire to tell one writer's story, and in her insistence on her own individuality—her own unquestionable uniqueness—Hurston's autobiography bears more resemblance to *One Writer's Beginnings* and *The Woman Within* than to *Black Boy* or, say, the autobiographies of Malcolm X and Angela Davis. This zealous defense of her individuality (a defense that often attempts to sublimate the historically shaping determinants of race, sex, and class) is something Hurston shares with each of the writers in this study and with a number of other southern women writers as well. In her analysis of autobiographies by both black and white women from the South, Elizabeth Fox-Genovese explains that this emphasis on individualism, often at the expense of the larger community, is an implicit rejection of the "southern conservative tradition, notably represented by Allen Tate and the Agrarians," which held that "the South embodied the last true community in the Western world precisely because it continued to combat the corrosive tendencies of individualism." For Tate and others who took his position, "the individual should, ideally, be understood as subordinate to and even constituted by the community to which he or she belonged" ("Between Individualism and Community" 21).[19]

All statements to the contrary notwithstanding, the fact remains that southern women writers have produced a great many autobiographies, memoirs, diaries, journals, and—like *Killers of the Dream*—other hybrid forms of self-literature. In her Foreword to *The Days Before* (1952), Katherine Anne Porter even noted that she preferred to regard her collected essays and reviews as her "journal," a reflection of her evolving thought, of her self-in-development (vii). Again, it should not be surprising that critics would (inadvertently?) write southern women writers out of the canon of southern autobiography; these critics are not unlike the historians who produce intellectual histories of the Southern Renaissance with little more than an obligatory chapter on one or two women writers.

When one compares the work and lives of southern women authors, one can detect not only conflicts between the individual conscience and that of the larger community; one can also detect some intriguing behavioral patterns, for women writers of the twentieth-century South have been pushed into a number of defensive postures. The southern woman of letters has had to defend the very integrity of her artistic vision, and this is especially true of writers like McCullers and O'Connor, whose names are for many synonymous with the southern grotesque, or of writers such as Lillian Smith who have taken unpopular positions on civil rights and the whole political value of modern literature.

Sometimes these defensive postures stem from accusations that make little sense. A writer like Lillian Hellman, who grew up in both New Orleans and New York, has had to confront the charge that she is somehow not southern enough, while a writer such as Eudora Welty has constantly had to explain her preoccupation with regionalism, or with what Welty would prefer to call "place" (a term that seems less pejorative and also less accusing). Lillian Smith was not accepted by most of her white southern male colleagues because they believed she was obsessed with race; by contrast, Zora Neale Hurston was rejected by most of the black male intellectuals of her day—both from the South and the North—because she was not obsessed with the issue of race (or at least not obsessed in what could be taken as a politically correct way). Both Carson McCullers and Katherine Anne Porter have been misjudged by critics who would prefer to comment on the slightness of their literary output—on their obsessions with single themes—than to confront the meaning of their art itself. In the same traditional sense in which a woman can be a cook but not a chef (a term generally reserved for male cooks), Porter seems to have sensed that rather than praising her as a "stylist," critics were in fact using this term to dismiss or to avoid confronting the real implications of her work. As she makes clear in her interview with the *Paris Review*, "stylist," and the same can be said of "craftsman," is a loaded term that should not be confused with "artist" (Givner, *Conversations* 92–93). The evidence suggests that southern women writers have understood all too well the social constructions of femininity and the effect of these definitions on the evaluation of what they as women artists might achieve.[20]

Rozsika Parker and Griselda Pollock have persuasively argued that the "economic, social, and ideological effects of sexual differences in a western, patriarchal culture" have required women to speak and act "from a different place within that society and culture" (49). In the South the traditions and ideologies of patriarchy have been given reinforcement even from outsiders; Leslie Fiedler, for example, referred to (and in effect dismissed) McCullers, Porter, and a whole group of southern women writers as "distaff Faulknerians" (*Love and Death* 475). Is it surprising that these writers have assumed postures that are not only defensive but also at times are subtly deceptive? Is it not understandable that the smiling exterior Ellen Glasgow displayed in her quest for acceptance in a male-dominated republic of letters turns out to be a pose that she deconstructs in the autobiography she would permit to be published only after her death?

When a major critic issues a charge such as Fiedler's, other critics, both male and female, will in time attempt to clear the air. Robert Drake says that he frequently offers a course on Welty, Porter, and O'Connor in part to "get out from under the shadow of Faulkner" (41). This in itself is a noble enterprise: Faulkner has dominated most college courses on southern writing if not most assessments of the renascent period itself. One justifiably suspects that the scope of his influence has been inflated. One cannot read Eudora Welty's collected interviews without an awareness of her deep respect for Faulkner and his great talent; neither can one miss Welty's impatience with interviewers who seemingly desire that she acknowledge more of an affinity with her fellow Mississippian than in fact exists (Prenshaw, *Conversations* 220, 299, 302, 321, 333–34). As Louise Westling has shown in her chapters on Welty in *Sacred Groves and Ravaged Gardens* (1985), to continue to compare Welty with Faulkner is to miss what makes her a distinctively southern feminist writer.

It is important, as Robert Drake concedes, to look at the work of southern women writers for its own indigenous features, but when it comes to providing a rationale for why he chooses to offer a course that links Welty, Porter, and O'Connor, Drake can only say that it is because they share a common background of place, time, and community; he then quotes Gertrude Stein's well-known remark that she could not write about her native city of Oakland, California, because "there was no there there" (47). The relation of the southern woman of letters to her region is complex, more so than Drake indicates. In *Tomorrow Is Another Day* (1981), Anne Goodwyn Jones gets to the core of the problem when she observes that the southern woman writer participates in, or at least responds to, "a tradition that defines her ideal self in ways that must inevitably conflict with her very integrity as an artist: voiceless, passive, ignorant" (39–40). The ideal that Lillian Smith devoted so much energy to deconstructing rests upon a woman's self-abnegation. The southern woman—at least the white southern woman—was to marry, produce children, and reify the rigidly engendered ideals of her region, ideals that most southern women writers have quite rightly rejected. Jones, like Smith before her, notes that the presence of lynch mobs well into the 1930s testifies to the persistence of the southern lady as an ideal, as do, of course, the more recent rejections of the ERA by the southern states (15, 17).

The great irony is that the South—despite the tenaciousness with which southerners have patrolled their ideals and traditions—has always accepted the woman writer within southern culture. To cite Jones once again, literature was one of the very few professions "that a Southern lady of good family not driven by dire economic necessity might pursue without being thought to have 'desexed' herself" (5); Jones reminds us that southern women writers have in fact been active throughout the full course of southern literature.[21] Yet as Ellen Glasgow makes clear in *The Woman Within*, southerners have not always set the highest criteria for judging their literary efforts: "I have known intimately, in the South at least, few persons really interested in books more profound than 'sweet stories.' My oldest and closest friends, with the exception of James Cabell, still read as lightly as they speculate, and this description applies as accurately to the social order in which I was born, from which I had escaped, and to which I had at last returned from a long exile" (216). Jones accurately equates Glasgow's attack on the South's "confederacy of hedonism" (*Tomorrow* 42) with her tacit rejection of the southern "patriarch's equation of woman, beauty, literature and irrelevance" (44).

The "new woman," perhaps best represented collectively by the figures in this study, never completely undermined the force of either the feminine or the southern mystique, but she did openly denounce the glaring constraints placed upon women, racial minorities, and political dissidents, as well as the constraints that white men have placed upon themselves. Nor is it insignificant that, when most of these writers finally produced their autobiographies, they chose to focus on their lives as writers, on their self-conscious and fully deliberate decisions as women to establish themselves as artists. Such was not the case with the generation of southern women writers before them, who, because of the boundaries between public and private utterance, could not be so forthright. Frances Newman claimed to have become a writer because she was not attractive; Margaret Mitchell because she was out of work with an ankle injury; Grace King because she was challenged by a man to portray the South more accurately than had George Washington Cable (Jones, *Tomorrow* 47–48). With the self-writing of Glasgow, Welty, Hurston and others, one is given, by contrast, the conscious, creative, female self who is offering her inner experiences to the public.

It is fair to say that each of the six writers included in this study were less restricted than their predecessors by the various penalties for making their real feelings known; without the conventional masks, each spoke out loudly and clearly on topics of personal, regional, and national concern. Censorship, when and where it existed, came from without. Zora Neale Hurston, for example, felt that the issue of American imperialism—both its deadliness and its hypocrisy—was important enough to warrant its own chapter in her autobiography. It was Hurston's editors and publishers who felt differently and who suggested that she omit any potentially offensive opinions and revelations.

As her self-writing demonstrates, each of the writers in this study helped to close the barrier between what a southern woman might think in private and what she might say in public. Each played her own part in defining and expanding the liberal tradition that Jones caught glimmers of in the work of previous writers but which she concluded was only part of the tradition in which "more often, anything that felt radical was suppressed, masked, or transformed into the familiar paradox of the strong southern women arguing for her own fragility" (*Tomorrow* 45), in which, in short, anything that felt out of place was carefully censored from within.

In one sense this study, with its focus on the southern woman of letters and her works of self-definition, supplements the work of Gray, O'Brien, King, Singal, and Hobson. Lillian Smith begins this study because her work is central to any reassessment of the Southern Renaissance, a conclusion with which King, Singal, and Hobson might concur even though they emphasize that element in Smith's work that most clearly pertains to their individual arguments. Of all the women writers of the Southern Renaissance, Smith represents the sharpest disruption of a conservative discourse and a narrow set of assumptions that until the late seventies were generally taken as adequate explanations of the origin and direction of a major body of twentieth-century writing. Smith is the one woman writer of the Southern Renaissance whose nonfiction is as widely regarded as her novels; much of what remains implicit regarding the intersection of gender, region, religion, and race in the work of her male and female contemporaries is made explicit throughout Smith's nonfiction and receives its fullest and most careful expression in *Killers of the Dream*.

2.

LILLIAN SMITH

The Confessional Tract

In 1960 Lillian Smith wrote to George Brockway of W. W. Norton about a revised edition of her 1949 *Killers of the Dream*. According to her biographer, Anne C. Loveland, Smith's interest in a new edition had been galvanized by the recent sit-in movement in the South. Smith felt that the same readers who had not been drawn to the race problem in the late forties were now willing, even eager to respond more constructively. Moreover, while Smith had praised W. J. Cash's *The Mind of the South* (1941)—the one analysis of the southern mind still in print and readily accessible in the early sixties—Smith also regarded Cash's work as "too distant from today's psychological problems to be of much help in giving insight" (quoted in Loveland 220). Smith believed that *Killers of the Dream* "should be *the* book on the southern mind and soul"; her self-reflexive analysis of this work indicates that she regarded it as the culmination of a personal quest to understand herself within the context of a tormented and guilt-ridden region: "Rarely in the history of Western writing has anyone chosen to write of moral and political and social affairs in direct terms of his own personal experience of them. This book is a kind of existential confession; this is life in a segregated culture as I saw it, heard it, felt it, experienced it, and was shaped by it. Therefore it has a lasting quality, as do honest memoirs, a lastingness that no other writer from the South or about the South has been able (up to now) to give a book" (quoted in Loveland 220).

Since Smith had been rushed to complete the book in 1949, she valued the opportunity in 1961 to bring out a slightly revised and expanded new edition that would reflect her reading, thinking, and observations during the intervening twelve years.

While critics were on the whole hostile to the first edition, the 1961 *Killers* was greeted with more enthusiasm—if not enough to satisfy Smith's deeply rooted need for both public and critical prestige. Unlike Porter, Welty, McCullers, or O'Connor, each of whom knew that she was highly prized by an admiring if sometimes small coterie of readers (and critics), Smith struggled throughout her career with the undeniable evidence that she was indeed a neglected writer. In an undated letter (ca. 1960), Smith said that it was probably inevitable that she be regarded as a defender of causes, though, as an artist, she wrote "to explore the unknown, to answer [her] questions or else find new questions" (*Winner* 217). In this letter, Smith reflects on *Now Is the Time* (1955), the book she wrote to help the South accept the 1954 Supreme Court decision to desegregate the public schools, the one work she freely admitted was pure polemic. Returning to this small book five years after its publication, Smith says she was "amazed at its simplicity, its good sense, even its wisdom," adding in a parenthetical aside that she had "to say these things even out loud, occasionally, to keep from blowing my brains out in my discouragement at the critics' and reviewers' refusal to accept me as a writer" (*Winner* 217). Smith was willing to have others disagree with her diagnosis of the South if they could indicate that they had read her at all. She realized, however, that her opponents had chosen another tactic—what she labeled elsewhere as a "conspiracy of silence": "I have been curiously smothered during the past nine years; indeed, ever since *Killers of the Dream*. When writers about 'race' are discussed, I am never mentioned; when southern writers are discussed, I am never mentioned; when women writers are mentioned, I am not among them; when best-sellers are discussed,

Strange Fruit (which broke every record for a serious book) is never mentioned. This is a curious amnesia; I have smiled at it, have laughed at it; but I know what it has done to me in sales and in prestige" (218). Conceding that she can still laugh at her dilemma, Smith begs her reader not to be embarrassed by her frankness. Still, "now and then" she is prompted to ask: "Whom, among the mighty, have I so greatly offended!" (218).

Smith's question is of course rhetorical; the exclamation point gives it away. Smith knew that she had offended, among others, the conservative Agrarian critics who with their various anthologies had in large measure defined the canon of twentieth-century southern literature and who with their New Criticism had come to dominate the way literary texts were treated in universities across the nation. Nor was Smith blind to the gender-based hostility to her work; in 1963 she told an interviewer, "The Boys—that's what I call the eight or nine foremost American critics—won't accept a woman writer if she writes strong, intellectual things. They can't. There's a tremendous woman hatred in America today: If you're a woman writer and write soft things, they like you. Anything else and they fight you" (Mollnow 7). Smith also knew that she had offended those readers who were not yet ready for a cultural transformation of their native South and who further realized—if only intuitively—that one way to silence a writer is to ignore her.

It is because she viewed this attempt to smother her work as the single great abuse of her life that Smith would have relished the recent academic interest in her writings. In the late seventies, critics began to reexamine the phenomenon known as the Southern Renaissance, defined as it had been by men like Allen Tate and his followers. Of these critics—among them Richard Gray, Michael O'Brien, Morton Sosna, Richard King, Daniel Singal, and Fred Hobson—all but Gray and O'Brien have made the work of Lillian Smith a part of their reassessments. Most of these men are self-acknowledged liberals who understand that Smith provides a unique refutation of assumptions that are too narrow, too deeply embedded in myth, to account for that mesh of contradictory attitudes commonly called the "southern mind"; for many of these writers, Smith represents at least one significant dimension of a movement that can no longer be defined as exclusively conservative and at times reactionary. Equally important, Smith's reflections on herself and her region provide a new context for examining the autobiographical nonfiction prose of other southern women writers of her generation—an approach to her work that Smith herself would have eagerly sanctioned. The focus here is primarily on *Killers of the Dream*, a book that is highly confessional, as Smith herself acknowledges, and that contains the essence of her thinking about the South.

Lillian Smith was born on 12 December 1897 (the year Ellen Glasgow published her first novel) and spent the first eighteen years of her life in Jasper, Florida. Her father, Calvin Warren Smith, was a successful businessman in the naval stores industry until the outbreak of World War I when the European market for such stores declined, at which time he relocated his wife, Anne Hester Simpson Smith, and nine children to Rabun County in the north Georgia mountains. Near the small town of Clayton, Calvin Smith opened at first a summer hotel and then, in the same location on "Old Screamer Mountain," a summer camp for girls.

Lillian Smith's formative years made a strong impact on her sense of self and her nascent social consciousness; their diversity helped to distinguish her from other southern women of her age and class. Smith attended the local Piedmont College on a scholarship in 1915 but declined a second year in order to help her father manage his new business. After a year at Peabody Conservatory in Baltimore and a brief stint with the Student Nursing Corps in 1918, Smith accepted a teaching post as principal of a two-room schoolhouse in the small mountain community of Tiger, Georgia. In 1919 she returned for three years to Peabody where, like Carson McCullers, she studied to become a concert pianist, a goal that she, again like McCullers, eventually abandoned, but perhaps most significant in terms of the writer she eventually became are the three years, 1923–25, that Smith spent in Huchow, China, as a music teacher at a Methodist mission school. As Anne Loveland points out, "The young woman who had shocked Clayton by being the first to bob her hair and wear short skirts was completely unprepared for the cultural and intellectual shock of China. . . . Her political consciousness was awakened for the first time as she observed the operation of European colonialism and the aftermath of the Chinese Revolution of 1911 and 1912 and as she heard and read about Mahatma Gandhi's fight for Indian independence" (11–12). In China, Smith had the opportunity to observe parallels between the Orient and her own southern home and to read widely in Eastern philosophy and in the literature by and on Freud, the man who would become germane to her own psychological approach to the South and its problems. Smith returned to Clayton in 1925 to operate her father's camp. Here she instituted a progressive mode of education that was by no means the order of the day; her techniques, which were rooted in experimental play acting, stressed creativity, downplayed competition, and sensitized her camper-students to the complexity of all human needs: sex, race, and the workings of Southern Tradition were not exempt from Smith's curriculum.[1]

In 1936 Smith and Paula Snelling began publishing a little magazine, *Pseudopodia*, which would become the *North Georgia Review* in 1937 and finally *South Today* in 1942.[2] Smith had hired Snelling, a native of Georgia, to teach at the camp but quickly realized that they shared the same interests in literature, psychology, southern history, and culture; Snelling would remain a close friend and companion until Smith's death from cancer in 1966. Though Smith's biographer believes that the relationship between the two writers was not sexual, one might conclude otherwise. Whatever secrecy she retained about her own sexual practices, Smith's writings—particularly her novel *One Hour* (1959) with its positive depiction of a lesbian relationship—are proof that she had no fear of homosexuality.[3]

In an introductory note to their small quarterly—which would eventually see a circulation of over ten thousand—Smith and Snelling explained the significance of the pseudopod as "a temporary and tender projection of the nucleus of the inner-self, upon the success of whose gropings the nucleus is entirely dependent for its progress and sustenance" (quoted in White and Sugg xii). Their concern with the self, with its human right to grow unfettered by the walls of segregation—racial or sexual—would be the guide in their endeavor to provide a forum for liberal dissent in the South. There were few dimensions of the southern experience that Smith and Snelling failed to address. They published both white and black writers and were especially receptive to writers who had yet to make their reputations.

In her own column, "Dope with Lime," as well as in many articles and reviews and subsequent books, Smith would isolate the splits she believed characterized the dominant thinking of the South's spokesmen—splits that she would define in *Killers of the Dream* as ruptures between the spirit and the body, between human rights and states' rights, between southern churches and Christianity, between people and humanity. Yet as Smith herself realized, she too was the victim of a similar split, a strong divided impulse within her own psyche that she would spend most of her adult life attempting to reconcile. In letters and interviews throughout her career, Smith referred to the conflict between the "Mary" and "Martha" sides of her nature: Mary was Smith's "creative daemon," Martha her conscience (quoted in Loveland 13).

In a different mood, and in another letter, Smith claims that she was "a creative writer, *not* a propagandist nor a reformer nor a person primarily interested in public affairs" (quoted in Loveland 141). Yet for all her protestations, Smith could not be content with producing only works like her second novel, *One Hour* (1959), in which the issue of racial segregation is sublimated into the skewed interpersonal relationships that form the drama and conflict of that book. She did not always want to admit it, but Smith was a propagandist, a reformer, and a person interested in public affairs, and she could never fully resist the inclination to address her concerns head on. It is probable, however, that this conflict was the very basis of Smith's strength as an artist, for it led her ultimately to formulate a theory of nonfiction prose that enabled her to produce works that fully demonstrated her insistence that nonfiction can be "as creative and full of art and poetry as fiction." This statement is taken from a letter in which Smith addresses the Mary/Martha split. "I must admit the 'Martha' in me . . . is always pushing the 'Mary' aside to clean up the messes, to feed the starving," Smith said to a writer with *The Atlanta Constitution*, "but sooner or later, Mary slips inside Martha and shows her how to take the human 'problems' and transmute them into poetry and art of a sort, at least; and maybe, now and then, into something really valid and enduring" (quoted in Loveland 235).

Smith wrote her best-selling *Strange Fruit* (1944) while editing *South Today*. She had previously produced other works of fiction, one a thinly disguised account of her stay in China which, because their explicit autobiographical elements had the potential to embarrass her family, she finally chose not to publish—a regrettable decision; the manuscripts were destroyed in a fire that burned her home in 1955. *Strange Fruit* is, of course, the work that made Smith's reputation. Set in the fictional town of Maxwell, Georgia (a.k.a. Jasper, the site of Smith's childhood), the novel presents the problematic love affair between a white man, Tracy Deen, son of a wealthy doctor, and Nonnie Anderson, a young African-American woman educated at a college modeled on Spellman in Atlanta. Tracy's dominating mother and his own lack of will lead him to abandon Nonnie for a more conventional arrangement. The novel culminates in a lynching. Left pregnant, Nonnie is avenged by her brother who kills Tracy and then flees north. By an ironic twist, the man lynched for the murder is Henry McIntosh, Tracy's foster brother.

This synopsis does not convey the force of Smith's narrative, nor does it suggest anything about the poetic quality of her prose. In his perceptive review for the *New Republic*, Malcolm Cowley noted that Smith "writes as a native Georgian, proud of her old and rather distinguished family, devoted to the South as a whole and fond of her neighbors in the little town where the crime took place. At the same time, her sympathies lie with the Negroes in their ramshackle houses beyond the railroad tracks. She violently rejects the myth of their inferiority, together with the whole social fabric it implies" (320). Cowley is right to read the novel as an indictment of a "whole social fabric" and to note further that Smith shows how "history, folkways, economics, religion, even the weather and pure accident" all converge in the moment of the lynching. In her review for *The Nation*, Diana Trilling made similar observations but focused more pointedly on the way the novel handles that "touchiest" of all race problems: miscegenation. Trilling says that Smith does not indicate that Tracy and Nonnie must marry: "They never do marry, of course; and Miss Smith knows they never could marry. . . . Yet as their love story unfolds, the issue forces itself upon us: why in the world can they not marry? What is this difference in color which is admittedly no bar to love but so unassailably a bar to marriage? And even our vaunted Northern liberalism begins to look unpleasantly like hypocrisy" (342).

Cowley and Trilling did not represent the entire chorus of critical comment. Shortly after *Strange Fruit* had become a popular and vehemently debated topic of conversation, having generated as much controversy as any work of its time, Smith provided a self-reflexive piece, "Personal History of *Strange Fruit*," for *The Saturday Review of Literature* in which, without naming names, she responded to the critics' charges before tracing the origins of the novel and the central impulse that prompted her to write it. "There are two forces in every reader that an author cannot long remain unaware of," Smith writes at the opening of this essay, "a resistance to knowledge of self and a consuming curiosity about people" (9). That Smith places such high value on the self in this early reflective piece is indicative of the importance it would assume in later works. After noting that she is not a writer who can produce the kind of literature that strikes a balance in which "knowledge of self rises no higher than one's toleration, and knowledge of others reaches no deeper than one's credulity," Smith then dissects, with a potent dose of irony, the chief objections to her novel: its dismissal by some white critics as protest literature, a "problem novel"; its "re-appraisals" by leftist periodicals that had published favorable reviews before offering their reconsiderations; its explosive meaning for "the lunatic fringe of the fascist groups and the White supremacy crowd" (Smith noted that Eugene Talmadge's paper, the *Hapeville Statesman*, called it a "literary corncob" and added in a parenthetical aside that "you may or may not know the varied uses to which the corncob is put in our South"); and its ban in Boston by men who were "not to be outdone by Dixie demagogues"—a ban lifted by Franklin Roosevelt at the urging of his wife Eleanor, a friend and early admirer of Smith's work.[4]

Smith's tone changes in the second part of this essay as she reflects on the genesis of the novel and its roots in her earliest memories of Jasper, Florida, with its "white mill town, colored mill town, little white church, little colored church—and one big commissary for all" (10). The music Smith heard as a small child from her own black nurse, she also hears as an adolescent from the unpainted black church. Alerting her to the "invisible wall between human beings" (10), it is a sound that accompanies Smith on the journey that enabled her to pierce the disguised meanings of terms like "segregation" and catchwords such as "Jim Crow" and the "Negro problem." Smith's travels bring her full circle to Maxwell: "And I wrote down in *Strange Fruit* what I found there. I thought of my book as a fable about a son in search of a mother [a significant variation on a well-known archetype], about a race in search of surcease from pain and guilt—both finding what they sought in death and destruction" (10).

Though Smith's "Personal History of *Strange Fruit*" is significant for what it implies about her own understanding of the novel that brought her to the general public's attention, one of its most intriguing components is the way it prefigures her work to come. With this piece one can see Smith moving in the direction that would lead her to *Killers of the Dream*. In the following passage, she seems to be anticipating the book that would follow *Strange Fruit*:

> To understand what is troubling the white race so deeply . . . one might have to take a long journey that would lead down interesting by-paths. We might have to look long and hard at certain road signs: at Calvinism, monogamy, at the Western small family, at the high esteem Nordic culture puts on "sex purity" which in practice becomes a regressive displacement of honor on autoeroticism instead of mature genitality. We might have to look also at the Protestant God-the-Father image in contrast to the Catholic Mary-Mother-of Christ; and we might need to travel to countries where love and mature sex life are honorable and race prejudice is dishonorable. . . . We might have to look at the whole of white culture and travel backward in time far beyond that date when the first Negro was enslaved by the first white Christian. (10)

These by-paths and others she discovered would become the focus of Smith's attention as she planned and wrote *Killers of the Dream*, a work that, like *Strange Fruit*, grew out of two intersecting journeys: the one that took her back to her life as a child and the one that led her forward, beyond the constrictions of her southern childhood world.[5]

Anne Loveland notes that Smith "was not unwilling to accept the value *Strange Fruit* conferred on her as an authority on the South and race relations—and to avail herself of the wider forum now open to her" (80). After she suspended publication of *South Today* in 1945, Smith began to appear more regularly in liberal periodicals like *The Nation* and the *New Republic*, and she found herself in demand as a lecturer. Smith expanded on previous themes during this period and she began probing even deeper into the psychology of racism, especially that of her native South. One article in particular deserves attention. In September 1944, Smith published a piece in the *New Republic* under the title "Addressed to White Liberals," a piece that should be read in conjunction with her self-reflective essay on *Strange Fruit*; like the earlier essay, Smith's subsequent "address" clearly anticipates the polemical feature of her writing that would be so pronounced in *Killers of the Dream*.

"There are many among us who think of segregation as merely a

Southern tradition, a Southern 'custom' that grew out of poverty, out of certain economic patterns, out of certain racial dilemmas, when in reality segregation is an ancient psychological mechanism used by men the world over whenever they want to shut themselves away from problems which they fear and do not feel they have the strength to solve" (331). Smith wants southern liberals in particular to understand the logic of her equations: segregation, which is southern tradition, is more a way of death than a way of life; it is not only "cultural schizophrenia, bearing a curious resemblance to the schizophrenia of individual personality" (331), it is also a form of "spiritual lynching" where both "the lynched and the lynchers are our own people, ourselves, our *children*" (333). Hence Smith urges other liberals, who must take the initiative, to do more than merely recognize the problem; she desires a radical shift in their attention from the so-called "Negro problem" to the white man's "deep-rooted needs that have caused him to seek those strange, regressive satisfactions that are derived from worshipping his own skin-color." The core of Smith's argument resides in her belief that "the white man himself is one of the world's most urgent problems today; not the Negro, not other colored races. We whites must learn to *confess* this" (331, emphasis added).

Killers of the Dream would become Smith's personal confession; it would also develop in fuller detail the antigradualist stance that she takes in her address to white liberals, as well as her belief—perhaps the one thing she shared with the influential Agrarians—that "man is not an economic or political unit," that "hard as it is to acknowledge, the simple truth is that the South's and the nation's racial problems cannot be solved by putting a loaf of bread, a book and a ballot in everyone's hand"; literacy, like the ballot, may be a mode of political and economic empowerment, but for Smith these things will mean little "so long as we refuse to acknowledge [African-Americans] as human beings in *need of that which makes them human*" ("White Liberals" 332). Smith knew that she was addressing men like Hodding Carter and Virginius Dabney who, unlike herself, could not find the courage to oppose segregation. Smith knew also that she was providing an alternative to the Agrarians, a group of writers who had failed to address the real meanings of segregation in their well-known social critique, and whose silence and complicity necessitated that liberals, too, take their stand.

At the conclusion of his review of *Strange Fruit*, Malcolm Cowley said, "Miss Smith seems to lack the specifically literary gifts of William Faulkner, let us say, or Carson McCullers; and it is possible that her talents will lead her eventually into some other field than the novel" (322). Cowley's observation now seems prophetic. Smith did return to the novel with *One Hour* (1959), a work that grew out of her dismay at the excesses of McCarthyism, but most of her work after *Strange Fruit* represents a new kind of literary nonfiction. Kathleen Miller is right to note that Smith's work often "defies easy categorization" and that this problem is one of several, including Smith's "intuitive, lyrical approach," that caused and perhaps still causes a confusion of reader response (278). Smith's last book, *Our Faces, Our Words* (1964), is a series of photographs and nine monologues by fictional men and women in the civil rights movement, plus an epilogue in which Smith speaks as herself. Some readers, as Loveland observes, thought the monologues were literal transcriptions of original sources, a reaction that annoyed Smith, who believed the book had been misread in a number of ways and, in a despondent moment, admitted in a letter to a friend, "Maybe I should have written it straight, not in the quite, half-creative way I used" (quoted in Loveland 253).

Whatever her misgivings about this late work, as an artist Smith savored the opportunity to experiment with literary forms, and her output is diverse. In addition to *Killers of the Dream* and her book of monologues, Smith's nonfiction includes *The Journey* (1954), a philosophical meditation that grew out of a trip she took back to the small Florida town of her youth; *Memory of a Large Christmas* (1962), a personal reminiscence of some of the less painful memories of her childhood; and, not the least significant, *Now Is the Time* (1955), a work Smith described as a "tract, deliberately written as one" (quoted in Loveland 121), a small book she intended "to change minds and behavior" as she prepared the South to accept the Supreme Court's 1954 decision to integrate the public schools. Smith's "pamphlet" is an explicit piece of propaganda; it provides her rationale for desegregation—"this ordeal of school integration can become for the entire nation a magnificent opportunity for growth, for soul-searching, for discovery of important things" (*Now Is the Time* 15)—and it includes Smith's answers to twenty-five basic questions, ranging from "Is not education better than legislation?" to "If God wanted the races to mix, why didn't He make us all the same color?" Smith's reply to the latter question is indicative of the relish she took in dismantling the traditional and unquestioned notions of her Bible Belt South: "If God had not wanted people of different colors to mate, why didn't He make it biologically impossible for them to do so?" (108).

Kathleen Miller reminds us that Smith had planned for *Killers of the Dream* to be an informative book much like *Now Is the Time*, but as it took shape it also "began to assume a different, more probing character, more of the nature of personal confession" (284). Still, as Miller and others have observed, the book, which appeared five years after *Strange Fruit*, firmly established Smith's status as a social commentator and, in Miller's words, "a crusader against racial injustice" (285). Miller makes an observation that is crucial to an understanding of Smith's subsequent reputation as a social reformer: "As a book of nonfiction which starkly revealed the roots of racism as well as its cultural manifestation, *Killers* could not be dismissed as fiction, and the difference was not lost on its readers" (286). In effect the book did something for Smith that she feared; it established her in the public mind as a "Martha" rather than a "Mary" figure.

Even those readers who accepted Martha's diagnosis did not always know how to classify her new work, and the same is true of Smith's recent critics. Louise Blackwell and Frances Clay, the two women Smith chose as her biographers, take a less admiring view of the work than subsequent critics; they see its elliptical structure as evidence of weak organization but claim that the book is nonetheless "valuable as Miss Smith's personal memoir, written when she was fifty-two years of age and while she was still enjoying fame and fortune as a result of publishing *Strange Fruit* (98–99). Morton Sosna calls *Killers of the Dream* a nonfictional sequel to *Strange Fruit*, "an autobiographical, historical, and psychological examination of the triumph of white supremacy of the New South," a work in which its author "became more explicit about what it meant to be a white woman in the South" (195). Richard King refers initially to the work as Smith's autobiography but later claims that, because it omits much of what usually goes into an autobiography—it is "strangely silent on her personal relationships and vague on the texture of family life"—*Killers* is only "an autobiography of sorts, or better a meditation upon the intersection of personal and regional experience" (*Southern Renaissance* 186, 192). Fred Hobson avoids both "autobiography" and "memoir"; rather, he says *Killers* is the first of Smith's major works in a personal, confessional, and non-dramatic vein: "Of all Smith's books, this is the boldest, the most starkly revealing—perhaps the harshest portrait of the South by a notable white Southerner since Hinton Helper's *Impending Crisis*" (315).[6]

Those critics who have focused on the confessional element of *Killers of the Dream* have taken note of at least one of the book's two most significant dimensions. Like Pearl Buck, who called it "confession at its deepest and highest" (n. p.), these critics seem to understand that the confessional feature is something that sets it apart from many autobiographies. Like the *Confessions* of St. Augustine or Jean-Jacques Rousseau, or even like Norman Mailer's *Advertisements for Myself*, the confessional element of *Killers of the Dream* is not an end in itself; it serves a much larger purpose, in this case Smith's psychological exploration of the destructive ideology of white supremacy and her polemic against the South's divided way of life. A few months before Norton published *Killers of the Dream*, Smith wrote another self-reflective piece that she knew would create anticipation for her new work. "Why I Wrote 'Killers of the Dream' " appeared in Irita Van Doren's *Weekly Book Review* of the *New York Herald Tribune*. Here Smith explains that her interest in the South is more than a personal obsession. Rather the South "has become a symbol of something that must never be again" (2). Smith outlines in detail what she wanted to know by confronting the symbolic and mental constructs that had come to define her native region and that had nearly undermined her own sense of self. Like W. J. Cash, Smith viewed the mind of the South as something that could be explored even if it had failed to explore itself. She goes on to say that she wants to know the nature of fantasies, the defense mechanisms and "psychic fortifications" of this mind: "I want to know, too, why the Southern liberal is weak and the Southern demagogue has access to energies that carry through mammoth tasks for evil. I want to know what kind of children we grow in the South; and who put the Southern woman on her pedestal and why she crept down from it again. . . . I want to know why our region has, proportionately, not only the most churches of any region in the United States but the most murders, the most poverty, the highest rate of illiteracy, the lowest wages and the poorest health (2).

The list goes on, but Smith is quick to note that what she has discovered about the South is, but to a lesser degree, true of the Western world in general. She believes the answer to her questions are "surely worth searching for"; and she acknowledges that her own search, rooted as it is in personal memory, will take her to the confessional booth. By demystifying segregation—an "abstraction" in the truest sense—Smith wants to sensitize her readers to the "pulsating whole" of life. She "writes the South" in order to understand herself and to effect change. Without using the term itself, Smith acknowledges that *Killers of the Dream* is her confessional tract.

Smith grew tired of those readers who wanted to categorize or dismiss her book as a "Freudian interpretation of the South" (Long 37), yet at no point in *Killers of the Dream* does she underplay the significance of Freud in what Fred Hobson would call her "rage to explain."[7] The first fifty years of the twentieth century saw "more change in men's ways" than in the previous thousand years, but southerners at the midpoint of the century still attempted to live as if Freud, Einstein, and Marx had altered nothing at all. If Smith was drawn especially to Freud, it is because she was confronting a "tight inflexible mind that could not question itself" (153). For Smith the southern mind is synonymous with the mythic mind; southern aristocrats and residents of tobacco road alike knew it best not to probe too deeply, for "the dread of the mythic mind is," Smith contends, "no respecter of classes and— as is the way of the Anglo-Saxon—nearly everyone preferred to keep a safe distance from the profound depths of his own or another's nature" (208). More than any other thinker of her time, Freud enabled Smith to understand and subsequently crack the southerner's protective shield. The rhetoric of *Killers*, with its many references to "psychic fortifications" and "childhood memories long repressed," is indicative of both Smith's temperament and her debt to Freud. In a sense, Smith assumes Freud's role as psychoanalyst, as therapist; she isolates the sources of the South's psychosis in order to offer, if at times obliquely, a way of healing.

Smith's Freudian approach accounts in part for the elliptical structure of *Killers of the Dream*. Though the book is organized into fourteen thematically linked chapters with titles that cue the reader's expectations ("Custom and Conscience," "The Women," "Tobacco Road Is a Long Journey" and so on), there is a free-associational quality to Smith's writing and the book is deliberately repetitive, a complaint

made by many of its early critics. Often Smith will off-handedly intro-
duce a theme in one context and then return to it in a subsequent chapter where she gives it a different emphasis or fuller development. In
"Distance and Darkness," she explains how the southern male's exploitation of the South's women, the topic of a previous chapter, is mirrored in his thoughtless exploitation of the land. In "The Lessons," she
presents the concept of the unpardonable sin and the ideology it embodied for most rural southerners before further exploring this ideology in "Trembling Earth," a chapter devoted solely to the South's
highly visible religious rituals. The Freudian approach requires that
Smith return repeatedly to the same subjects in search of connections
that will enable her to understand the "sex-race-religion-economics
tangle" (146) and to position her own personal past within that of the
region.

An inward journey thus becomes the book's central motif (one that
Smith would balance by a literal journey in the subsequent book of that
title). Smith's memories take her first to the world of her childhood:
"In this South I lived as a child and now live. And it is of it that my
story is made. . . . Out of the intricate weaving of unnumbered threads,
I shall pick out a few strands, a few designs" (*Killers*, 27). What Smith
gives the reader is a distillation of her childhood world, a synthesis of
the contradictions she and others internalized. Smith learned, for instance, that she would have to outgrow her feelings for the black nurse
she loved as much as any other figure in her family (29); she learned
that it was "possible to be a Christian and white southerner simultaneously; to be a gentlewoman and an arrogant callous creature in the
same moment . . . to glow when the word *democracy* was used, and to
practice slavery from morning to night." Smith's explanation of how
she learned such things undergirds almost all her memories of the
South; she came to see that such behavior can be learned only if one
closes "door after door after door" until the mind is segregated from
the heart—and from reality (29).

   Since Smith's goal was not to produce an intimate autobiography
like Ellen Glasgow's *The Woman Within*, she says little about her parents. Smith prefaces the revised *Killers* with a dedication to the memory
of her mother and father "who valiantly tried to keep their nine children in touch with wholeness even though reared in a segregated cul-

ture" (7). What Smith discloses in her text, however, is that neither parent was plagued by the kind of self-criticism that unmasks moral contradictions: "The mother who taught me what I know of tenderness and love and compassion taught me also the bleak rituals of keeping Negroes in their 'place.' The father who rebuked me for an air of superiority toward schoolmates from the mill and rounded out his rebuke by gravely reminding me that 'all men are brothers,' trained me in the steel-rigid decorums I must demand of every colored male" (27).

In the one passage in which Smith does provide a more personal glimpse of her parents' lives, she draws a picture that resembles Glasgow's more detailed memories of her parents. The two writers delineate a pattern that, as Smith was well aware, defined a great many southern homes. Smith says that her mother, Anne Hester Simpson Smith, "was a wistful creature who loved beautiful things like lace and sunsets and flowers in a vague inarticulate way, and took good care of her children. We always knew this was not her world but one she accepted under duress. Her private world we rarely entered, though the shadow of it lay heavily on our hearts" (33). The reader recalls this account of Smith's mother when in a later chapter Smith analyzes the South's rigidly defined gender norms and the expected behavior of southern women who are or aspire to be southern ladies. As for her father, Calvin Warren Smith, he too was an example of the society that molded him and that he in turn had helped to maintain. Before relocating his family from north Florida to north Georgia, Smith's father had "owned large business interests, employed hundreds of colored and white laborers, paid them the prevailing low wages, worked them the prevailing long hours, built for them mill towns (Negro and white), built for each group a church, saw to it that religion was supplied free, saw to it that a commissary supplied commodities at a high price, and in general managed his affairs much as ten thousand other southern businessmen managed theirs" (33).

Smith does not fully understand the forces that brought her to an awareness of the contradictions in the South's way of life, nor does she understand exactly how she managed to open doors that either she or others had previously closed; her journey does not carry her that far: "Why I had the desire or the strength to open them, or what strange accident or circumstance opened them for me would require in the answering an account too long, too particular, too stark to make here"

(29). What she provides instead is one particular incident—a "paradigmatic moment," as Richard King would have it (*Southern Renaissance* 186)—that marked a significant change in her response to the customs of her native region. It is an incident very much in keeping with the confessional tone of Smith's book.

"A little white girl was found in the colored section of our town, living with a Negro family in a broken-down shack" (*Killers* 34–35). The women in Smith's mother's club decided that the child, Janie, must have been kidnapped, so, with the assistance of the town marshal, the child was taken from the black family and brought to live in Smith's home. She wore young Lillian's clothes, played with her dolls, and became her constant companion—for a brief period of time. Janie turned out to be black and was, of course, returned to the house where she was found. Smith knows that such an incident, which lay buried in her memory for thirty years, and which did not square with her conscience even at the time it occurred, is admittedly rare in the South or elsewhere; yet she also discerns that the incident with Janie was "an acting-out, a private production of a little script that is written on the lives of most southern children before they know words. Though they may not have seen it staged this way, each southerner has had his own private showing" (30).

Smith's theatrical metaphor is significant, and it connects this first chapter, "When I Was a Child," to the one that follows, "Custom and Conscience," in which Smith recounts the time when, many years later as director of the Laurel Falls Camp, she and her student-campers staged their own morality play "about Every Child who makes a journey through the universe to collect new experiences he may need in order to grow up" (43); but Every Child eventually discovers that his chosen companions—Conscience, Southern Tradition, Religion, and Science—cannot resolve the dilemma he creates when he states his desire to play with all of the earth's children. Religion and Science, seated in their separate balconies, are ineffectual forces in the face of custom and Southern Tradition, the clear antagonists of Smith's drama. Though the play concludes with the children banishing Southern Tradition to the wings of the stage before forming a circle and dancing together (a vivid contrast to the image of a rotted framework that opens the chapter), Smith acknowledges, "It was make-believe and we knew it. But we could not let our play die as so much that is young has died on that old wall, segregation" (50). Later the same evening, one of Smith's most dedicated students accuses her of teaching ideals that cannot be lived; the student tells her outright: "You've unfitted us for the South" (54).

This comment is Smith's indirect way of defining the goal of her confessional polemic. In response to the student, Smith offers a lengthy explanation of how the South came to be the way it was at the midpoint of the century. She provides a history of the Civil War and its legacy as the story of two brothers, "two bad consciences, each covering up its guilt and its greed, each insisting on its right to sin in its own way, each having economic and religious and psychological reasons for doing so" (62). Smith explains that she and her family were implicated in a way of life in which hostilities between the two regions were taken for granted. Phrases like "human rights" were "as remote as the moon on a blazing hot day to these white men stricken by their hatred for each other" (62).

· In her historical survey, Smith moves through the era of reconstruction to the development of the South's odious sharecropping system and on to what she calls a sort of "gentlemen's agreement" that emerged between the North and South, a tacit pact that called for a suspension of morals in the areas of race, money, and politics. Looking back on its past, Smith says that "it seems as if the whole white South suffered a moral breakdown." There were no gas chambers as in Germany, but Smith refuses to ignore the fact that "in those eighty years after the Civil War nearly five thousand human beings were *lynched*" (68). The lynchings became the symbolic ritual of white supremacy, an ideology reinforced by the silence of men—newspaper editors, ministers, and others—who had the resources and public forum to speak out more forcefully. Smith aims for balance in her reflections; there are things she loves about her native region, and she understands the inclination to remember only those features. She can also sympathize with the student who tells her it would be easier to do the right thing if only "you hated your family," for Smith sees in this statement the essence of something "the tortured southern liberal knows so well" (72–73).

The entirety of this chapter, "Unto the Third and Fourth Generation," is written as a direct address to the student who approaches Smith the night of the morality play; that is, Smith's allegorical condensation of southern history is presented within the framework of a teacher-student setting. A student of child psychology, Smith knew the didactic value of parables, fables, extended metaphors, and other such devices. As one of her earliest and best critics, Margaret Sullivan, has noted, Smith never uses allegory for its enigmatic qualities or as a way of disguising her views; rather, Smith's "subsequent ostracism" is an irrefutable indication that her message was always clear (13). In "The Role of the Poet in a World of Demagogues," a speech she gave in 1965 when she accepted the first Queen Esther Scroll awarded by the Women's Division of the American Jewish Congress, Smith claims that "only the poet can look beyond details at the total picture" (*Winner* 161); her analogical devices are a way of getting perspective on the larger picture. Though generally regarded as primary tools for the moralist, these devices do not work against Smith's psychological approach; they are, rather, the expression of what her inward journey has taken her to see.

The four chapters that comprise Part I of *Killers of the Dream* confront the problems and questions of childhood in "a region that values color more than children" (75). Smith concludes this introductory section of her book with a brief discussion of those young adults who lost faith in the ability of the South's politicians to affect change and who, as a result, turned to communism as a way out. Though she cannot approve of their decision to trade one mode of authority or one form of totalitarianism for another she finds equally appalling, Smith understands that some students have chosen this route because "in the strongest democracy on earth they were not free to live their ideals" (77). At this point in her narrative, Smith abandons her figurative devices and lets the words of ten southerners, all white men, speak for themselves. Included are passages from writings and speeches by men such as Senator Richard Russell, William Alexander Percy, and Hodding Carter, a self-proclaimed southern liberal who, as the following passage reveals, could nonetheless accommodate racial barriers: "I cannot emphasize one point too strongly. The white South is as united as 30,000,000 people can be in its insistence upon segregation. Federal action cannot change them. It will be tragic for the South, the Negro, and the nation itself if the government should enact and attempt to enforce any laws or Supreme Court decisions that would open the South's public gathering places to the Negro" (79).

Such comments expose the insidiousness of an ideology that men have chosen to defend even when it costs them poverty and jobs to do so, not to mention self-respect. These passages form a suitable preface to the subsequent chapters in which Smith moves from the global-regional picture to the particularities of sex, religion, race, gender, and economics—the tangle that constitutes her native South.

Each of the chapters in Part II, "The White Man's Burden," focuses on a specific issue or problem, though again, there are many repetitions, many cross-references. Smith begins Part II with a psychoanalytical probe of the lessons that undergird the life of a segregated culture. Her rhetorical device in this chapter is to give a firm but bleakly humorous voice to these lessons, each of which bleeds into and draws from the other. Hence, she concentrates not just on the segregation of races but also on the segregation of certain parts of the body from others: "By the time we were five years old we had learned, without hearing the words, that masturbation is wrong and segregation is right, and each had become a dread taboo that must never be broken, for we believed God, whom we feared and tried desperately to love, had made the rules concerning not only Him and our parents, but our bodies and Negroes" (83–84).

It is the first lesson, the one about God himself, that Smith says made the most significant impression: "We were told that he loved us, and then we were told that He would burn us in everlasting flames of hell if we displeased Him" (85). God in this lesson becomes another manifestation of authority—always the enemy for Smith—another embodiment of the forces that restrict creative maturation. It is here that Smith introduces the concept of the Unpardonable Sin, or rather the notion that all sins can be forgiven save one: blasphemy against the Holy Ghost. "What this sin was, what the 'Holy Ghost' was, no one seemed to know. Or perhaps even grown folks dared not say it aloud. But the implication was—and this was made plain—that if you did not tread softly you would commit it; the best way was never to question anything but always accept what you were told" (86). In the same vein, Smith notes that children were told not to question where babies come from—a command that does not sit well with Smith the budding feminist who sensed the fear that "little females might over-value their role in this drama of creation and, turning 'uppity' as we say in Dixie, forget their inferior place in the scheme of things" (88). With another pungent dose of sarcasm, Smith paraphrases the lesson on skin color: "Remember this: Your white skin proves that you are better than all other people on this earth. Yes, it does that. And does it simply because it is white—which, in a way, is a kind of miracle. But the Bible is full of miracles and it should not be too difficult for us to accept one more" (89).

At the heart of these lessons—Smith's clever way of demonstrating that ideology is something that must be taught and learned (and learned again and again)—is the necessity that "everything dark, dangerous, evil must be pushed to the rim of one's life"; segregation thus becomes "a logical extension of the lessons on sex and white supremacy and God" (90). All these lessons were reinforced for Smith and her generation by a simple configuration of "signs" placed above bodies as well as doors, bus stations, theatres, and drinking fountains. Such repression is evident in what Smith calls the "gothic curves" of southern emotions (85); less apparent, she implies, is the way repression on such a grand scale accounts for the lingering predominance in the South of names like *honey*, *sugar*, and *sweetie*. Those parents, rich and poor alike, who might have taken a less rigid mode of child rearing had it not been for the reinforcement of religion and southern tradition, were nonetheless human, Smith writes, and often indulged their children in "a startling fashion." She adds that "we were petted children, not puritans" and that "sugar-tit words and sugar-tit experiences too often made of our minds and manners a fatty tissue that hid the sharp rickety bones of our souls" (93).

Like Ellen Glasgow and Eudora Welty, Lillian Smith was drawn to the white revivalists who populated the landscape of her southern childhood; like these writers, Smith also rejected the anti-intellectual, excessively emotional, and often violent mode of religion that characterized the fundamentalist churches of the South and that reached an emotionally charged peak during their summer camp meetings. While Welty was attracted especially to the comic and larger-than-life dimension of the circuit-riding evangelists (a characteristic that also intrigued Flannery O'Connor, who nonetheless used their distorted behavior to show the essence of what she believed to be a genuine religious quest), Smith, once she worked through her childhood fear of a literal Hell, attempted to penetrate the ideology at the heart of a belief system that could condone segregation but dared not question itself. In her chapter

on the lessons about God and race, Smith uses the geological occurrence of "trembling earth" as a metaphor for her interpretation of the
South's religious rituals, of its alarming religiosity.

Smith notes that she was no different from other southerners for
whom going to church was the "long troubled journey" rather than the
transforming inner journey and "seemed never to end but went on
from Sunday to Sunday" (100). What stands out in Smith's memory is
the brush-arbor summer revival meeting with its combination of entertainment and terror. Sanctioned by almost all of the South's major denominations, these meetings provided a much-needed break from
small-town boredom and from the isolation of a society cut off from
the outside world. For Smith, the evangelists were not unlike the
South's political demagogues who also "enjoyed people" and who
"won allegiance by bruising and then healing a deep fear within men's
minds" (103). Unlike the hypocrites they became in most of the literature devoted to them, the revivalists "were men whose powerful instincts of sex and hate were woven together into a sadism that would
have devastated their lives and broken their minds had they acknowledged it for what it was. Instead, they bound it into verbal energy and
with this power of the tongue they drove men in herds toward heaven"
(104).

Smith's memory of these men also includes the ironies that highlight
the significance of religion in the South's tangle of sex, race, religion,
and economics. While the summer revivalists were "unafraid to explore the forbidden places of man's heart," they nonetheless espoused
a narcissistic religion that concerned itself solely with the body and the
soul. "Wherever their answers came from," Smith writes, "that place
did not send them answers to the problems of poverty, of race segregation, unions, wages, illness and ignorance, war, and waste of forest
and soil and human relations" (105). With irony Smith remembers the
importance of the altar call that concluded a nightly service, an event
that could go on for hours. "Strangely enough," Smith recalls, "I cannot remember one time when the banker or millowner or principal of
the school, or cotton broker or politician went to the altar. They were
always among 'the saved' " (106). Smith's analysis moves in and out of
the confessional mode; she remembers, for example, how difficult it
was for her personally to feel saved: "My younger sister, more certain
of her place in the family, was naturally more certain of her place in

heaven, and rarely went to the altar. I remember how I admired her restraint" (110).

Near the beginning of this chapter, Smith says it is not easy to understand the hypnotic power of the revival meetings "unless we let our minds fill with echoes of distance and darkness and ignorance and violence and worn-out bodies and land" (101). She concludes the chapter with an evocative description of the little town and the swamp that served as a physical setting for these communal dramas of fear, sin, and guilt. With its snakes, alligators, water lillies, cypresses, underground rivers and quicksand, and with its earth that literally trembled, the swamp became "a giant reflection of our own hearts" (112). It provided the symbolic backdrop against which Smith learned and, more significantly, unlearned her lessons.

Smith uses another extended metaphor in the pivotal chapter that follows, "Three Ghost Stories." Here she explains how the lessons of her region undermined one another: "The raveling out of what had been woven so tightly was usually a slow process. . . . However it happened, it was not long in the little southerner's life before the lessons taught him as a Christian, a white man, an American, a puritan, began to contradict each other" (114). Again Smith draws from her own childhood experience to illustrate the unraveling. As she points out, it was not uncommon for southerners of the middle to upper class to employ a black nurse, or Mammy, a woman who "always knew her 'place,' but neither she nor her employers could have defined it" (128).[8] Smith's nurse was her beloved Aunt Chloe:

> In my home, our nurse lived in the back yard beyond Mother's flower garden in a small cabin whose interior walls were papered with newspapers. Much of my very young life was spent there. I was turned over to her when a new baby took my place in the family. And because I seemed not to have the stamina to adjust to this little intruder I protested by refusing to eat and kept up a food strike so long that they grew alarmed and called in the doctor although Aunt Chloe looked on, they say, with obvious scorn at their panic. . . . The story is that Aunt Chloe tried food after food all of which I rejected, then studying the pale young face before her for a little, she took the food, chewed it first in her mouth, put it in mine and I swallowed it promptly. (130)

Smith adds that she soon flourished on "this fine psychological diet" and that "such a relationship with such a woman is not to be brushed off by the semantic trick of labelling her a 'nurse' " (130).

Yet to conceal the true nature of such a relationship is exactly what southern tradition demanded; and such a demand took its toll on the southerner's psyche. Again Smith alludes to Freud: "this dual relationship which so many white southerners have had with two mothers, one white and one colored and each of a different culture that centered in different human values, makes the Oedipus complex seem by comparison almost a simple adjustment" (131).[9] Of course this relationship, that of the white child and his or her "surrogate" mother—the beloved black nurse—is only one of the three "ghost" relationships that Smith explores; she gives equal attention to the relationship between the white man and the black woman, and the relationship between the white man and his "colored" children, the physical evidence of these unacknowledged liaisons that, as Smith notes, were nonetheless pervasive throughout the South.

It is generally agreed that Smith is the first of the South's analysts to grapple with the full complexity of the powerful link between race and sex in maintaining segregation. In figurative terms, she contrasts the puritanical and patriarchal "front-yard" world of the white man to the matriarchal and less sexually guilt-ridden "back-yard" world of the black woman. It is her belief that the South's white men "succeeded in developing a frigidity in their white women that precluded the possibility of mutual satisfaction" (120); and further, "The more trails the white man made to back-yard cabins, the higher he raised his white wife on her pedestal when he returned to the big house. The higher the pedestal, the less he enjoyed her whom he had put there, for statues after all are only nice things to look at" (121). Such a passage indicates why Smith did not endear herself to her fellow southerners, who could or would not accept white supremacy and segregation and their attendant evils as the fundamental facts of southern tradition.

Smith did not stop here, however. A repeated emphasis of her Freudian approach is that "no part of this memory can be understood without recalling all of it" (136). Thus in the chapter that follows "Three Ghost Stories," she turns her attention to the South's white women. Even the region's liberals, Smith argues, "did not see what segregation had done to the South's women, pushed away on that lonely pedestal called Sacred Womanhood" (137). Smith presents herself as someone who can see—who has taken the effort to see—and whose depth of vision enables her to categorize, in the manner of a sociologist like John Dollard, whose *Caste and Class in a Southern Town* (1938) she greatly admired, at least five different types of white southern women who had emerged by the midpoint of the century. From hindsight one can see that Smith paved the way for later historians whose subsequent studies have in the main verified Smith's ground-breaking if less academically motivated considerations.[10]

Smith's aim in "The Women" is to show the disparity between the idealized southern lady—genteel, innocent, dependant, submissive, the ultimate representation of racial purity—and the reality of southern women's lives in the face of a Victorian ideal that took root in the North as well as the South but that lingered longer and with even graver consequences in its southern setting. Smith's subject thus becomes not the gender norms themselves but the different reactions and behavior patterns of southern women whose lives have been "culturally stunted by a region that still pays rewards to simple mindedness in women" and provides them with little defense against such blandishment (141).[11]

Smith first identifies the women who could not cope with a blatant sexual double standard and the demands it placed on their lives: "It was as if these women never quite left the presence of the dead but mourned gently and continuously a loss they could not bear to know the extent of. Unable to look at the ugly fact of their life, they learned to see mysterious things the rest of us could not see" (139). It is a description that echoes Glasgow's depiction of her mother. Such women, though still visible, were actually few in number. Smith contends that the bulk of the South's women "turned away from the ugliness which they felt powerless to cope with and made for themselves and their families what they called a 'normal' life" (141). These women created homes where "food and flowers were cherished, and old furniture, and the family's past (screened of all but the pleasing and the trivial)," homes where neither sex nor segregation was ever mentioned (141). Though she does not identify her own mother as one of these empty or hollow women, it seems clear from Smith's description in her opening chapter that Anne Hester Simpson Smith was herself the model for Smith's analysis. "With their gardens and their homes," Smith observes, "these women tried to shut out evil, and sometimes succeeded only in sheltering their children from good. . . . It was as if one question asked aloud might, like a bulldozer, uproot their garden of fantasies and tear it out of time, leaving only naked bleeding reality to live with" (142–43).

Though she devotes only one paragraph to those southern women who rejected their "womanly qualities" in an attempt to be treated like men—she notes that "there was no comfortable place for such women in the South, though a few lived in every town" (140–41)—Smith gives significant attention to her fourth group, the reformers (what she calls the "lady insurrectionists"), women like Dorothy Tilly, who dared to vacate the pedestal and who "went forth to commit treason against a southern tradition set up by men who had betrayed their mothers, sometimes themselves, and many of the South's children white and mixed, for three long centuries" (144). Smith is drawn to these women because she herself is an inheritor of their goals. Church women who would have denied any taint of radicalism in their behavior, these women held what Smith perceived to be combative devices, including the power of "spiritual blackmail." "All they had to do was drop their little bucket into any one of numerous wells of guilt dotting the landscape and splash it around a bit" (145).

Of the many progressive organizations formed by southern women during these early decades of the twentieth century, Smith is drawn especially to the Association of Southern Women for the Prevention of Lynching, founded in 1930, the same year the Agrarians published their manifesto. "It may seem incredible," Smith points out, "but the custom of lynching had rarely been questioned by the white group" (146). She adds that few could have been prepared for the shock of a visible protest against "the sleazy thing called 'chivalry' " and a blatant attack on the Ku Klux Klan at a time when little protest had been raised against "this group from whom Hitler surely learned so much" (147). Like Anne Firor Scott, who traces the beginnings and evolution of southern women's activism in her seminal *The Southern Lady: From Pedestal to Politics, 1830–1930* (1970), Smith views the many women reformers of the South as evidence of a widespread if not always vocal dissatisfaction with the region's patriarchal structures.

Yet Smith knows that, unfortunately, she has not yet exhausted the full range of reactions to the male-authored ideals of southern womanhood; she makes no attempt to disguise the presence of a fifth group, not so few in number, that, like many of the South's men, "found it easier to cultivate hate than love" (149–50). These women "armored their children against their fantasies and feelings, preparing them for human relations as if for a cruel medieval battle"; these were the women who, ironically, became the "vigilant guardians of a southern tradition which in guarding they often, unbeknownst to their own minds, avenged themselves on with a Medea-like hatred" (151).

It is productive to read this chapter on the South's white women in conjunction with an essay Smith and Paula Snelling coauthored for *South Today* in 1941. As the nation entered World War II, the two editors turned much of their attention to international matters. In "Man Born of Woman," Smith and Snelling maintained that it is man's natural proclivity to make war. Women, they argued, "are less given to symbolism" and do not partake in "the sacrifice of tree to forest which man in his allegiance to abstraction has incorporated into his soul" (*Winner* 182, 183). Smith's and Snelling's essay took a harsh view of man's destructive energies as well as the civilization man has made, and they insisted that "the sex which has to spend nine months in the begetting of each human being would have less time to devote to the service of death, were it equally inclined, than the sex of whom nine minutes are required" (182). Yet while the two authors claimed that woman "will perish with her host unless she can aid him in liberating himself from his seductor death" (183), they also believed that women have not learned much during the course of modern time. "It is an indictment of woman in her role of mother," they argued, "that millions upon millions of her sons today turn to war and violence as the 'way out' of their deep trouble" (184). A more surprising indictment was their contention that it was a man, Sigmund Freud, rather than a woman who discovered the secrets of and articulated much of our knowledge about childhood. Smith and Snelling urged modern woman to use the knowledge of psychoanalysis and "learn again the ancient ways of the female, the subtle strengths of her sex—birthrights she has sold for the pottage of a specious 'equality' in a man's world" (185).

Much of this argument Smith extends in her discussion of the South's women in *Killers of the Dream*. Here Smith argues, "Colored and white women stirring up a lemon-cheese cake for the hungry males in the household looked deep into each other's eyes and understood their common past" (144). White women, Smith claims, knew intuitively "that all a woman can expect from lingering on exalted heights is a hard chill afterward" (143). The key difference between this treatise and the earlier essay is that Smith is more reluctant in 1949 to blame women for cooperating with their oppressors or for the part they have played in "splitting the soul in two" (153). Southern women and men alike were born into "a culture that lacked almost completely the self-changing power that comes from honest criticism" (152). In *Strange Fruit*, Smith had been particularly harsh on Alma, the dominating and obsessive mother of Tracy Deen; in *Killers of the Dream*, she presents a revised perspective and adds a new twist to the phrase that provided her with the title of her first novel. "Sometimes we blame Mom too much for all that is wrong with her sons and daughters. After all, we might well ask, who started the grim mess? Who long ago made Mom and her sex 'inferior' and stripped her of her economic and political and sexual rights? Who, nearly two thousand years ago, said, 'It is good for a man not to touch a woman. . . . The patriarchal protest against the ancient matriarch has borne strange fruit through the years" (153, Smith's ellipses). These remarks, which anticipate a speech Smith gave at Stetson University in 1963, "Woman Born of Man" (*Winner* 201–11), also anticipate the work of later feminist theorists who would turn to Jacques Lacan rather than Freud to explain the rift between feminine desire and the "law of the fathers."

The chapters that comprise the second part of Smith's book, especially "Three Ghost Stories" and "The Women," are the ones that have generated the most debate and perhaps the most emotionally charged response from Smith's readers and critics. Caroline Dillman has complained that one of the chief methodological impediments to the study of southern women is the frequent absence of both miscegenation and a victimizing sexual double standard in their works. These are, however, the topics that Smith places at the very center of her analysis. As Dillman observes: "Lillian Smith—considered a deviant and stigmatized because of it—was one of the few women prior to the 1970s to write about the continuation of repression of women's sexuality and exploitation of Southern women in the 20th century. Most female writers did not write about women and sexuality at all. If they dared to do so, ostracism and stigmatization were the results" (5).

Richard King, in *A Southern Renaissance*, is right to focus on the value of Smith's confrontational and psychoanalytic approach in what he calls her effort to change the "essential mind set" of her native region (183). As King points out, Smith's approach emerged from her gradual understanding that southern tradition amounts to little more than "a composite of denial, avoidance, splitting, rationalization, idealization, resistance—the classic compendium of defense mechanisms which masked the past and present of the region and the self" (184). King argues that, while one cannot expect to verify Smith's analysis with "proof in any common meaning of the term," there is enough evidence to suggest that "the individual and collective fantasies of white Southerners did point to a rough plausibility in her analysis" and that "at best she offered a powerfully suggestive understanding of the incredibly complex vicissitudes of desire in the Southern cultural-social order" (190).[12]

What King objects to in Smith's analysis of the southern woman is what he labels an "inverted sentimentality" in her image of the black mother; like Fred Hobson and Morton Sosna, King believes that even though Smith is right to reject the tradition of the white fathers, she did not "do justice to the psychological and emotional damage that blacks had suffered" (191). Fred Hobson for his part rightly complains that Smith "may, finally, in her eagerness to indict the Southern man for his lack of sensitivity, have overestimated the wisdom and sensitivity of Southern woman. Not all Southern women in 1962 [a year after Smith published her revised edition of *Killers of the Dream*], not even most, 'smelled the death in the word *segregation*' " (322).

The last two parts of *Killers of the Dream* are somewhat less confrontational and present fewer episodes from Smith's own childhood. The four chapters that comprise Part III, "Giants in the Earth," address the historical forces that produced a segregated way of life in the South along with the loss of human potential that has been the result of the South's divided culture. Again Smith reiterates how difficult it is to understand the southerner's way of thinking without a willingness "to look for not 'one cause' but a series of causes and effects spiralling back through the centuries" (166). Smith knows that it would be foolish to write about the South without an understanding of its physical setting. Thus in "Distance and Darkness," she provides a psychological exploration of the southern landscape while highlighting the complexity and force of the mythic mind. Though this chapter takes the reader through a world of southern demagogues and corrupt politicians with their "drug of white supremacy" (165) and their manipulation of the poor southern white, and though it denounces the South's early settlers as an "aggressive, wasteful and greedy" group of men who "stripped the soil and the forest of richness"—an "outward expression, an acting out, too often, of their secret feelings about women" (168–69)—Smith nevertheless concludes the chapter by expressing her belief in the power of men and women to find new ways of life and to bring about cultural renewal. "There is toughness of mind in Southerners, and tremendous vitality," Smith insists. "Most are not sick people nor cruelly perverse; they are starved. Most are conformists rather than idol worshippers. They can be appealed to on a moral level" (174).

In light of this comment (one that is consistent with the guarded optimism expressed in the book's closing section), it is difficult to accept Fred Hobson's conclusion, "Despite her occasional profession of love for her homeland, the fear and the shame are what one finally is left with" (322). It is important to remember that Smith could easily have chosen to live outside the South and not confront its most alarming excesses, but unlike many of her fellow southern writers (even the Fugitive-Agrarians, most of whom migrated North), Smith chose to remain and live as an artist and citizen activist in her home state. If she is as harsh on her fellow southern liberals as she is on the southern demagogues, it is because she believes the liberals, with the exception of notable examples such as Franklin Roosevelt, have failed to provide effective moral leadership. Her conclusion to "Distance and Darkness" expresses what may be her deepest belief in the rural South and its people: "I fear the wool-hat boys and girls far less than I do the educated leaders who fear them and therefore desert them in their need—and the demagogic leaders who shoulder the people intimately but exploit them ruthlessly" (174). Smith knows of course that her book would not be read by the "wool-hat boys and girls" but that her real audience would be those "educated" readers who would either accept, defy, or—worse—ignore her challenge.

Smith follows "Distance and Darkness" with a reprint of an article she wrote for *South Today* in 1943, "Two Men and a Bargain." Smith's grimly humorous parable focuses on "Mr. Rich White" and "Mr. Poor White" and their tacit agreement to divide one another's labors. Better educated than his counterpart, Mr. Rich White will control the economy while Mr. Poor White takes on his black brother; in his miserable poverty, Mr. Poor White must believe that he is better than someone.

Such a bargain ensures a demented form of psychological gratification for the poor white as he or she is manipulated into carrying out the rituals that sustain the ideology of white supremacy. Here is the voice of Mr. Rich White: "If you don't have much to do, and begin to get worried-up inside and mad with folks, and you think it'll make you feel a little better to lynch a nigger occasionally, that's OK by me too; and I'll fix it with the sheriff and the judge and the court and our newspapers so you won't have any trouble afterwards; but *don't expect me to come to the lynching, for I won't be there*" (177). Though she flatly rejected communism as a solution to the South's social inequities, what her parable provides is something close to a witty Marxist critique of an exploitative social structure, though one editorial writer for *The Atlanta Constitution* preferred to call it Smith's "orgasm."[13]

In the chapter that follows, "Tobacco Road Is a Long Journey," Smith offers a more straightforward history of the Jim Crow system, but her thesis is still the same, only here she indicts the North as well as the South for its complicity in a nationwide sacrifice of American democracy. She gives particular attention to what she calls the Compromise of 1876, the goal of which "was to return white supremacy to the South eleven years after the war to free the slaves, in payment for political and economic concessions to the North" (194). The poll tax, the white primary, the one-party system—all emerged from a compromise that led ultimately to an authoritarian regime in which the region's institutions "defended the ideology of white supremacy and the constellation of skin-color-purity concepts that fixed and supported it and kept the mind of the people from questioning its 'truth' " (203).

Smith concludes Part III with a chapter called "Southern Waste," her variation on Mencken's "Sahara of the Bozart," published almost three decades before. It is likely that Mencken would have concurred with Smith's analysis, though her tone—that of profound sorrow—is decidedly different from his. Smith acknowledges that, though southerners valued beautiful objects (oil portraits, expensive rugs and chandeliers, china, silver, and the like), and though a few southerners even enjoyed books and ideas, the culture as a whole did not sanction the kind of self-scrutiny that is indigenous to the literary imagination. The values of the upper-South aristocracy were evident in its preference for "the esthete rather than the creator, taste rather than truth, erudition rather than critical intelligence" (208). Indeed, it was not strange for southerners to "believe in the immorality of the creative process, for their preachers—from circuit-rider to revivalist—had warned them that art, dancing, novels, and curiosity pandered to the evil in men's natures" (206). Smith moves beyond Mencken in her analysis of the violence that was so pervasive yet rarely questioned in the South before the writers of the Southern Renaissance, including Smith herself, could no longer ignore the violence as a major fact of southern life. Smith echoes Ellen Glasgow when she says that prior to the twenties most writers, either "in devotion or despair," chose to "write down the official daydream" (211). She concludes her "Sahara" with one trenchant remark: "Perhaps the wasting away of our people's talents and skills has been the South's greatest loss" (215).

The most substantial additions in the revised edition of *Killers of the Dream* appear in Part IV, "The Dream and Its Killers." According to her biographer, Smith thought the last two chapters of her book were "eloquent and moving, but also somewhat muddled and so worked to make them clearer and more cogent" (Loveland 221). Of the additions Smith made for the revised volume, none has been more remarked upon than her indictment of the Fugitive-Agrarian critics in the penultimate chapter, "Man Against the Human Being."

With the exception of Donald Davidson, the Agrarians had by the late thirties moved from Vanderbilt to other institutions, and many had either abandoned or substantially modified their original views. Still, that Smith found it necessary to dismantle their collective social philosophy as late as 1961 is itself an indication of how influential the Agrarians had become. Smith was alarmed by the conservatism of their social philosophy and the limitations of the formalist literary criticism espoused by Ransom, Tate, and Warren in their subsequent incarnation as New Critics. She was also disturbed that the Agrarians had in the minds of many critics expressed the only important intellectual movement to emerge from the modern South. Their dominance had all but silenced the liberal opposition, and in the words of Smith, "No writers in literary history have failed their region as completely as these did" (223).

Actually, Smith's attack is more evenhanded than the preceding remark might indicate. Acknowledging that "their books, their talks, their lectures were woven of the valid and the false" and that "it is difficult to unbraid the strands," Smith makes the following assessment: the Agrarians recognized the excesses of an industrialized society, but in urging a return to a medieval pattern, "they ignored evils of the Middle Ages and what is worse the cultural and political dynamics that made the period what it was" (223). Though they were right to denounce "the increasing anonymity of men's activities" as well as "the overesteem of the scientific method," they did not see that we "need not succumb to material values because the machine age has made them conspicuous, nor to a worship of science because it has become too powerful" (224).

Smith could not forgive the Agrarians for their dominant influence in the nation's universities; instead of urging their students to commit themselves to a difficult future, the Agrarians "urged their students to busy themselves with literary dialectics, to support the 'new Criticism' instead of a new life . . . to search the pages of contemporary turgid writing for secret symbolic meanings where no meaning existed" (224). Smith took great exception to the Agrarians' insistence that the artist does not use his or her work to inspire political action. "They are wrong," she insists, "a glance at the history of the European artist shows that the mainstream of art has always involved itself with the profound experiences of its age and man's commitment to them. An artist has to be that hard thing: a human being who is artist" (225–26). In 1960, only a year before, Smith had issued what is in effect her culminating defense of a didactic literature devoted to liberal ideals, "Novelists Need a Commitment." Here Smith wrote, "One hears, 'Of course you can be a great poet and still be a Fascist; you can write a great novel and still cling to nihilism or to segregation.' I don't believe a word of it" (19). In a piece that can be seen as a response to the Agrarians (and to Leslie Fiedler, whose negative review of *One Hour*, "Decency Is Not Enough," appeared earlier in the same year), Smith urged artists to "pool their talents and skills, their imagination and knowledge, their hope and their compassion" in order to "create a new kind of person, a new kind of life on earth" (18).[14]

Smith's chief complaint against the Agrarians and their social philosophy bears her unmistakable stamp:

The basic weakness of the Fugitives' stand, as I see it, lay in their failure to recognize the massive dehumanization which has resulted from slavery and its progeny, sharecropping and segregation, and the values that

permitted these brutalities of spirit. They did not see that the dehumanization they feared the machine and science would bring was a *fait ac-
compli* in their own agrarian region. They knew of the dual system of
sharecropping and segregation, but something had blunted their imaginations for they had only a contactless association with it. By overlooking
the gaping wounds and fissures of the present and the corruption of the
spirit that had occurred in their region's past, they missed the major
point in the Twentieth Century dialogue which has to do *not with systems*
but with men's relationships. In a philosophical sense, they were a left-
over from the Nineteenth Century. (225)

To be identified as a remnant of the previous century might have
surprised the Agrarians; Allen Tate, for example, identified the nineteenth century as the age that saw the rise of social liberalism. In a
letter to Ellen Glasgow, whose *Sheltered Life* he greatly admired
(though he cared little for Glasgow's early works), Tate wrote: "It has
always seemed to me that you were very hard on Virginia and the
South, but I suppose that the failure of the liberal ideas of your generation has shown you that any alternative system is likely to be no better,
and possibly worse; so that now you see that human nature itself is the
real trouble" (Watson 9). Smith did not deny the frailty of human nature, but she could not understand the value of an intellectual system
that purported to confront the social needs of men and women and yet
ignored the very real problems of race.[15] The core of her attack is exactly what the many apologists for the Agrarians have tried to downplay; here, for example, is Louis Rubin in his 1977 Introduction to *I'll
Take My Stand*: "There was the chance, even the likelihood, that, as in
the early 1930s the obvious impracticalities of a return to subsistence
farming in the age of the tractor, the supermarket, and the television
set, as well as the political sectionalism and the defense, implied and
stated, of racial segregation, might serve to distract the symposium's
readers from what was and is the book's real importance: its assertion
of the values of humanism and its rebuke of materialism" (xvii). Apologists for the Agrarians—and they are many in number[16]—have made
much of the southern Agrarian/New Critic's fear of abstraction, but as
Richard King argues, the Agrarian critics and their successors, despite
their "confessed concern with history and tradition," have failed to understand that "if there has been a massive violative abstraction in this
century—or the last several for that matter—it has been the extermi-

nation of a major part of European Jewry and the enslavement of millions of Africans." Like Smith, King distrusts any social vision that ignores or fails to adequately address these "concrete facts," be it the aesthetic organicism of the Agrarian/New Critics, the Christian humanism of Eliot, or the Anglo-American modernism of Pound and Eliot which, as King reminds us, "has provided no opposition at all to the racism that runs not just through the southern but also the Western tradition" ("The South and Cultural Criticism" 706). In a review of Loveland's biography, Louise Westling has persuasively evaluated Smith's critique of agrarianism: "Lillian Smith's impact as a critic of Southern life in the twentieth century may well turn out to be more lasting than that of the Nashville Agrarians. While they looked backwards and championed an intensely elitist code of behavior, Smith spent her life attacking traditional patterns of racism and social privilege. . . . [Smith's] vision was progressive and prophetic where theirs has come to seem embarrassingly reactionary" (121).

Killers of the Dream is in a sense "The Portable Lillian Smith." It contains the essence of her thinking about the South and its segregated life, which, few will deny, still lingers in many rural (and urban) communities. *Killers of the Dream* also contains many of Smith's most tersely articulated expressions of her continued need for self analysis. Not only does it synthesize and expand upon material Smith had previously published in *South Today* and elsewhere, its revised edition reveals something significant about the turn in Smith's philosophical development between 1949 and 1961, years during which she read extensively including the works of the French philosopher and paleontologist, Pierre Teilhard de Chardin.

In what is probably his most widely read book, *The Phenomenon of Man* (1959), Teilhard interprets Christianity in light of science and presents his theory that scientifically and spiritually humankind will continue to evolve until it reaches its destiny—its ultimate spiritual unity. Having discarded the rigid fundamentalism of her youth, Smith was drawn to the intellectual basis of Teilhard's philosophical vision. In a late interview, she said *The Phenomenon of Man* had influenced her "more than any other book on the face of the earth" (Long 36).[17] Teilhard's theory of evolution accommodated one of Smith's key metaphors, that of the slow and measured journey we take as we create ourselves and attempt to make sense of what we have created. Smith's writings from the midfifties, which reflect her new religious quest, show her embracing the optimism she would applaud in Teilhard. In *The Journey* (1954), she wrote, "It is man's role in this evolving universe . . . to create the new from the debris of the old. And he is beginning, today, to have spectacular success in doing so" (254). Smith concluded this work—her own sustained philosophical meditation—with a rationale for her life-long liberal commitments: "To believe in something not yet proved and to underwrite it with our lives: it is the only way we can leave the future open . . . to lay down one's power for others in need; to shake off the old ordeal and get ready for the new; to question, knowing that never can the full answer be found; to accept uncertainties quietly, even our incomplete knowledge of God: this is what man's journey is about, I think" (256).

The revised edition of *Killers of the Dream* contains this new element in Smith's thinking, though here Smith is somewhat more guarded. Racial segregation is not the central subject of *The Journey*; when Smith returns to this issue in the revised edition of *Killers of the Dream*, her acceptance of Teilhard's vision is still intact, but she has become less optimistic about man's "spectacular success." The nonviolent protest movement of the early sixties had given her great hope for change, but Smith appears to have tempered some of her earlier optimism. In the concluding chapter, "The Chasm and the Bridge," she says, "It is as if God has brought the Earth people through a long, labored journey of slow growth and evolvement beginning four billion years ago and now has put everything into their hands—even their relationship with Him" (237). In a bold and audacious stroke, Smith herself assumes the voice of God:

> From now on, you do it; use your own culture, the knowledge you have accumulated, your own ideas and dreams, your skills and technics and inventiveness—and become what you like. As a human being, you are only partially evolved; if you want to, you can continue changing yourself. But it is up to you. . . . Call yourself modern, if you like, but you cannot stand still because you are not nearly completed. You are now in a dangerous state of flux: you could with ease become a monster or destroy yourself and your earth, but you cannot move backward. You are only a broken piece of life, remember, and cannot live without The Others. To live as a man you must somehow find ways to relate to Me, to past and future, all you have made: your art, your science, your things,

your understanding; and you must somehow learn to bridge your mythic to your rational mind, you must somehow learn the difference in merging and relating. . . . You can never become one with what you love or hate or fear or long for: only related; therefore your loneliness will always, like your shadow, be with you. (237–38)

Like Alfred, Lord Tennyson, who concluded *In Memoriam* with praise for the man he believed represented a new rung on the evolutionary ladder, Smith concludes the revised *Killers* with praise for Martin Luther King—a man "with nerves of iron and emotions that lie down like lambs with him" (251)—and the students and protestors he had inspired. Yet she also noted that "a virulent campaign is now on, worthy of Joseph McCarthy, to throw heavy suspicion on their loyalty and affiliations" (252). The great pity is of course that Smith died only two years before King himself and did not live to see the full scope of his significance in the social evolution that absorbed a great part of her thinking in the years before her death—an evolution that she herself had helped to bring about.

It is easy to see why Lillian Smith has become a major figure in the reassessments of southern intellectual history by men like Morton Sosna, Richard King, and Fred Hobson. These men have responded to the passion of Smith's convictions as they were displayed during an era of reactionaries and social gradualists. It is not always so easy, however, to accept the image of Smith that emerges from the works of these men. Morton Sosna, who is right to stress the significance of her travel and experience outside the South on the development of Smith's social consciousness, nonetheless exaggerates what he calls Smith's "evangelical conception of the artist's role" (180). While Smith may at times sermonize and may even speak with the "fervor of a fundamentalist" (197), surely the nature of her discourse and the range of her self-scrutiny keep Smith a safe distance from the southern evangelicals. Sosna claims that "moral judgments predominate over psychological ones in *Killers of the Dream*" (196), and in *A Southern Renaissance*, Richard King argues that Smith is a writer with "a moral rather than a historical imagination" (185). Aside from setting up illicit contrasts— as George Brockway has remarked, "Everything Lillian Smith wrote was informed by a profound psychological insight that was at the same time a profound moral insight" (53)—these judgments say more about

Sosna, King, and their preferences than they tell us about Smith. As Anne Loveland observes, the intellectual historians have each focused too narrowly on one or more influences on Smith's development to the exclusion of others (King, for example, illustrates the importance of Freud but says little about the influence of Teilhard). Yet in her final summation of Smith's achievement, Loveland herself does little better: "Regrettably, [Smith's] philosophical thinking was generally derivative and superficial and her literary effort unexceptional. Her primary significance lies in the role she played in the southern civil rights movement of the 1940s, 1950s, and 1960s" (262). In his review of Loveland's biography, Leslie Dunbar calls Loveland's evaluation "too blunt, too harsh"; he adds, "A writer surely can be 'derivative' without being superficial. [Smith] was never the latter, ever, and all Southern writers I can think of (and nearly all anywhere) have been philosophically derivative." Dunbar calls *Killers of the Dream* "as fine as any book interpretive of the pre-1965 South, and *Strange Fruit* a very good novel, better than several of Faulkner's" (205).

Daniel Singal provides one of the most provocative explanations of Smith's significance to the literary and intellectual life of her time. In *The War Within*, Singal traces the South's evolution from Victorianism with its "evasive idealism" (the phrase is Ellen Glasgow's), to the modernist perspective with its acceptance of human imperfection and its ability to probe beneath the smiling exteriors. "Perhaps the clearest articulation of these tendencies in the 1940s appeared in the writings of Lillian Smith, who, more than anyone else," Singal claims, "brought the issues of race and segregation into the open. With her, the assault against the Victorian ethos reached maturity. Her account of the psychic forces sustaining segregation identified the Victorian dichotomy, with its separation of mind and body, as the chief culprit" (374). As a modern artist, Smith employed a number of genres to do more than merely replicate the fragmentation she believed to be the definitive characteristic of the modern self and of modern life in toto; for Smith, " 'integration' meant more than a racial strategy; it meant the effort to restore man's 'wholeness' in the deepest modernist sense" (375). Singal's analysis does justice to the nature of Smith's self-defined goals. Given her centrality to his paradigm, one wonders why Singal devotes less than two full pages to Smith and her work. Is it because her influence has been felt most forcefully in the sphere of public rather than literary affairs?[18]

The time has come to understand and evaluate Smith in new ways, to place her within the context of her female contemporaries. Critics have tended to define Smith as an anomaly; rarely have they linked her work to that of other southern women writers. Kathleen Miller is an important exception: "[Smith's] was a 'spirit of rebellion' in the tradition of activists like Jessie Daniel Ames and Dorothy Tilly of the Association of Southern Women for the Prevention of Lynching and writers like Evelyn Scott and Carson McCullers who dared conceive of the South and Southerners in new ways" (281). It may be significant that of the writers included in this study, Smith became friends only with Carson McCullers, who, like Smith, saw segregation as a symbol of the barriers people erect between themselves. Other similarities are worth noting. Both women trained to become concert pianists; both were highly sensitive to the social problems of their native region and could evoke with poetic images the desperation of lonely rural southerners who try in odd and sometimes violent ways to solve the problem of their isolation; and both formed many of their most significant relationships with other women.[19] Most important, however, may be the two writers' use of the same metaphor to describe the artist and his or her ability to undermine the force of tradition and symbolic barriers. There is an apparent if not immediate affinity between the definition of the artist that McCullers formulated in her self-reflective essay, "The Flowering Dream: Notes on Writing" (1959), and the following passage from *Killers of the Dream*: "in the artist is the seed of a dream growing into a book, a painting, a poem, which awakens in the one beholding it another shadowy dream that, like a reflection in a pool, takes on mysterious shape and substance. . . . This is art's power over us; and its terror, for there are dreams we do not want aroused, ash that must remain ash" (154).

On the subject of relationships between men and women, Smith has echoed Katherine Anne Porter's theory of a "necessary enemy." In an intriguing chapter on Smith's relationships with both men and women, Anne Loveland claims that Smith's "notion of an inherent enmity between the sexes"—a sentiment she and Snelling presented in "Man Born of Woman"—was perhaps "the result rather than the cause" of her generally tense relationships with men (208). Loveland cites a letter in which Smith claims she never married because she had all her life "felt burdened by having to make promises that extend too far into the future" (quoted in Loveland 209). Perhaps more to the point is a speech Smith gave just a few years before her death. Addressing students in 1963, Smith recalls that the women of her generation "wanted two things": "we wanted an interesting career and we wanted an interesting man to live with. It was easier to find the interesting career than the interesting man. . . . we discovered men did not want their women to have brains; or if they had them they mustn't use them, and it hurt, it hurt like hell if I may say so, to find that the interesting men liked us in the office and laboratory and on the stage but most of them didn't want women like us in their home. So we finally had to swallow hard and admit that while we had won the battle we had lost the war" (*Winner* 206–7).

In a late interview, Katherine Anne Porter made a similar observation: "It is a disaster to have a man fall in love with me. They aren't content to take what I can give; they want everything from me" (Givner, *Conversations*, 165). Porter adds that there was little about her upbringing to encourage more creative relationships: "I was brought up in such ignorance, you see. Although that had more to do with the time, which was the Victorian age, than the fact that it was the South. Such ignorance. All the boys were in military schools and all the girls were in the convent, and that's all you need to say about it." (164). This, of course, is not all Porter said on the subject; her letters indicate the intensity of her belief that men make creative relationships a seldom-realized possibility. Though Porter married four times—she was willing to confront the "necessary enemy" and make the marital commitment that Smith avoided—she shared Smith's desire to define herself apart from men (only one of her four marriages figures significantly in her collected letters). While both women were reluctant to call themselves feminists, both subscribed to what Loveland calls "a kind of private feminism," an intense need for "personal autonomy and self-fulfillment" (191).

Smith's affinity with Lillian Hellman is perhaps more immediately apparent. Like the famous playwright, Smith boldly decried social inequalities and regarded herself as a leftist even though—unlike Hellman—she never supported Communist causes. Smith distrusted Communists even during the 1930s when, as Loveland points out, many other southern radicals like Lucy Randolph Mason and Claude Williams identified themselves with the Popular Front and hoped to implement Marxist solutions to the South's problems. If Hellman was slow to realize the state of affairs in Stalin's Russia, Smith was perhaps too eager to pronounce the shortcomings of American Communists and too quick to denounce European colonialism without also denouncing the United States for its own colonial enterprises. On the other hand, it is important to note that Smith was never a militant anti-Communist on the order of Sidney Hook. In fact, when Hook held a counterrally to protest the 1949 Cultural and Scientific Conference for World Peace—a conference Hellman was instrumental in organizing—Smith refused to participate (Loveland 91).[20]

Though both Smith and Hellman denied that they were organizational persons, each remained an active participant in various social organizations until the time of her death. Smith's involvement with groups such as the Southern Conference for Human Welfare and the Congress of Racial Equality has been well documented; less written about is her participation on behalf of the Americans for Democratic Action, a nonpartisan political organization that supports progressive candidates for public office. (It was, incidentally, the President of the ADA, Joseph Rauh, who represented Hellman when she appeared before the House Committee on Un-American Activities.) Many of the organizations that Smith and Hellman worked for—the Student Nonviolent Coordinating Committee, for example, or Hellman's own Committee for Public Justice—appealed to the young, the social group each writer believed would be the most likely to effect social change. When asked to explain the nature of their social activism, their sometimes avant-garde and even "unlady-like" social views, both writers, ironically, turned to the South as a source of inspiration. In *Scoundrel Time*, Hellman claims that whatever their other shortcomings, southerners have been brought up to believe that they could do essentially as they please; in a letter to Robert Evett, Smith says simply, "What I do in the realm of race relations is because as a citizen of the South I feel compelled to bow to my values and take a stand for 'the right to be different' and the right to breathe freely with one's mind and spirit" (quoted in Miller 273).

Even more important than any of these similarities is the fact that Smith, Hellman, and Porter were all drawn to one primary theme: the dangers of a passive collusion with evil. In *Scoundrel Time* and *The*

Never-Ending Wrong Hellman and Porter vent their scorn on those who through passivity and ignorance of their own motives allow evil to take place. Smith puts this theme at the center of *Strange Fruit* and *Killers of the Dream* (see Bolsterli) and many of her other writings as well. In 1957 Smith presented a speech, "No Easy Way—Now" (subsequently published in the *New Republic*), where she elaborated her theory of mob psychology. Actually, Smith identifies three distinct mobs in this piece, beginning with Mob No. 1, which initiates the violence and whose members are, in effect, "riff-raff with no visible source of strength at all." To find the source of their strength, Smith says that one must be willing to take two journeys, the first to Main Street where "sitting at their desks" one will find Mob No. 2, or, rather, "the men who quietly protect the rabble and give it its hidden power." Even if these men refuse to dynamite houses and churches, through their boy-cotts, their hushed threats, their economic reprisals, their censorship and cover-ups, they tacitly sanction the violence of Mob No. 1. To find out why these genteel, community-minded men have nonetheless pro-tected the street mobs, Smith says we must search for Mob No. 3, a search that entails an inner journey, for "Mob No. 3 lives in the depths of every man's mind" and, as such, "is nourished on anxiety about the body image, on anxiety about our personal relationships, and on an-cient myths of birth, death, blood, heredity, animals, darkness, and much else" (*Winner* 79–80). This is, of course, the journey Smith takes in *Killers of the Dream*; it is a journey that entails a direct confrontation with the irrationality of the mythic mind. Lillian Hellman and Kath-erine Anne Porter record similar journies in *Scoundrel Time* and *The Never-Ending Wrong*; and like Smith, each writer agrees that the group Smith identifies as Mob No. 2 is to be feared more than Mob No. 1. Each writer puts the issue of ethics—and particularly the limits of our responsibilities to one another as human beings—at the center of her own self-definition.

In 1955 Smith received an award from the Georgia Writers Associ-ation for *The Journey*, a nonfiction work "of the highest literary value" (Loveland 111). Also present at this awards ceremony was Flannery O'Connor, who delivered a speech that Smith praised in a letter to her Viking editor, Denver Lindley, noting that it was "witty, here and there; sardonic, now and then plain nasty about Georgia and full of good sense and sensitive understanding of the role of the writer." O'Connor's speech led Smith to observe that writers of the fifties could "now say things out loud without any realization, actually, of how one or two of us down in the South opened the way for them" (quoted in Loveland 111–12).[21] Lindley, who became one of O'Connor's editors at Harcourt, passed Smith's praise on to the younger writer, who was pleased that Smith had enjoyed the speech (*Habit* 123).

The differences between Smith's and O'Connor's social views should not be downplayed. O'Connor was at heart a social gradualist; her refusal to entertain James Baldwin at Andalusia, her Milledgeville home, provides a telling contrast to Smith, who, even in the late thirties, used her camp to bring the two races together for the expressed purpose of breaking down racial barriers. Still, Smith and O'Connor refused to romanticize or sentimentalize the South, and the two women, for all their differences, shared a number of intellectual interests and many of the same beliefs about the purpose of fiction. Most important, both writers held that mystery, which they took to be the true concern of the artist, could be approached only through a presentation of concrete particulars—or, as O'Connor would have it, through "manners." Both maintained that it was the artist's responsibility to apprehend and convey the mysteries of life, and both were drawn to many of the same thinkers—most notably Jacques Maritain and Pierre Teilhard de Chardin—who deepened their understanding of the interconnections between the spiritual and the physical. Attention has already been drawn to the influence of Teilhard on Smith's intellectual development; not only did she consider him a great scientist, she also regarded him as a great poet who could speak with the simplicity of a child (*Winner* 162). Readers of O'Connor's letters are aware of her attachment to the Jesuit paleontologist; the title of O'Connor's last collection of stories, *Everything That Rises Must Converge* (1965), is itself a measure of the importance she gave to Teilhard and his writings. In a review of *The Divine Milieu* (1960), O'Connor claims that collectively Teilhard's works "may have the effect of giving a new face to Christian spirituality" (*Presence* 108); and in a review for *The American Scholar* (the only review she produced for a secular publication), O'Connor isolates those features of *The Phenomenon of Man* (1959) that also intrigued Smith. This review is brief enough to cite in its entirety:

> *The Phenomenon of Man* by P. Teilhard de Chardin is a work that demands the attention of scientist, theologian and poet. It is a search for

human significance in the evolutionary process. Because Teilhard is both a man of science and a believer, the scientist and the theologian will require considerable time to sift and evaluate his thought, but the poet, whose sight is essentially prophetic, will at once recognize in Teilhard a kindred intelligence. His is a scientific expression of what the poet attempts to do: penetrate matter until spirit is revealed in it. Teilhard's vision sweeps forward without detaching itself at any point from the earth. (*Presence* 129–30)

Only at first glance is it puzzling that the work of a French paleontologist would appeal so strongly to, on the one hand, a Roman Catholic fully devoted to the teachings of her church and, on the other, a secular humanist who defined God as a creative force, a divine center, and who liked to repeat Paul Tillich's saying, "God is a symbol for God" (quoted in Loveland 172). Is it because Teilhard has never been embraced by either the liberal or the conservative community that critics of Smith and O'Connor have often misunderstood or slighted his influence on their artistic development?[22]

A reverence for mystery—for the ultimately inexplicable nature of human existence—undergirds the body of nonfiction prose by women writers of the Southern Renaissance, and *Killers of the Dream* is no exception. Smith's book is more than an account of the South's sense of racial guilt; it is a meditation on the differences between false and therefore destructive mysteries and those that affirm and bring meaning to human experience. In a series of notes she prepared for an interview, Smith wrote: "To reduce the wonder and mystery and fascination of the human experience to a matter of epidermis seems to me the height of absurdity. In a sense, this is total nihilism. Even Sartre has not thought of a more devastating form of Nothingness" (quoted in Miller 274–75). Southerners have too often made themselves slaves to mysterious prohibitions regarding the body and race, mysteries that, as Smith argues in *Killers*, "have to do with sin" (92). These seemingly impenetrable prohibitions do not cultivate a "reverence for the Unknown," nor do they encourage hearts and minds to stretch "to something bigger than the mind can find words for" (99). *Killers of the Dream* is Smith's personal attack on traditions and mysteries that feed on the mythic mind and are the enemy of the true mystery—"that complex mass of tingling life with its millions of relationships that we call a 'human being'" (171).

Like most of the writers in this study—particularly Glasgow, Hellman, Porter, and Hurston—Smith was not without her share of contradictions. She firmly held, for example, that segregation is a psychological problem and that any political solution would be only partially adequate. This view, however, did not prevent Smith from giving sound political advice to local and national leaders, including John F. Kennedy; nor did it keep her from working throughout her long career to bring about basic political reforms. Often she worked behind the scenes, as when she convinced Eleanor Roosevelt to make a contribution to Grace Thomas in her bid for the Georgia governorship in 1954. Smith doggedly refused to define herself as a political person—a refusal she shared with both Hellman and Porter—but she never underestimated the power of political structures. In a 1947 article in *The Nation*, "Pay Day in Georgia," she revealed just how astute a political commentator she could be. Addressing liberals once again (many of whom she knew to be conservatives at heart), Smith said, "We have not yet learned the fundamental principle of politics: you have to give people something to believe in with all their hearts, or something to hate with all their hearts; and plenty of bread" (119).

In a 1945 letter to Clark Foreman of the Southern Conference for Human Welfare, Smith wrote: "My talent is that of clarifying the issues; is that of telling the stark truth as I see it, with as much compassion of spirit as I am capable of" (quoted in Loveland 56). Smith would admit that her own special talent did not come without effort, that she had to struggle to see not just the South but also the nation as it is—just as she had to struggle to balance the Mary and Martha sides of her own complex psyche. Smith's correspondence makes it clear that she was aware of the tensions in her life and art; yet like poet Adrienne Rich, Smith knew that she had to work with what she had been given. In "Split at the Root," an essay whose title itself echoes Smith's many writings on the self and its sense of fragmentation in the modern world, Rich, like Smith, calls for both psychic and cultural renewal before insisting that "we can't wait for the undamaged to make our connections for us; we can't wait to speak until we are perfectly clear and righteous" (*Blood, Bread, and Poetry* 123).[23]

One could safely argue that Smith, one of the most self-reflective of modern writers, prefigures the intense need for self-exploration now associated with a later generation of feminist authors like Rich. When

Smith revised *Killers of the Dream*, she could not resist the opportunity to reflect once again upon the book she believed had turned the South against her. Consequently she included as a Foreword a letter she had written to her publisher George Brockway. Here Smith reflects upon the self-transforming power of the work she had produced twelve years before: "Coming back to the book after these years, I opened it wondering if what I was about to read would seem authentic to me. For I have changed since writing it. I am different. Because I wrote it. In the writing I explored layers of my nature which I had never touched before; in reliving my distant small childhood my imagination stretched and enclosed my whole life; my beliefs changed as I wrote them down. As is true of any writing that comes out of one's own existence, the experiences themselves were transformed during the act of writing by awareness of new meanings which settled down on them" (14).

In this Foreword, Smith does not shy away from the bold claim, nor does she apologize for the confessional tone, though she does acknowledge that some readers might object to this feature of the book. "Too much feeling?" she asks: "Perhaps. I could snip off a little of the pain, rub out a few words. But no; let's leave it; for it may be the most real part of the book" (21–22).

In 1954 Smith quoted Ernst Cassirer on the title page of *The Journey*: "If I put out the light of my own personal experience I cannot see and I cannot judge the experience of others." In her Foreword to the revised edition of *Killers of the Dream*, Smith consciously echoes Cassirer's remark: "I realize this is personal memoir, in one sense; in another sense, it is Every Southerner's memoir" (21). In the late thirties, Smith had the opportunity, through a fellowship awarded by the Rosenwald Fund, to tour the South and closely observe its variety of people and their customs (it was an experience not unlike Eudora Welty's WPA travels through her own home state of Mississippi). The director of the Rosenwald Fund, Edwin R. Embree, believed that Smith had the ability to bring southerners together by writing a novel about the failure of the South's one-crop agricultural system; he suggested something on the order of John Steinbeck's *Grapes of Wrath*, insisting to Smith, whose talent he much admired, "If we are to move the region and the nation we must state the case in more powerful terms than a sociological treatise" (quoted in Sosna 182). Smith did not produce another Steinbeck novel, but it seems apparent that she took Embree's call to action seriously. Her response was a form of nonfiction that blended confession and polemic, a work that moves backward in time—to the world of her childhood—in order to "write the South," to understand its past, and to project a vision for its future.

Smith said she came to know more about herself through writing *Killers of the Dream*; like any confession, it was a form of therapy. Less easy to gauge is the extent to which the book as a personal polemic has affected others. In an obituary for the *Saturday Review*, George Brockway said that Smith was a "master" of four genres—the novel, the parable, the essay, and the oration—and that with *Killers of the Dream* she produced "the acknowledged—or, often, the unacknowledged—source of much of our thinking about race relations" (53). In *Personal Politics: The Roots of Women's Liberation in the Civil Rights Movement and the New Left* (1979), Sara Evans compares Smith to Virginia Durr of Alabama and Anne Braden of Kentucky, other southern women of Smith's generation who publicly denounced the South's segregated culture. Smith in particular, Evans writes, "offered a pioneering analysis of the intertwined racial and sexual repression in the South" (28); her work established her as an important adult role model for younger southern women activists. Even more indicative of Smith's influence may be the comments made by those African-American students who on 3 February 1960 began the sit-in movement at a Woolworth store in Greensboro, North Carolina. When asked to identify their sources of inspiration, the four freshmen named the writings of Gunnar Myrdal, Gandhi, and Lillian Smith (Waters 73). In her Foreword to the revised *Killers*, Smith does not dwell on the book's polemical influence, though she does note that its continuing relevance astonishes her: "For what was based on intuition, on a kind of prophetic guess, is now boldly acting itself out on a world-size stage" (15). Beyond the value of the book as a personal/regional confession, Smith emphasizes its universal significance; segregation, she insists once and for all, is "a word full of meaning for every person on earth. A word that is both symbol and symptom of our modern, fragmented world" (21).

One might guess that Smith would have understood the opposition to multiculturalism in colleges and universities as yet another indication of a "modern, fragmented world" that refuses to heal itself. A writer silenced not only for her strong stand on civil rights but also for her disdain of the New Critics and their damaging refusal to historicize texts, Smith knew the penalties for taking unpopular or progressive positions, especially in a region in which progressives have been vastly outnumbered.

Nonetheless, in her conclusion to the revised *Killers*, Smith takes one more opportunity to distance herself from those southerners who have devoted their intellectual energy to the burden of the southern past. Implicit in her concluding remarks is a reaffirmation of her own liberal vision and an exhortation to others. "And now," she writes, "I must break off this story that has not ended; a story that is, after all, only one small fragment, hardly more than a page in a big book where is being recorded what happened to men and women and children of the earth during the Great Ordeal when finally they separated themselves a little way from nature and assumed the *burden* of their own *evolution*" (253, emphasis added). *Killers of the Dream*, like Smith's other autobiographical works, documents the outcome of her personal evolution, the journey she took to self-realization in a culture that has traditionally pitted reality against the comfort – and power – of myth.

3.

ELLEN GLASGOW AND
EUDORA WELTY

Writing the Sheltered Life

At the end of her autobiography, *One Writer's Beginnings* (1984), Eudora Welty attempts to summarize all that she has implied up to this point in her narrative: "As you have seen, I am a writer who came of a sheltered life. A sheltered life can be a daring life as well. For all serious daring starts from within" (104). It is a slightly defensive statement: Welty is willing to admit that as a woman growing up in the South, she has had her share of well-intentioned protection, but she is not willing to concede that her upbringing has in any way constrained her. It is possible that Welty knew her concluding paragraph would remind readers of Ellen Glasgow, a writer who explored the problematic nature of the sheltered life in what many consider her most successful novel of that title, and who chose to call her own autobiography, appropriately enough, *The Woman Within* (1954). As with Lillian Smith, southern women writers have been pushed into positions in which they have had to defend their artistic visions and choice of subject matter; it is not surprising to see them showing people within and outside their region that a sheltered existence need not stifle one's sense of self, that—on the contrary—it can be the very impetus for discovering that "self within the self" that Glasgow refers to in her other autobiographical work, *A Certain Measure* (1943).

One might easily question the appropriateness of linking Lillian Smith to Ellen Glasgow and Eudora Welty; each writer is associated with the Southern Renaissance, but the polemical nature of Smith's work—both her fiction and nonfiction—make her something of an anomaly. Certainly Welty's essay "Must the Novelist Crusade?" indicates that she and Smith are diametrically opposed on the question of the modern southern writer's social obligations to her reader. Smith's didacticism may distinguish her from both Welty and Glasgow, yet she too has delineated the distinguishing features of a sheltered upbringing at a time when a southern woman's role was clearly prescribed for her. The three writers have each shown how a voice from the "woman within" led them to define and thereby understand their own sense of vocation. Their angles of vision differ—tensions Glasgow and Welty hint at, Smith will often explore in detail—but in their need to define the self, the three writers converge on common ground.

Though Smith acknowledges that *Killers of the Dream* is not an autobiography in any traditionally accepted sense, she nonetheless toyed with the idea of producing a "real" autobiography and even lectured on the subject, the text of which was published during the decade after her death. Actually, Smith is one of the first women to theorize about the nature of autobiography and to speculate on the differences between autobiographies by men and those by women. As a feminist and a southerner, Smith offers perspectives that help to illuminate the problems Glasgow and Welty solved as they confronted themselves in *The Woman Within* and *One Writer's Beginnings*.

Above anything else, Smith made it her goal to describe the difficulty of the autobiographical project. Her purpose was missionary as usual; she wanted others to see, perhaps for the first time, that autobiography is an unstable literary genre and that one does not find the truth about one's life—"one creates it" (*Winner* 200). In the following passage from a fragment she had planned to include in *The Creative Uncertainty* (a work she never completed), Smith suggests the indeterminate nature of a genre that must not become rigidly codified:

The mysteries of autobiography are so deep rooted, so hidden and hard to come by, that one cannot name them easily. Perhaps a better word to use than mystery is paradox. For this is obvious: when one earnestly searches for one's self, when one calls the word *I*? immediately six, seven, or eight voices answer: *Here*! There is a power struggle among the aspects of one's nature, as would-be selves suddenly claim a dominant role in the story. If the story concerns a matter as subjective as one's belief about the human condition the difficulties grow. For not only is there the subtle problem of whose belief, which part of the self's belief, and the cruder problem of the public self holding a hand over one's secret mouth; there is also the almost inescapable betrayal of belief by one's vocabulary. (*Winner* 199)

The mystery and paradox of selves that compete for attention but are betrayed by the inadequacies of language—Smith's view of autobiography is not a comforting one, and it becomes even less so as she links the autobiographic impulse to problems of gender.

Writing before the full impact of Jacques Lacan on feminist literary theory, Smith made the following observation in her 1962 lecture, "Autobiography as Dialogue Between King and Corpse": "We have no record that Adam was aware of himself before Eve gave him that first long look. She was his primal mirror. It must have been quite a shock to discover himself in a female's eyes" (*Winner* 187). In the same manner, Smith adds that "women, themselves, have never written much about what Eve saw when she looked at Adam," nor have women been inclined to write about the way they look to one another for to tell the truth about themselves "might radically change male psychology" (188). Smith empathizes with "women's conspiracy" to keep their secrets but concludes, sadly, that "great autobiographies are not written by people who have conspired to keep silent" (189); "With all their talent for the specific and concrete, with their capacity for passion and for disloyalty to conformity, women have not, as yet, written autobiographies that deserve the word 'great' " (192). Smith noted that women have been "exceptionally good" with less self-assertive forms of self-writing—the memoir, the diary, the journal—but that even here most women have avoided telling the truth "about their sex experiences or their most intimate relationships, nor do they spend much time asking the unanswerable questions about the meaning of human life since they have never been too sure they were human" (189).

Smith's small but significant body of writing on this topic adumbrates more recent feminist considerations of women's self-writing. In " 'Saying the Unsayable': An Introduction to Women's Autobiography," Norine Voss provides a brief but useful summary of recent goals and trends in the reexamination of autobiographies by women. Voss begins with an attack on what she accurately labels the androcentric bias of traditional autobiographical criticism—the work of men like Georges Gusdorf, Wayne Shumaker, Roy Pascal, and Barrett John Mandel—and the effect this bias has had on the evaluation of women's self-writing. Not only have the traditionalists upheld a masculinist ideal of public life, they have formed definitions of autobiography that are dangerously prescriptive. In their hands, autobiography becomes an attempt to impose order and to construct, through retrospection, a coherent account of a life that has been lived. As Lillian Smith observed, this coherent, shaping ideal is at best dubious; it does not appear to typify women's experience and, as Voss notes, the traditional critic's view of the autobiographer as aloof and capable of recollecting life in tranquility "may be an artificial construct not representative of men's lives either" (219).[1]

Carolyn Heilbrun is the first feminist critic to note that Smith was ahead of her time. Heilbrun accepts Smith's analysis yet thinks she "missed, perhaps, what was most important, the degree to which women had internalized the 'facts' dictated to them by male psychology" ("Women's Autobiographical Writings" 19). Smith's goal was to revise our thinking about autobiography. If she missed implications of her argument that would be apparent to subsequent critics, she nonetheless gave eloquent expression to the demands that are placed upon the female autobiographer, demands that are compounded not the least by the many different selves that vie for her attention, by man's tendency to "choose [the public self] and tell only that self's story," and by women's silence in the face of a public ideal that male autobiographers and critics have constructed as "the bedrock of the autobiographical project" (*Winner* 194). Glasgow's and Welty's decision to focus on the inner self is a firm response to the demands Smith articulated; it is the inner self—the solitary core of their identity—that makes the strongest claim to their attention as artists.

Though scholars have relied heavily on Glasgow's autobiography for insights that affect their arguments regarding her fiction, little has been said about *The Woman Within* as a text itself.[2] By contrast, *One Writer's Beginnings*, which was recently the basis of a BBC special on Eudora Welty, was eagerly awaited by the community of Welty scholars and several important studies have already appeared. While *The Woman Within* cannot boast anything resembling the popularity of *One Writer's Beginnings*, a number of similarities between their life stories make Glasgow and Welty especially suitable for comparison. Each writer traces and attempts to understand the enormous influence of her family in shaping her own vision; each came from a home with parents who represented different sensibilities and, in Glasgow's case, sometimes different moral approaches to life; each confronted a society in which, Glasgow remarked on many occasions, the writer's art is held in no great esteem; each had to resolve an inner conflict over a painful shyness that affected her sense of vocation; and each had to work her way through to the realization that her art would depend for its strength upon the region in which she was reared and that, for all its contradictions and failings, she knew best.

That Welty's autobiography is less painful for many readers than Glasgow's is also significant, and it is worth noting that while Welty chose to publish her autobiography during her own lifetime, Glasgow, who does not omit her romantic involvements, left strict orders that hers not be made available until well after her death. The connection between the two works is, however, more than a matter of the two women's similar or dissimilar circumstances. The ultimate concern of each writer is the same—the need to trace the sources of her art, to seek out the essence of her creativity as a writer who has followed the promptings of a voice from the "woman within"—the need, finally, to define in order to understand.

When in 1988 Julius Raper published *Ellen Glasgow's Reasonable Doubts: A Collection of Her Writings*, readers could trace under one cover the evolution of Glasgow's thought on topics such as feminism, southern politics, and philosophy. Raper's collection, which presents the image of a very public woman of letters, is a vivid contrast to the autobiography in which Glasgow reflects on her family, lovers, and private life. Glasgow began work on her autobiography in 1934; it was a project she returned to intermittently throughout the thirties and the early forties. Published posthumously in 1954, *The Woman Within* represented a triumph for many reviewers (see reviews by Edel and Free-mantle) but came as a surprise to others, both locally and nationally, who must have expected a less intensely personal book (see reviews by Caperton and Prescott). For her part, Glasgow thought the book to be a real achievement; in a letter to Frank Morley, 28 February 1943, she made this assessment: "My autobiography, even if it requires rather drastic editing in certain chapters, may be the best that was in me" (*Letters* 312). Glasgow is not off the mark. Though *The Woman Within* creates a number of tensions and poses problems for contemporary readers, it does represent a significant achievement, the nature of which can be understood only by looking closely at the ways in which Glasgow both defines and unmasks herself in this complex work.

Glasgow opens her book with a technique that characterizes many of the great first-person narratives of the nineteenth century. Like the opening of Dickens's *Great Expectations* or *David Copperfield*, her introductory chapter, "I Feel," contains the major motifs that she will develop incrementally throughout her narrative. She begins by attempting to capture her first remembered sensations in images that set the tone for the chapters that follow: "Light flickers out of fog. Nothing but this wavering light is alive in my world . . . I feel myself moved to and fro, rocked in my mother's arms, only I do not know that I am myself" (3). Emerging from this pattern of light and dark is a bodiless face staring at her from a window—"a vacant face, round, pallid, grotesque, malevolent" (4). Glasgow's emphasis in this introductory chapter is upon her first conscious images, and though she claims to have been made aware of beauty, delight, and wonder at an early age, her very first impressions are bathed in pain, and what the reader is likely to retain from this opening chapter are those images that convey her early sense of fragmentation and separateness, her empathy for the hunted and helpless, her sense of life's victimization and ultimate ephemerality. Glasgow refuses to falsify these early impressions, and in an initial statement of her autobiographical intentions, she insists upon speaking the truth as she knows it "because the truth alone, without vanity or evasion, can justify an intimate memoir . . ." (8, Glasgow's ellipses).

As she recounts episodes of family life in a provincial southern town during the last two decades of the previous century, Glasgow speaks of misgivings about presenting her book to strangers: "So I am recording these episodes chiefly in the endeavor to attain a clearer understanding of my own *dubious* identity and of the confused external world in which I have lived" (130, emphasis added). She acknowledges the difficulty of writing about a painful experience such as her affair with the man she calls "Gerald B—" but concludes that no honest account of her life could be given without acknowledging this relationship, and in an often cited remark, she asserts that "the only reason for this memoir is the hope that it may shed some beam of light, however faint, into the troubled darkness of human psychology" (161). These two statements clarify Glasgow's central aims, yet while she admits that others will see more about the workings of her psyche than she herself might understand—indeed, she invites psychoanalysis—Glasgow is not content merely to chronicle the events of her life, to recapture earlier impressions, or even to convey the workings of her mind as she understands them. One of the most self-critical of modern writers, Glasgow continually questions the nature of her autobiographical enterprise itself.

Running throughout *The Woman Within* is a critique of its limitations as a self-reflexive document that confronts the dilemmas lying at the root of all self-writing. Though her autobiography is organized within a broad chronological framework—she moves from Part One, "The Child and the World," to Part Six, "What Endures"—Glasgow nonetheless finds it almost impossible to stay within the present of a given episode. For example, she presents her mother's death at the conclusion of Chapter Seven, "The Search for Truth," and then in the following chapter, "The Search for Art," she backtracks two years to her first trip to New York. Occasionally she will catch her digressions and remind the reader—as well as herself—that she is running too far ahead, that a certain event actually occurred years later. Certain chapters even come to resemble a series of notes.

As her sense of time becomes increasingly fluid and her "quest for reality" distinctly meditative, Glasgow will interrupt the flow of her narrative to apologize for her essentially associational method, for what she finally calls her "more or less incoherent memoirs" (214). In her early study of women's autobiography, Elizabeth Winston notes that Glasgow fluctuates between the loose style of a journal and more formal means of expression: "The often-used ellipses and question marks seem at times to signal a genuine inability to complete the thought, a diary-like looseness of form to express tentative content; at other times they seem the mannered pause, the feigned interrogative of a knowing narrator who wants us to fill in the spaces and answer the questions ourselves" ("Women and Autobiography" 107–8).

Like any other writer of prose fiction, Glasgow understands the tendency to dramatize key incidents in her life, and she also understands that the imagination can merge with memory to reshape what may have happened, or to remold one's responses to what did happen. Hence, she is never fully unaware of how she is defining herself. When, for instance, she recounts her twenty-one year affair with Henry Watkins Anderson (the man she calls "Harold S—"), she underscores her wish to avoid the easy rhetoric of the Freudian era—this despite her pride in being one of the first fiction writers to consciously employ the insights of both Freud and Jung (see Goodman). In a passage that suggests a great deal about the nature of self-reflexive writing in general, Glasgow explains her fear of suggesting a resolution that is too pat, or of coming to a conclusion about experience that would betray the experience itself; in reference to her affair with Anderson, she writes: "Although, in after years, this whole episode exercised a profound influence over my work, in the immediate present my creative mental processes remained in a trance. . . . Instead of molding both causes and effects into a fixed psychological pattern, I have tried to leave the inward and the outward streams of experience free to flow in their own channels, and free, too, to construct their own designs. Analysis, if it comes at all, must come later. I am concerned, now, only with the raw substance and the spontaneous movement of life, not with the explicit categories of science" (227).

Of course Glasgow cannot resist the tug of analysis, nor can she dismiss the fear that in seeking to understand her own identity and in defining it for herself and others, she may have told too much or may have presented an image that is somehow distorted. This fear is given clear expression in another statement that is fundamental to her whole self-reflexive undertaking: "But when I reflect that I may have included too much, I remind myself of the rest—of all the things I might have included—and did not" (227).

Glasgow's concern may be the "raw substance and the spontaneous movement" of life, but she understands that the autobiographical impulse is of necessity a shaping impulse—that ultimately one defines the self by writing the self. Thus after acknowledging the futility of her obsession with Henry Anderson, she wistfully asks, "Doesn't all experience crumble in the end to mere literary material?" (226). All that any autobiographer has to work with are the resources of the literary artist—language with all its limitations.

In its concern with the process of its own making, *The Woman Within* prefigures a major trend in postmodern literature: the tendency to make the act of creating the work an important subject of the work itself. Still, Glasgow would not subscribe to the view, given perhaps its most terse expression by Paul de Man, that the "self" an autobiographer sets out to discover is in the end a linguistic construct.[3] She may question the ability of language to convey the complexity of her mind's inner workings, particularly as it confronts something so awe-inspiring as, for example, a near-death experience, but her questioning stops short of a radical departure from the belief that the self does in fact exist and that it can be defined with the resources of the literary artist. Glasgow claims that everything about her life, even "the very elements" of her own identity, had required a struggle. Her trenchant response to this awareness is worth citing: "I was willing to struggle" (113).

If this study stresses the *autos* in addition to the textuality of Glasgow's autobiography, it is in part because critics have focused most of their attention on the facticity—the *bios*—of Glasgow's book rather than her keen awareness of how she has chosen to define what she perceives to be her most intimate self. Edgar E. MacDonald speaks for many others when he notes, "Ellen Glasgow may have intended the work to be a truthful recounting of her life as she experienced it, but she was accustomed to writing novels. As for many writers, her emotional life and her career were the same. Seeing people and events through a 'filter,' she gives accounts that are not always in accord with the facts as recorded in letters and the observations of others" (172).[4] MacDonald points specifically to Glasgow's less than flattering account of her engagement with Henry Anderson. While it is not the intention here to suggest that facts are unimportant, recent academic interest in the nature of autobiography has encouraged many scholars to explore those psychological and textual features that rely less upon facticity than upon the images and designs that undergird the autobiographer's deepest sense of self, a self whose "boundaries" are "limited to" but not circumscribed by "the close horizon" of what Glasgow views as one's more superficial personality (232). Glasgow claims to speak the truth as she knows, feels, or imagines it; she does not subordinate one to the other—the three are, rather, inextricably connected. Glasgow's fear of evasion recurs throughout her autobiography, yet her distrust of mere facts to convey anything of value is so deep that she appears to regret the intrusion of any empirical reference, even the date of the year.

As if to illustrate her disdain of dwelling on what can be immediately verified, Glasgow only briefly alludes to the fact that she was active in one of the first American societies for the protection of animals, yet a predominant feature of her autobiography is its many images of hunted and abused animals. Though she does not linger over the feminist implications, Glasgow makes the early observation that boys are the natural enemies and plunderers of the animal world (*The Woman Within* 56–57), a realization that adds meaning to her later anger over her father's callous disposal of a pet dog. "Rage convulsed me," she writes of this incident, "the red rage that must have swept up from the jungles and the untamed mind of primitive man." Glasgow cannot recall uttering words in her father's presence after this incident; she remembers only that she "picked up a fragile china vase on the mantelpiece and hurled it across the room" (70).

Animals are emblematic of Glasgow's complex sense of victimization. With no hesitation, she, like O'Connor, Welty, Porter, and Mc-Cullers, declares that her natural sympathies are with the social outcast, the inarticulate, the "underdog" (228). The crucial irony is that Glasgow conflates her sense of oppression and victimization with the experience of creatures who do not have her resources to articulate themselves. Animals solicit Glasgow's sympathy, but in another sense they reflect her fear of being misunderstood, of articulating herself in a society that has defined a place for her that she cannot accept, a society that is understandably hostile to its pets (animals or women) who outgrow their usefulness, or who, like Glasgow, never agreed to be useful in the first place—at least not in any socially sanctioned manner. During her last trip to Europe, Glasgow recalls a visit to the Luxembourg Gardens: "The gate of the Conciergerie is opened for us, and we give our card to a man in a small dark room where a bird lives in a cage. The bird in the cage is the first thing I notice; for whenever anything is caged, either in the prison of facts or the prison of memories, I am there" (262).

Significantly, Glasgow can see herself "without shelter," to use Julius Raper's phrase, at the same time that she delineates the contours of a very sheltered upbringing. *The Woman Within* shows that there is more than a hint of autobiography in Glasgow's depiction of Jenny Blair, the young heroine of *The Sheltered Life* (1932), who at the end of the novel is left to confront the meaner features of reality that others have attempted to shield from her. The critical reader of Glasgow's autobiography will recognize that much of its interest resides in the tensions that underlie such confrontations, and surely none of these tensions is more pronounced than the victim/rebel struggle that resides at the heart of *The Woman Within*. The many images of helpless animals with which Glasgow identifies must be weighed against the more forceful projections of a woman who exists and defines herself in opposition to those very forces that would shelter, oppress, or destroy—forces that include a rigid Calvinistic conscience, an overbearing patriarch of a father (defiance of whom offers the author a sense of liberty), and a society that prefers evasive idealism to truth and accountability for one's actions. Glasgow is not content with her victimization; implicit in her search for art is the awareness that language is a means to empowerment for the rebel within, a way of creatively transforming the defiance and anger that would prompt her to destroy a vase in her father's presence. Without denying the sense of victimization that plagued her throughout life, Glasgow implies in her own way that she, like Jane Eyre, a character she greatly admired, was no Helen Burns.

Still, if one accepts Glasgow's invitation to psychoanalyze the self she has defined, one sees moments when her self-presentation appears to be at odds with itself. To cite a particularly striking example, Glasgow claims to have been much like her beloved brother Frank in recoiling from experience and drifting deep into herself: "I was still a child when I learned that an artificial brightness is the safest defense against life" (67). What one cannot avoid asking is this: is not such a posture itself a kind of evasive idealism? Glasgow speaks disparagingly of William Dean Howells's genteel realism and the "rash of refinement" it spawned in his followers (as an author, she defines herself in contrast to Howells), yet Glasgow herself is attached to manners and the refinement they embody, so much so that she mourns the loss of her society's "finest creation, a code of manners" (140–41). Glasgow's ambivalence toward the protective rituals of her society is apparent; in one sentence she speaks of giving her first party at age seventeen—an event that would have been expected of a young southern woman about to enter society—and in the same winter of joining the City Mission and becoming "the youngest 'visitor' in its membership" (81). At an early age, Glasgow is aware that her quest for reality does not accommodate itself to certain traditions, yet while she "put aside, indifferently, the offer of the usual 'coming-out party' and the 'formal presentation to Richmond society,' " she cannot dismiss the pleasure of her first ball: "I was made, according to the gracious courtesy of old Charleston, one of the belles of that brilliant and unforgettable evening" (78–79).

An equally vexing subject for Glasgow is her encroaching deafness, a problem she first mentions in Chapter Eight as something that a New York doctor had told her she would never have to worry about but that becomes a more prevalent concern as her autobiography progresses, and she recounts instances in which she felt it better to pretend to hear than to display her infirmity. Towards the end of *The Woman Within*, Glasgow asserts that physical weakness can lend warmth to the inner life (a view expressed by Porter, McCullers, and O'Connor as well), yet she depicts her deafness as a "secret wolf," linking it to the pervasive animal imagery, an "impenetrable wall," and a "closing barrier." Similarly, she can say that life had "defrauded" her of "something infinitely precious" but that she "was not disposed, by temperament, to self-pity" (113). A few chapters later, she undercuts the force of this assertion by recounting a comment made by one of her doctors: " 'You are the only one of my patients who is not depressed by deafness,' one of the leading aurists in New York said to me a few years ago. I smiled that faintly derisive smile. If only he could know! If only anyone in the world could know! That I, who was winged for flying, should be wounded and caged!" (139).

Maureen Howard has written, "In *The Woman Within* Ellen Glasgow presents herself as a southern grande dame, demure about personal details yet self-regarding, given to defensive overevaluations of her work and then spilling the beans of self-doubt much like Norman Mailer" (*Seven American Women Writers* 9). Howard does not probe the various tensions or contradictions, but she does insist that readers allow Glasgow the same degree of complexity and contradiction that they expect of a more flagrantly self-absorbed writer like Mailer. Glasgow responded to the challenge of her undertaking; implicit in her belief that an intimate memoir can justify itself solely by the light it sheds on human psychology is an awareness that human psychology is itself never simple, never reducible to formulaic expressions, never anything less than a mystery. She gives eloquent expression to this belief in "Fata Morgana," the chapter in which she introduces her affair with Henry Anderson: "We boast of our discoveries in psychology, of our arbitrary and inelastic categories; but all that we have acquired is a general framework for the more obvious reactions. Of that finer essence, by virtue of which one individual differs from another, which responds and recoils, not according to scientific rules and measurements, but in obedience to its own special nature, which arouses the waning embers of love—of all these secret sources of behavior, we know as little in this epoch of electricity as we knew in the candlelit ages of faith" (213–14).

Her sense of life's ineluctable mystery is something Glasgow felt at a very young age; in "Early Sorrow" (a chapter that deals primarily with the parental conflicts of her childhood), she draws herself in contrast to her two closest friends: "I felt that I had changed beyond understanding and recognition. They lived happy lives on the outside of things, accepting what they were taught, while I was devoured by this hunger to know, to discover some meaning, some underlying reason for the mystery and the pain of the world" (73).

Like other southerners, male and female, Glasgow's early reverence for mystery made her skeptical of dogma; she understood even as an adolescent that in her search for a personal destiny she could never acquiesce to the rigid beliefs of her father with his Calvinistic world view. Glasgow's self-depiction may recall Jane Eyre, but her search for truth is more like that of another nineteenth-century British fiction heroine, George Eliot's Dorothea Brooke, whose quest for a "binding theory" grows out of the same kind of dissatisfaction Glasgow outlines in her own search: "I was looking for a purpose, for a philosophy that would help me to withstand a scheme of things in which I had never felt completely at home. I wanted a reason, if not for creation in general, at least for the civilization which men had made, and were still making. The truth was, I suppose, that I still needed a religion. Though I was a skeptic in mind, I was in my heart a believer. I believed even in the art of fiction, and one who believes in that can believe almost anything else" (140).

What makes Glasgow a modern heroine is what distinguishes her, finally, from a character like Dorothea Brooke—her willingness to remain faithful to her disbelief. "I had never known a person, certainly not in the Solid South," she writes, "who believed as little as I did, for I doubted the words of man as well as the works of God" (141). Glasgow moves beyond Dorothea, who never abandons her belief and who finds limited happiness through marriage, to what she identifies as a state of inner self-sufficiency where "the life of the mind alone . . . contains an antidote to experience" (296).

Glasgow is concerned primarily with her interior life—with the evolution of her psyche as it confronts the external world—but submerged in her story of the woman within is a critical commentary on her own work, as well as an extended reflection on the nature of her region and her role as a woman writing within the sheltering restrictions of that region. Glasgow did not ignore or downplay her work in her autobiography; too many commentators have overlooked the extent to which *The Woman Within* is in fact a sustained reflection on the sources of and events that shaped Glasgow's art. Even Estelle Jelinek, in her important survey of women's autobiography, claims that Glasgow provided "almost no discussion of her writing career." Jelinek praises Glasgow for the sensitivity of her "inner search for self-clarity" but concludes too hastily that she can be placed in that group of women autobiographers who have in fact shied away from their own writing careers and have consequently left out a significant part, perhaps the most significant part, of their experience (*Tradition* 148).[5]

The truth is that Glasgow felt her vocation so intensely she could not have focused on the woman within and ignored her own art, her overwhelming need to create; nor could she dismiss the circumstances that surrounded her work life as an artist, including the patronizing (and sexist) publishers who greeted her first book and the critics who subsequently misunderstood her and praised what she found to be inferior fiction. It is clear from the chapter she calls "I Become a Writer" that Glasgow's need to write was deeply rooted in her need to rebel; in fact, the themes of rebellion and self-expression are so closely interwoven that it is difficult to separate them even for the purpose of analysis.

At the age of seven, when her first attempts at poetry were read aloud by an older sister for the amusement of her guests, Glasgow decided to write only in secret and began to "live two lives twisted together" (38). She defines her external life—"delicate but intense"—as one "devoted to my few friends, Mother, Mammy, my brother Frank, my sister Rebe, Carrie Coleman, and Lizzie Patterson" (38). Conspicuously absent are her father and her older sisters. By contrast, there is the interior world, "that far republic of the spirit" where Glasgow says she "ranged, free and wild, and a *rebel*" (40–41, emphasis added). With the recognition of these two states of being Glasgow discovered her vocation to be the "single core of unity" at the center of a divided nature; and with the wide perspective of age, she is able to detect what she calls "a solitary pattern" that has characterized the maverick spirit of each creative effort: "Always I have had to learn for myself, from within" (41).

Glasgow gives sustained attention to the genesis of *The Descendant* (1897), her first published novel. She does not disguise its crudity as an apprentice work, but she does underscore its thematic significance—it grew out of her need to confront life without its protective shelters— and she suggests the ways in which it functions as a precursor to her mature work. Her early hatred of the "inherent falseness in much Southern tradition" (97) is embodied in the central male character, Michael Akersham, the illegitimate working man who becomes a radical spokesman for his class and whom Glasgow uses as an expression of her disdain for the cruelty as well as the insidiousness of sentimentality. "If only I had learned to write before writing," she notes, "my first book might have been not entirely unworthy of my idea" (98).

In Chapter Ten, "Alone in London," Glasgow considers various influences on her writing, including that of James, Flaubert, Maupassant, and Tolstoy. At one point, Glasgow felt *Madame Bovary* to be the "most flawless novel" she had encountered but concluded, finally, that "something was wanting. The hand of the master [a term she never uses for herself] was too evident. . . . Life is a stream, it is even a torrent; but it is not modeled in clay; it is not even dough, to be twisted and pinched into an artificial perfection" (124). Though she admits to modeling her second novel, *Phases of an Inferior Planet* (1898), after Maupassant, she ultimately rejects his influence as well and asks, "Was it possible that literary 'realism' was not an approach to reality, but a pattern of thought, with no close relation to the substance of life?"

(125). Glasgow has great respect for the Brontës, and she notes that one of her regrets is that she never met Virginia Woolf, yet she mentions no women in this chapter: the greatest self-perceived influence on her approach to art, if not on her work itself, is Tolstoy (an influence that other southern women writers have claimed as well), and what she says about the Russian author bears on the perception she has of herself as a regional writer: "From the beginning I had resolved to write of the South, not, in elegy, as a conquered province, but, vitally, as part of the larger world. Tolstoy made me see clearly what I had realized dimly, that the ordinary is simply the universal observed from the surface, that the direct approach to reality is not without, but within. Touch life anywhere, I felt after reading *War and Peace*, and you will touch universality wherever you touch the earth" (127–28).

As for the influence of Glasgow's contemporaries, her comments are less flattering and take a distinctive feminist slant. Though she had longed to experience the New York literary scene, she ultimately found it "scarcely less flat and stale than the familiar climate in Richmond, where social charm prevailed over intelligence." Glasgow's remarks on the most influential authors of her time, especially William Dean Howells (a nemesis of sorts), are unusually acerbic: "At the Authors' Club I met the various authors who would soon become, by self-election, the Forty Immortals of the American Academy. They were important, and they knew it . . . They had created both the literature of America and the literary renown that embalmed it" (139). Glasgow's general disdain for literary coteries—a distaste for following the leader as intense as that of Katherine Anne Porter's—is combined here with her understanding that more than gender determines one's ability to master an art. She admits to finding these men agreeable: "The trouble was that I thought of them as old gentlemen, and they thought of themselves as old masters. There was an insuperable disparity in our points of view" (141).

Rarely does Glasgow relate an event or feature of her life without punctuating its significance with her self-perceived role as artist. Her quest for self-understanding led her to explore those periods, often following the death of someone she loved, during which the creative impulse would briefly die, only to be followed by a period of creativity that was apparently stimulated by her keen sense of loss. In Chapter Sixteen, "Heartbreak and Beyond," Glasgow confronts the death of her sister Cary in 1911, the woman who had been instrumental in Glasgow's developing feminist consciousness. If Glasgow does not escape the nineteenth-century language of concealment that evaded the reality of women's physical problems, she does astutely grasp the implications of Cary's death to her own art and life. Though she would move on to the "unseen future" of her best work to come, she could do so only by escaping a personal past that had become a "present enemy" (194).

Throughout *The Woman Within*, Glasgow is candid about the tensions that are part of her creative powers. She admits that intellect and emotion never "shone with equal light at the same instant," that consequently her "best books have all been written when emotion was over and the reflected light had passed on. My deepest feelings have responded only when my intellect was obscured" (214). Scholars have puzzled over the fact that Glasgow, unlike Porter, Gordon, or McCullers, produced what has generally been regarded as her best work in the latter part of her life. Glasgow does not ignore this feature of her career, nor does she hesitate to identify her best efforts: "in spite of physical odds against me, I had begun to write my best books in the middle of the nineteen-twenties. After *Barren Ground*, which I had gathered up, as a rich harvest, from the whole of my life, I had written and published two comedies of manners: *The Romantic Comedians* (surely, as many critics have said, a flawless work of its kind) and *They Stooped to Folly*. In the early nineteen-thirties, I wrote *The Sheltered Life* and *Vein of Iron*. As a whole, these five novels represent, I feel, not only the best that was in me, but some of the best work that has been done in American fiction" (270).

By the time she wrote *The Woman Within*, Glasgow had come to uphold the view that a writer must experience life in order to write about it. Yet before *Barren Ground* (1925), she had not been able to put the whole of her distilled experience into her writing. Her explanation of her later success may be too vague to satisfy some readers, but it is in keeping with her intensely personal approach, and it again suggests the extent to which writing was part of her continued need to rebel: "My physical weakness, after the heartbreaking strain of a divided life, appeared to lend light and warmth to my imagination. Pain had not defeated me. It had made me *defiant* and more confident of my inner powers" (270, emphasis added).

Fearful that readers would think she had given only cursory treatment to her creative work, Glasgow refers them to *A Certain Measure* (1943), her "book of self-criticism" (270). There is in fact some overlap between this collection of revised and expanded prefaces and *The Woman Within*, for Glasgow worked on both books at the same time. Her literary executors, F. V. Morley and Irita Van Doren (editor of the *Weekly Book Review* of the *New York Herald Tribune* where many of Glasgow's occasional pieces had appeared), note in a preface to *The Woman Within* that, eleven years before her death in 1945, Glasgow had planned "what might be called two companion autobiographies. One was to be her mature comments on the life of the workshop; the other, which in her lifetime she wished to keep completely private, was the life of the woman within" (vii). Morley's and Van Doren's distinction is perhaps too neat; the life of the workshop, a useful term as far as it goes, is not really separate from the life of the woman within. Glasgow the woman is Glasgow the artist, and she would have disparaged such a split. Still, Morley and Van Doren are correct to note that Glasgow, in effect, produced two separate autobiographical works, and within the context of this study one might justifiably question why.

Glasgow is, as already shown, a clear exception to the tendency Estelle Jelinek has observed in women writers who produce autobiographies; Glasgow had no reservations about analyzing her work and commenting on its value for others and herself. Yet the existence of *A Certain Measure* in Glasgow's oeuvre suggests that, though she had no anxiety about producing a large body of self-criticism, she still experienced a strong sense of dividedness when it came to coupling analysis of her work with those more personal disclosures about the nature of the psyche that produced this work. Was Glasgow aware that her sense of life's sorrow might be construed as self-pity and therefore blunt the potential force of her fiction? Or did she realize that though she might avoid the pain of public ridicule for too much self-exposure during her lifetime, she knew that such pain would mean little after her death? Or, more likely, did she decide to publish *The Woman Within* not only because, as she says, it might shed some understanding on the nature of human psychology but also because she knew it contained some of her best prose? These are speculations. What is clear is that Glasgow's sense of fragmentation accounts in part for the fact that, ultimately, she produced two autobiographical works—*A Certain Measure*, a public work intended for readers during her lifetime, and *The Woman Within*, written chiefly for her own self-clarification, a private work but one that could be made public after her death. Attuned to the stress a woman writer experiences as she attempts to make public her private experiences, and sensitive to the curious myths that surround the woman writer (she devoted an essay to this subject and then expanded it for *A Certain Measure*), Glasgow cultivated what she called the smiling, ironic pose. The different emphasis of her two autobiographical works is a significant expression of this pose, a posture within itself, but one that she among women writers was not alone in displaying before a public not yet ready for the intimate disclosures that would characterize a later generation of women artists.

The more obvious reason for Glasgow's decision not to publish *The Woman Within* during her lifetime is that she chose to make a number of confessions about her family and her romantic involvements. The family theme is singled out by Alfred Kazin in a frequently cited review of *The Woman Within*. Kazin links the work to Faulkner's *The Sound and the Fury* (1929), and the comparison is not without pertinence. Glasgow does reveal a family in decay, at the head of which is a father with an iron will—more patriarchal than paternal, as Glasgow puts it— and a ghostly figure of a mother, a woman who withdrew into her own inner world, but whom Glasgow calls the center of her childhood: "I have two images of her, one a creature of light and the other a figure of tragedy. One minute I remember her smiling, happy, joyous, making gaiety where there was not gaiety. The next minute I see her ill, worn, despairing, yet still with her rare flashes of brilliance" (13). Her mother's doctors failed to understand her inner illness, and though Glasgow does not specify this illness by name, she gives enough information for the contemporary reader to see that Anne Jane Gholson Glasgow, though she may have at once possessed the southern "vein of iron" that Glasgow would memorialize in a number of works, reached the stage where she could no longer function as both exemplar and victim, the dual pressures that have traditionally defined the nature of southern womanhood.

Glasgow re-creates her father in a decidedly different vein. He is the enemy, the other, and he comes to embody all that she detests about life's cruelty:

Father gathered us about him, and read aloud his favorite belligerent passages from the Old Testament. What comfort he could have found in the slaughter of Moabites or Amalekites, or even of Philistines, it is hard to imagine. Certainly, he could have had no special grievance against any one of these tribes. But, I think, he needed comfort as little as he needed pleasure; and a God of terror, savoring the strong smoke of blood sacrifice, was the only deity awful enough to command his respect. He never read of love or of mercy, for, I imagine, he regarded these virtues as belonging by right to a weaker gender, amid an unassorted collection of feminine graces. (85)

Glasgow relates little about the relationship between her mother and father, nor does she make explicit the damage to her mother's psyche that was caused by her father's ongoing affair with his mulatto mistress. She does claim that for many reasons, among them his "iron vein of Presbyterianism," her father and mother should by no means have married. "Though he admired her," Glasgow charges, "he never in his life, not for so much as a single minute, understood her. Even her beauty, since he was without a sense of beauty, eluded him" (14–15). Her love for her older brother Frank is mixed with Glasgow's admiration for his devotion to their mother; twice she remarks that of ten children he alone never failed her. Glasgow is vague about her own sense of failure, and one wonders what she might have done differently for a woman who would gather her children around her during periods of anxiety and depression.

One of the most intriguing features of Glasgow's autobiography is the hierarchy of significance she devises for the members of her family, with her father taking the final, but only seemingly least important, position. At one point, Glasgow recounts a dream in which she is approached by all the "beings" she had valued in life, the order of which is not random: "On they came, walking singly or in twos and threes, and as they drew nearer the distance changed from light into ecstasy. Mother, Cary, Frank, Walter . . . then my childhood's 'Mammy' . . . and then Emily, Annie, Father" (239, Glasgow's ellipses) Understanding and evaluating the significance of one's family are the tasks of a lifetime. While Glasgow does not attempt to solve the mystery of her family's tragedies—her mother's nervous condition, her father's intolerance and lack of affection, her brother's suicide, and her sisters' early deaths—her hierarchal dream-visions indicate her attempt to discern the relative importance of personal loss. The figures appear in an order that indicates Glasgow's degree of affection. She could not bring herself to love her father; and yet his emphasis of final place also suggests the significance of such a presence—sentimental, intolerant, patriarchal, and ambitious—to Glasgow's sense of self; she could not condone his view of life, but neither was it a view she could escape.[6]

It becomes clear that certain experiences are awkward or painful for Glasgow to relive. Disclosures about romantic involvements as well as family affairs cause anxiety, and with the romances she admits to skirting the issue for as long as she can without, finally, suppressing the affairs altogether. Glasgow tells about three involvements, one of which she describes in Chapter Fifteen as an "experimental engagement" that "lasted for three chequered years" despite her "sound conviction" that marriage was not for her (178). Glasgow admits that all she felt for this man—she does not identify him even with a disguised name—was gratitude, and that "gratitude, though noble in sentiment, is without madness; and madness is the very essence of falling in love" (179). Here Glasgow reveals her essentially romantic temperament, but, ironically, she claims to prefer "the second best in emotion" just as her "fellow countrymen so often preferred the second best in literature" (179). Nevertheless, the intense emotion she claims not to have felt for this man whom Julius Raper identifies as Frank Ilsley Paradise, an Episcopal minister and author (xviii), is exactly what does characterize the two other affairs—that with "Gerald B—" in Chapter Fourteen and that with Colonel Henry Watkins Anderson ("Harold S—") in Chapters Eighteen and Nineteen. No one to my knowledge has commented on the fact that these two romances are strategically placed in the autobiography: the affair with "Gerald B—" concludes with a mystical naturistic encounter followed by a summary at the half-way point of the book; the affair with Anderson is in effect the climax of the autobiography: the two chapters devoted to him are followed by the final part of Glasgow's journey inward, "What Endures."

"Without warning, a miracle changed my life. I fell in love at first sight" (*The Woman Within* 153). With this remark Glasgow recounts her affair with "Gerald B—," but one notes that the chapter itself is titled "Miracle—or Illusion?"[7] In describing the relationship, Glasgow is willing, at least temporarily, to see it as a miracle that occurred in her twenty-sixth year. Glasgow is unusually aware of her effect on others in this chapter. Where romance is an issue, she tends to behave and envision herself in terms of what she perceives to be the reactions of others. Hence she resorts to a technique that, in general, she uses only occasionally; she describes herself obliquely through comments others make about her, including a remark that "Gerald B—" made to a friend: " 'She is so lovely, how could anyone help loving her?' The words shone in my mind, ringed with light, when they were repeated. Even now, they gleam with a faint incandescence, and I shall always remember and treasure them" (158).

Glasgow must realize that though such perceptions are true to her own experience, she knows that some readers will find them excessive and sentimental; thus she writes: "All this, it must be remembered, occurred, not in the mental upheaval of the Freudian era, but in that age of romantic passion, the swift turn of the century. If only we had read Freud and the new wisdom, we might have found love a passing pleasure, not a prolonged desire" (163). Glasgow's aim, however, is to express the truth (it is in this chapter that she claims the truth alone can justify an intimate memoir), and she knows that some of her emotions will appear to undermine one another. Thus while she proclaims herself a feminist—"for I liked intellectual revolt as much as I disliked physical violence"—and while she admits that women have "gained, immeasurably, by the passing of the old order" (163–64), she still finds herself "so constituted that the life of the mind is reality, and love without romantic illumination is a spiritless matter" (163). In a brief essay for *Good Housekeeping*, published three decades before she completed *The Woman Within*, Glasgow defined feminism as "a revolt from pretense of being," as "a struggle for the liberation of personality" (683). She never negated or challenged this definition, but what *The Woman Within* makes clear is that her feminism was more at home in the romanticism of a former era: "The modern adventurers who imagine they know love because they have known sex may be wiser than our less enlightened generation. But I am not of their period" (163).

These remarks prepare the reader for the experience that follows. After seven years in which their relationship matured, Glasgow, on a tour of the Alps, received a letter from "Gerald B—" confirming her worst suspicions about his health; she learned of his death from a Paris edition of *The New York Herald* on her return to the United States. After receiving this last letter, Glasgow describes a naturistic vision that she refers to again in the conclusion as her "moment." Couched in the romantic discourse of the premodern era, Glasgow's description is an emotional high point of her narrative:

> Many days later (I cannot be more exact concerning the time) I went up on the hillside, and lay down in the grass, where a high wind was blowing. Could I never escape from death? Or was it life that would not cease its hostilities? . . . Then, after long effort, I sank into an effortless peace. Lying there, in that golden August light, I knew, or felt, or beheld, a union deeper than knowledge, deeper than sense, deeper than vision. Light streamed through me, after anguish, and for one instant of awareness, if but for that one instant, I felt pure ecstasy. In a single blinding flash of illumination, I knew blessedness. I was a part of the spirit that moved in the light and the wind and the grass. I was—or felt I was—in communion with reality, with ultimate being. . . . (165–66, Glasgow's ellipses)

Glasgow acknowledges that the vision may have been "a fantasy of tortured nerves," that it may have been "communion with the Absolute, or with Absolute Nothingness," but she does not doubt its intensity as an event that helped to sustain her spiritually for years to come. It was, she concludes at the close of her narrative, her one "far-off glimpse of the illumination beyond," her one glimpse "of the mystic vision. . . . It was enough, and now it is over" (296).[8]

In the years between the affairs with "Gerald B—" and Henry Anderson, Glasgow had time to cultivate what she calls her ironic pose. At the age of forty-three, she came to this conclusion: "I had found nothing to which I could hold fast and say, 'Here, at last, is reality' " (215). This "protective ironic coloring" (224) is ultimately where her quest for reality takes her, and it is a pose that colors her re-creation of the romance with Henry Anderson. In recalling the past, Glasgow confronts a problem that faces any autobiographer: she must convey a self in an earlier phase through the perspective of a self that is still evolving. Just as her account of the affair with "Gerald B—" is colored by her youthful romanticism, her remembrance of Henry Anderson is filtered through her more mature and cynical perspective: "Long before I knew him, he had reached the top of his ladder and the ground below was liberally strewn—or so malice remarked—with the rungs he had kicked aside. If there is any social top in Richmond, he was standing upon it" (219). Glasgow says that she refused to be impressed by his postures, but she nonetheless found herself caught up in an "attraction of opposites," and, even more important, she admits that Anderson provided her with a release from a painful personal past. Despite their many differences—his love of everything she detests: "Trivial honors, notoriety, social prominence, wealth, fashion, ladies with titles, an empty show in the world" (225)—Glasgow writes, with tongue in cheek, "For the moment at least, until a more important personage—a queen, perhaps—appeared on his horizon, I held undisputed possession" (225).

In her reflection on this episode of her life, Glasgow presents herself as a woman fully in control of her emotions, as someone who can see the irony, even the absurdity, of relationships. This is not, however, the self-image she presents in the last few pages of her narrative where she transcribes part of a letter from her friend Marjorie Kinnan Rawlings. Glasgow rarely presents herself by way of "alterity"; a strategically placed exception is her quotation of a letter in which Rawlings recounts in vivid detail a dream she had of the older writer. Glasgow felt an immediate spiritual rapport with Rawlings (see Ribblett), and it is well known that after Glasgow's death in 1945, Rawlings attempted to write her biography, but her notes were later incorporated by Stanly Godbold in his *Ellen Glasgow and the Woman Within* (1972). Glasgow includes the letter in her Epilogue for what its images convey about the nature of her innermost experience. In the dream, Glasgow has come to live with her friend. Here is how Rawlings describes the encounter:

> I was away when you came, and on my return, to one of those strange mansions that are part of the substance of dreams, you were outside in the bitter cold, cutting away ice from the roadway and piling it in geometric patterns. I was alarmed, remembering your heart trouble, and led you inside the mansion and brought you a cup of hot coffee. You had on blue silk gloves, and I laid my hand over yours, and was amazed, for my own hand is small, to have yours fit inside mine, much smaller. You chose your room and suggested draperies to supplement a valance. The valance was red chintz and you showed me a sample of heavy red brocade of the same shade. I told you that from now on I should take care of you, and you must not do strenuous things, such as cutting the ice in the roadway. (294)

On one level the dream suggests the life of the woman artist who must take the raw substance of reality and shape it into her art, an activity practiced at one's own peril. On another level its inclusion at the end of her autobiography suggests Glasgow's awareness of her own physical and spiritual delicacy, her need, finally, for another kind of shelter—a shelter she envisions here as the protection and support of another woman.[9]

Marilyn R. Chandler has drawn attention to the therapeutic features of *The Woman Within*; similarly, Elizabeth Winston has commented on the affirmative vision of Glasgow's autobiography, a work which, for all its tensions, can be viewed as marking a major step in the history of women's self-assertion. Glasgow, Winston writes, "considered the satisfaction of her needs an acceptable aim in writing an autobiography for publication. This stated purpose distinguishes her from women autobiographers writing before 1920" ("The Autobiographer to Her Readers" 104). Linked to her need for self-affirmation is Glasgow's need to unmask herself, to revise an image she had created for others, and perhaps for herself. As a result, some reviewers were surprised to learn that her deepest sense of self had little connection with the woman they had observed at One West Main Street, the famous Richmond author who had also been a delightful hostess. In the end, Glasgow rejects not only the sheltered existence she had been born into—those restrictions on her personality that were imposed from without—but also the smiling pose she had acquired for her own self-protection—the shelter she herself imposed from within.

Like Ellen Glasgow, Eudora Welty also confronts the sheltered life, presenting another perspective from within. Yet while *The Woman Within* explores the various dimensions and constrictions of Glasgow's shelters on her sense of self-development, Welty's *One Writer's Beginnings* is about the nurturing possibilities of a sheltered upbringing, and as such the two works at times form antithetical poles between which women writers have often fluctuated as they have defined and accounted for the shape of their personal and artistic development.

No one has questioned the value of Welty's book as a factual record, nor has anyone implied that it is a work in any way at odds with itself. Separated in time by forty years, *One Writer's Beginnings* is one third the length of *The Woman Within*. Welty's book is more clearly focused, certainly more tightly concentrated than Glasgow's self-story. It was, of course, Welty's intention to narrow her concerns: nowhere in her autobiography does she declare that she is writing to achieve self-identity. The title indicates that her identity—that of writer—has been achieved and that her book is an attempt to trace the origins of this identity. Welty is guarded about what she reveals; she mentions nothing about romantic involvements, and she draws no attention to her relationships with other women writers such as Katherine Anne Porter or Elizabeth Bowen to whom she dedicated *The Bride of the Innisfallen* (1955). Nor does she invite the reader to psychoanalyze the self she has defined. Her final purpose is, however, the same as Glasgow's; each writer demonstrates, to use Welty's terms, that "all serious daring starts from within" and that the product of this daring is the "solitary core" of their identity.

One Writer's Beginnings was originally delivered as the first William E. Massey, Sr., Lectures in the History of American Civilization at Harvard in April 1983. Welty subsequently revised the three lectures that comprise the units of her book: "Listening," "Learning to See," and "Finding a Voice." The organizational scheme is not rigid and the categories are not exclusive of one another. The units are perhaps best seen as the author's way of taking a necessary pause, of coming up for air. Thus while she moves from early childhood to early adulthood, her method is largely associational and only semichronological. A comment Welty makes about childhood learning is relevant to the somewhat elliptical structure of her book: "Learning stamps you with its moments. Childhood's learning is made up of moments. It isn't steady. It's a pulse" (9). By extension, tracing one's origins, as earlier observed with Glasgow, is not a steady process; it too is a pulse, a matter of looking back and seeing connections in what Welty calls "a continuous thread of revelation," a thread that is anything but linear.

One Writer's Beginnings does not lend itself to easy summary, and though one might pinpoint the concerns that are predominant at any given point in Welty's narrative, these concerns within themselves do not suggest the complexity and power of her self-representation. Welty's autobiography is like a musical composition: themes appear, disappear, and then reappear in later sections, and any detail is enriched by the way it plays off one that precedes or follows it.

Sometimes Welty makes the connections for the reader. She begins "Learning to See," for example, with an account of a summer trip she and her family made to Ohio and West Virginia in a five-passenger

Oakland. Among many observations, she describes the effect of their native states on her parents' psyches; she speaks of towns with their own identities that "one's imagination could embrace"; she describes a naturistic experience on a West Virginia mountain top that helped to crystallize her love of independence (a moment that bears comparison to Glasgow's experience in the Alps); and she provides a brief history of her family tree. Then at the end of this section of the book she writes:

> I think now, in looking back on these summer trips—this one and a num-
> ber later, made in the car and on the train—that another element in them
> must have been influencing my mind. The trips were wholes unto them-
> selves. They were stories. Not only in form, but in their taking on direc-
> tion, movement, development, change. They changed something in my
> life: each trip made its particular revelation, though I could not have
> found words for it. But with the passage of time, I could look back on
> them and see them bringing me news, discoveries, premonitions, prom-
> ises—I still can; they still do. When I did begin to write, the short story
> was a shape that had already formed itself and stood waiting in the back
> of my mind. Nor is it surprising to me that when I made my first attempt
> at a novel [*Delta Wedding*], I entered its world—that of the mysterious
> Yazoo-Mississippi Delta—as a child riding there on a train. (68)

Early on Welty notes that she grew and developed out of her parents, and if any theme is central to *One Writer's Beginnings*, it is the need to make sense of what her parents knowingly and, more important, un-knowingly contributed to her development as an artist. She may shift attention from one parent to the other, but the two figures are never far removed from the focus of her self-representation.

In "Listening," Welty sets out to trace the roots of her early love for the narrative quality of southern conversation; she tells of how as a child she would sit between two grown-ups in a car and instruct them to "talk." She points out, however, that this love of gossip is not some-thing she had in common with her mother, who did not believe in wast-ing words and who was even contemptuous of southern conventions that prompted idle talk. Although not a particularly striking contrast, it becomes more significant as the book progresses and Welty recounts other instances of ways in which their relationship prompted her to make discoveries that were essential to her future role as an artist who tells stories.

She presents one such discovery in an episode that is itself structured like a brief short story. Here Welty describes one of the "trials" she presented to her mother—the time she asked her where babies come from. Welty's mother is evasive and ultimately tells her "the wrong secret—not how babies could come but how they could die, how they could be forgotten about" (17). Welty had found two nickels that, for some mysterious reason to her as a child, had lain on the eyelids of a brother who had died as a baby. Remembering her discovery, she came to two realizations. She wonders how her mother could have kept these coins but concludes that it would have been against her nature to give them away; like Glasgow's mother, "She suffered from a morbid streak which in all the life of the family reached out on occasions—the worst occasions—and touched us, clung around us, making it worse for her; her unbearable moments could find nowhere to go." Even more important, Welty the artist sees, "The future story writer in the child I was must have taken unconscious note and stored it away then: one secret is liable to be revealed in the place of another that is harder to tell, and the substitute secret when nakedly exposed is often the more appalling" (17). This incident has great resonance when the reader recalls that it follows immediately upon Welty's assertion that as a child she loved "scenes" and had learned to listen for stories as well as to them. In a key reflective moment she writes: "My instinct—the dramatic instinct—was to lead me, eventually, on the right track for a storyteller: the *scene* [such as this one with her mother] was full of hints, pointers, suggestions, and promises of things to find out and know about human beings. I had to grow up and learn to listen for the unspoken as well as the spoken—and to know a truth, I also had to recognize a lie" (15).

Welty never implies that her mother lied to her, but she admits to maternal conflicts that subsequently shaped her artistic vision. "When my mother would tell me that she wanted me to have something because she as a child had never had it, I wanted, or I partly wanted," Welty confesses, "to give it back" (19). Thus when Chestina Andrews Welty allows young Eudora to go to the Century Theatre with her father—"I'd rather you saw *Blossom Time* than go myself" (19)—Welty says that her response to the performance would be a mixture of pleasure and guilt, but she does not stop here: "There is no wonder that a passion for independence sprang up in me at the earliest age. It took me a long time to manage the independence, for I loved those who protected me—and I wanted inevitably to protect them back. I have never managed to handle the guilt. In the act and the course of writing stories, these are two of the springs, one bright, one dark, that feed the stream" (19–20). Welty indicates that the "unclouded perfection" her mother had outlined for her caused some anxiety (25) and that part of her objection to the grade school principal, Miss Duling, "a lifelong subscriber to perfection" (22)—and a presence that figures prominently in Welty's childhood memories—was that she did not need this woman's coercion in order to learn, that her affair with words and books transcended institutional requirements. It is clear from her portraits of both Miss Duling and her mother that Welty admires strong-minded women but that such women, though they may be sources of inspiration, also impinge on her own sense of independence.

It is not surprising that after noting her mother's strong sense of perfection, Welty says that her father "was much more tolerant of possible error" (25). By this point in her narrative, the reader has come to expect such a contrast, for a dominant pattern in Welty's autobiography, the contrasts between her parents and the importance of these differences, is established very early in her narrative: "My father had the country boy's accurate knowledge of the weather and its skies. He went out and stood on our front steps first thing in the morning and took a look at it and a sniff. He was a pretty good weather prophet. 'Well, I'm *not*,' my mother would say with enormous self-satisfaction" (4).

What follows in the subsequent pages is a clear outline of differences. Welty's father distrusted fiction and would read chiefly for information; her mother read as a hedonist with a passion for Dickens (7). Her father held a strong belief in the rights of the majority; her mother, having been born left-handed into a family of five left-handed brothers, held no great stock in the opinions or privileges of the majority. Her father, a man of logic, firmly committed to progress and the future, had no great interest in the past or in ancient family stories; her mother's mind "was a mass of associations" where events from the past would be forever linked with others, each event becoming the occasion of a "private anniversary" (19). Her father was essentially an optimist, her mother a pessimist with a streak of morbidity; her father came from a small family, her mother from a very large clan; her father's heart belonged to Ohio, her mother's to West Virginia. Welty shows her readers that understanding her beginnings as a writer is in part a matter of seeing these parental contrasts, for while both parents were united in their desire to procure the future for her, each gave a special gift. Like Glasgow, she singles out her mother's emotional support in her desire to become a writer; yet she notes that, though her father had just cause to fear this generally unlucrative profession, he and she also shared something that was nonetheless indispensable to her later artistic development—a love of journeys and an affinity for losing themselves "in the experience of not missing anything, of seeing everything, of knowing each time what the blows of the whistle meant. . . . Each in our own way, we hungered for all of this: my father and I were in no other respect or situation so congenial" (73).

Travel is an important theme of *One Writer's Beginnings*; it is, as Welty says, "part of some larger continuity" (97), and of course her central aim, as the conclusion of her book makes clear, is to discover and illuminate the larger continuities in her own inner life. The last part of her narrative is full of excursions—to the University of Wisconsin where Professor Ricardo Quintanna helped her to understand the nature of passion; to New York where she experienced the excitement of the theatre and publishing worlds; and to the many small towns and hamlets of Mississippi, where, with the WPA, she wrote brief news stories and took photographs—an activity that would impress upon her the necessity of understanding that "every feeling waits upon its gesture" and that she as a writer must be ready to recognize this moment when she saw it (85). These journeys, real and important, are subsumed into a more significant inward journey, a journey that Welty describes as leading "us through time—forward or back, seldom in a straight line, most often spiraling. Each of us is moving, changing, with respect to others. As we discover, we remember; remembering, we discover; and most intensely do we experience this when our separate journeys converge. Our living experience at those meeting points is one of the charged dramatic fields of fiction" (102).

Like Glasgow, Welty ranges over a number of her own "dramatic fields of fiction," identifying their sources and shades of meaning to her as their author. "Finding a Voice" is in many ways a meditation on the relationship between the creator and her art. At one point Welty claims not to "write by invasion into the life of a real person," that her "own sense of privacy is too strong for that. . . . On the other hand, what I do make my stories out of is the *whole* fund of my feelings, my responses to the real experiences of my own life, to the relationships that formed and changed it, that I have given most of myself to, and so learned my way to a dramatic counterpart" (99–100). One of the ironies that comes out of her self-reflections is the understanding that, though she is generally antipathetic to teachers and teaching, the character of hers she most fully identifies with is Miss Eckhart, the piano teacher from *The Golden Apples* (1949). Welty's description of her affinity with this character is surely one of the most affirmative passages from any self-reflexive work produced by a woman in this century:

> As I looked longer and longer for the origins of this passionate and strange character, at last I realized that Miss Eckhart came from me. There wasn't any resemblance in her outward identity: I am not musical, not a teacher, not foreign in birth; not humorless or ridiculed or missing out in love; nor have I yet let the world around me slip from my recognition. But none of that counts. What counts is only what lies at *the solitary core*. She derived from what I already knew for myself, even felt I had always known. What I have put into her is my passion for my own life work, my own art. Exposing yourself to risk is a truth Miss Eckhart and I had in common. What animates and possesses me is what drives Miss Eckhart, the love of her art and the love of giving it, the desire to give it until there is no more left. (101, emphasis added)

Most reviewers of *One Writer's Beginnings* noted upon its publication in 1984 that it is in many respects a companion piece to the highly autobiographical *The Optimist's Daughter* (1972), which Welty had published as a long short story in 1969 and as a novel three years later. Welty herself was aware that in *One Writer's Beginnings* she was providing a nonfictional account of many events that appear in the earlier novel. As if to underscore the connection—in fact, to show that the two works are different manifestations of the same concerns: memory, desire, and self-realization—Welty concludes her autobiography by quoting eight full paragraphs from the novel, that section of the work in which she presents Laurel's discovery that a life is "nothing but the continuity of its love" (103). She prefaces these paragraphs with a remark that unites the fictional and nonfictional experience: "I'm prepared now to use the wonderful word *confluence*, which of itself exists as a reality and a symbol in one. It is the only kind of symbol that for me as a writer has any weight, testifying to the pattern, one of the chief patterns, of human experience" (102). She follows the lengthy quotation with another remark, one that unites the fictional passage with the impulse that has led her to produce an autobiography: "Of course the greatest confluence of all is that which makes up the human memory—the individual human memory. My own is the treasure most dearly regarded by me, in my life and in my work as a writer" (104).

Welty does not provide a full account of her life, as if such an account were possible. Though she has taken great pleasure in reading and reviewing the personal letters and journals of, among others, Woolf and Faulkner, she has also expressed disapproval of critics and historians who poke into other writers' lives. Like O'Connor, Welty takes a slightly self-deprecating stance and insists that there is really nothing significant about the day-to-day details of her life. She sketches enough of her personal experience to illuminate her understanding of the art she has produced, and this sketch, she implies, is enough to solicit imaginative responses from her readers as well. Her disclosures are deliberate and the identity she affirms at the conclusion of her narrative is that of an artist, not a woman who is also an artist, but a woman who, again like Glasgow, insists that her art is the very core of her identity.

Perhaps Welty anticipated the response of contemporary readers who have become accustomed to autobiographies that attempt to tell all and who might feel that *One Writer's Beginnings*, even with its restricted scope, presents only a guarded, public view. At the end of "Listening," she makes it clear that writing the self is not the most secure of intellectual pursuits. After admitting that her mother's love was at times overbearing, that she "could not help imposing herself between her children and whatever it was they might take it in mind to reach out for in the world," Welty says that, like her two brothers, she solved this problem in a way that was complicated but respectful; she then adds that her mother was "relieved" when Welty decided to become a fiction writer, "for she thought writing was *safe*" (39, emphasis added). What Welty goes on to reveal in her autobiography is that, if taken seriously, writing is anything but safe, for it entails a confrontation with life that is always a matter of great courage:

> It seems to me, writing of my parents now in my seventies, that I see continuities in their lives that weren't visible to me when they were living. Even at the times that have left me my most vivid memories of them, there were connections between them that escaped me. Could it be because I can better see their lives—or any lives I know—today because I'm

a fiction writer? See them not as fiction, certainly—see them, perhaps, as even greater mysteries than I knew. Writing fiction has developed in me an abiding respect for the unknown in a human lifetime and a sense of where to look for the threads, how to follow, how to connect, find in the thick of the tangle what clear line persists. The strands are all there: to the memory nothing is ever really lost. (90)

For Welty, as for Glasgow, writing an autobiography is one more way of confronting the mystery that is the self.

Two years after its publication, Welty was asked if she was "trying to find a new vocabulary in *One Writer's Beginnings.*" She responded by noting that the book was quite unlike anything else in her body of work: "My mind was entirely on what I was trying to convey, but I never have written about myself as myself. Nonfiction to begin with is hard for me. But I'm glad I did it. I at least learned what the writing of it taught me." Welty further noted that, in the end, she excluded a great deal of material once she found the right construction: "the things that didn't magnetize I threw out. But it was so much fun putting my life together, so much enlightenment. I advise everybody to do it" (Devlin 24–25).

By all accounts, *One Writer's Beginnings* has been a highly successful book. It was reviewed (favorably) by most of the nation's major newspapers and many of the better weeklies, not to mention the various literary journals (see Brookhart). Welty's book was also a coup for Harvard University Press: the first best-seller in its then seventy-one year history. This may not surprise anyone who understands how much pleasure Eudora Welty has brought to readers since the midthirties. One could easily argue that readers want to know more about Eudora Welty because she is who she is: an icon on the southern literary scene.

In the chorus of praise accorded to *One Writer's Beginnings*, there have been noticeably few voices of dissent. One important exception is Carolyn Heilbrun, who, in a 1986 essay on women's autobiographical writing, questioned the honesty of Welty's book. Heilbrun repeated her reservations, in somewhat lengthier form, in her 1988 book, *Writing a Woman's Life*:

> I do not believe in the bittersweet quality of *One Writer's Beginnings*, nor do I suppose that the Eudora Welty there evoked could have written the

stories and novels we have learned to celebrate. Welty, like [Jane] Austen, has long been read for what she can offer of reassurance and the docile acceptance of what is given; she has been read as the avatar of a simpler world, with simpler values broadly accepted. In this both Austen and Welty have, of course, been betrayed. But only Welty, living in our own time, has camouflaged herself. Like Willa Cather, like T. S. Eliot's widow, she wishes to keep meddling hands off the life. To her, this is the only proper behavior for the Mississippi lady she so proudly is. (14)

Heilbrun who contends that Welty sublimates her pain as a woman artist, finds *One Writer's Beginnings* to be a potentially harmful book for the very reason that it has been admired by so many readers since it appeared in 1984.

Because of her status as an icon with a devoted following of professional critics and general readers alike, there is the danger, as Heilbrun suggests, that Welty will be read solely on her own terms. One can thus appreciate Heilbrun's honesty in confronting Welty's autobiography, while simultaneously questioning her central premises.

It is more than a bit shocking to hear that Welty has appealed to readers for her "docile acceptance of what is given" or that "to have written a truthful autobiography would have defied every one of her instincts for loyalty and privacy." That Welty has guarded her privacy no one would deny; but from whom has she demanded loyalty? It is puzzling to read that *One Writer's Beginnings* is flawed by the kind of nostalgia for childhood that masks an "unrecognized anger" on the part of its author (*Writing a Woman's Life* 14–15).

It is by no means surprising that one of Welty's best critics would set out to counter Heilbrun's charges. (Heilbrun is, after all, a major feminist critic and herself an author of fiction.) In a spirited defense, "Eudora Welty and the Right to Privacy," Ruth Vande Kieft takes Heilbrun to task—and rightly so—for assuming what she should have proved: a childhood that is somehow inconsistent with the facts and emotions as Welty presents them. Vande Kieft shows that Heilbrun dismissed the facts or, rather, the reality of Welty's family background and, in the process, "turns Welty into a proud Mississippi lady engaged in a cover-up of unsavory personal experiences of the rigid Southern social codes which give rise to pain and anger" ("Eudora Welty and the Right to Privacy" 477). Using simple logic, Vande Kieft exposes a fundamental fallacy in Heilbrun's argument:

We cannot expect that all modern women writers will have suffered kinds and degrees of thwarting experiences such as were endured by Virginia Woolf, Willa Cather, May Sarton, or Carolyn Heilbrun. An honest writer cannot be asked to *invent* such experiences, or lay off the faintly tinted rose-colored glasses of loving memory in order to put on the more obviously distorting dark glasses of anger and resentment, for the sake of young women in need of liberated role-models—as though a woman should feel guilty about having enjoyed a happy and protected childhood, or cheated of some obligatory misery, some authenticating agony, if she is to achieve maturity and stature as a woman writer. (477)

Of equal importance is Vande Kieft's realization that Heilbrun's "attack" stems in large measure from the differences between her temperament and that of Welty's, differences that are crystallized in contrasting accounts of their early reading habits. Instead of "Welty's avowed hedonism and promiscuity in reading, her special delight in fantasy, fairy tales, myth and legend, we have Heilbrun's account of how as a young girl of about ten years, she began to read biography, 'working her way along the shelves' . . . 'denying [herself] an attractive book in *R* because [she] had reached only *G*' " (478).

In short, Vande Kieft effectively dismisses the substance of Heilbrun's argument. Vande Kieft is less successful, however, in the second part of her article when she attempts to do the same with a brief but noteworthy remark made by Frank Lentricchia in the pages of the interdisciplinary journal *Raritan*. In a 1989 essay concerned with Don Delillo's politically motivated fiction, Lentricchia calls Welty the "Cumean Sibyl of the new regionalism, who declares that fiction must have a 'private address' " (quoted in Vande Kieft 480). Vande Kieft is intrigued by the "partly honorific" connotations of this remark; yet she also contends that Lentricchia's epithet "makes out of [Welty's] sibylline power something dangerous, again misguiding of younger writers, leading them down restricted paths and into limited perceptions or off into the transcendent, toward evasion and retreat into private and personal realms, away from engagement in compelling public matters formative of American character and destiny" (480–81).

It seems inevitable that critics, Vande Kieft among them, would discuss Welty's autobiography in conjunction with her earlier essay, "Must the Novelist Crusade?"—the basis of Lentricchia's remark. The first deals with what Welty perceives as having gone into the making of her fiction, the later with what she has consciously excluded from the creative process. Yet while *One Writer's Beginnings* is a personal document (in the best sense of the term), "Must the Novelist Crusade?" is a manifesto—a political pamphlet, as it were. The difference between the two works is crucial and Lentricchia is correct to imply that Welty is here attempting to persuade others—even impressionable younger writers—to accept her argument. With "Must the Novelist Crusade?" Welty is doing something beyond writing about her own beginnings as a writer. Vande Kieft downplays this feature of Welty's polemic, and though one can agree with her that Welty's fiction may be far more political than frequently acknowledged (Vande Kieft draws attention to Louise Westling's excellent work on this dimension of Welty's writing), it seems necessary to let Welty's words speak for themselves. Welty answers her partly rhetorical question, must the novelist crusade? with a resounding No: "The novel itself always affirms. . . . It says what people are like. It doesn't, and doesn't know how to, describe what they are *not* like, and it would waste its time if it told us what we ought to be like, since we already know that, don't we?" (*Eye of the Story* 152). Welty's essay is beautifully written and elaborately argued, and yet one might find it necessary to pull back from the force of her prose and ask why the novel must always affirm, or why the "crusader-novelist must inevitably leave out the mystery and wonder of life" (150–51)—such is not the case with *Strange Fruit*, for instance—or why, for that matter, writing fiction is and must remain for all authors "an interior affair" (153).

To the extent that Welty is arguing for a literature that is not crudely explicit—that respects the full complexity of human existence—one can easily accept her argument. In interviews, Welty is often asked about the views she presented in "Must the Novelist Crusade?" In 1986 she agreed with Peggy Whitman Prenshaw that during the 1980s the nation "embarked on a new era of dogmatism." Though she finds the new sociopolitical climate alarming, Welty still refuses to let it dictate the shape of her art. Again she noted her well-known aversion: "I wouldn't like to read a work of fiction that I thought had an ulterior motive, to persuade me politically. I automatically react the other way. Is that just *perversity*?" (Devlin 29, emphasis added). Though this comment may not indicate a softening of her earlier stance, it does allow for a certain quirkiness of response, the same quirkiness or perversity that kept Welty as a child from reading Dickins when her mother suggested that she do so (18). Perhaps impatient with readers who might see her as the chief apologist for a "new regionalism," Welty acknowledged that no writer is governed by a set of rules, "Anybody can exhort us that wants to" (26). Despite her own aesthetic preferences, she even acknowledged the pointlessness of condescending to literature with an openly didactic purpose.

At the end of *One Writer's Beginnings* Welty makes it clear that, while she herself is no crusading novelist, her fiction is still a risk-taking venture. The danger of "Must the Novelist Crusade?" is that readers, taking this essay as their cue, might overlook Welty's risks—the ways in which her work is at times genuinely subversive. Welty may prefer an indirect or oblique approach, but her art is not without an instructive intent, as Peter Schmidt has recently shown in a provocative study of Welty's major short fiction. In *The Heart of the Story* (1991), Schmidt draws attention to the complex ways in which Welty uses myth to show her women readers in particular the value of challenging the community and its traditions. Her many "references to sibyls and to the Medusa teach her readers to identify and change the cultural texts that confine them—to evolve from identifying with Medusa [an image often used "to stigmatize women who transgress accepted conventions in society or in literature"] to identifying with a sibyl, from self-destructive rage and guilt to empowering acts of disguise and revision" (262–63). *One Writer's Beginnings* is itself an affirming yet subversive book. As Michael Kreyling has observed, Welty's autobiography documents the process by which she became aware that "words are the means of moving from passive object into the freedom of the subject." Kreyling further shows that Welty's act of self-affirmation is intricately linked to her many images of Perseus and Medusa: "Perseus slays the universal beholder, the face that seals the self into eternal 'alterity.' Each act of the subject, then, is the stroke of Perseus—an 'endless' rhythm. Perseus is the patron of all writers; perhaps the woman writer knows how deep is the debt" (Devlin 224).

While *One Writer's Beginnings* is Welty's one book-length attempt to write about herself as herself, it is not her first self-reflective work. Earlier pieces include such reminiscences as "A Sweet Devouring" (much of which found its way into the autobiography) and "The Little Store," both of which are included in *The Eye of the Story* (1978). On the surface, a piece like "The Little Store" might appear inconsequential (Welty merely recounts the adventure of a favorite childhood errand), but a careful reading reveals that she is using the reminiscence to define her major preoccupations as a writer, not the least of which is, again, her need to take risks. It is a piece that works through hints and pointers. Though it contains little of an intimate nature, it suggests a great deal about Welty's life as an observer, and for readers in the midseventies it was an indication of the kind of autobiography she might eventually produce.

It is likely that commentators will continue to ponder Welty's reservations about self-writing. As Sally Wolff, among others, has noted, "The autobiographical nature of Eudora Welty's art is difficult to discern fully, partly because the writer is an extremely private person who believes that knowing the life is not essential for understanding the fiction. Like William Faulkner, who wished to be remembered by the words, 'He made the books and he died,' Welty maintains that successful fiction conveys the writer's feelings apart from any biographical context" (79). Welty seems most doubtful that anything significant can be expressed through the bald personal detail, as she makes clear in a review of Elizabeth Bowen's uncompleted autobiography, *Pictures and Conversations* (1975). Peggy Whitman Prenshaw cites the following passage from Welty's review before demonstrating the ways in which Welty aligns herself with Bowen's autobiographical method: "Instead of the 'personal' (in the accepted sense), we were to be given the more revealing findings she herself could bring out of her life and her work, calling for the truer candor, the greater generosity—a work to do reader, as well as writer, proud" ("Antiphonies" 232). It is clearly these larger, more revealing findings that Welty is after in *One Writer's Beginnings*. It is these findings, she would argue, that best focus the reader's attention.

Glasgow's and Welty's autobiographies are examined here primarily in terms of what they say about the inner self. This is the approach that each author invites, and it is one that yields the most intriguing results. It is not uncommon for critics to take another tack: to probe self-stories for what they imply or say about a given culture from the perspective of someone who is strongly identified as part of that culture. As writers who are firmly linked in the public's mind with the renascent period of southern letters, Glasgow and Welty have commented at some length, especially in interviews and essays, on the nature of their native region. They may not place the South and its problems in the foreground in their autobiographies, but the region is part of the texture of their lives; and while their purpose is not to write social commentary, the commentary is nonetheless there and bears some comparison.

Glasgow's attitude toward the South can be summed up in a phrase she applies to southern customs of death, dying, and burial: "impressive unreasonableness" (159). At a later point in *The Woman Within* she writes that the whole structure of the South, at least as she knew it, depended "upon an invaluable sense of reality in illusion" (217). Her famous remark that what the South needs is blood and irony must be seen in the context of her disdain for the "inherent falseness" in southern tradition (97), or as she says at the end of Chapter Eight, "in the South there was not only adolescence to outgrow, there was an insidious sentimental tradition to live down. I had been brought up in the midst of it; I was a part of it, or it was a part of me" (104).

There is very little apology for the South in Glasgow's autobiography, though she does attempt to give her region its due in relation to other sections of the country. Like Welty she notes that southerners seem to have been born with the gift of talk, but she does not display Welty's great affection for this habit: "I was born in the South. I was part of the South. And, in the South, where conversation, not literature, is the serious pursuit of all classes, I continued to write as I must . . ." (152, Glasgow's ellipses). Earlier she had written that southerners did not publish, write, or read, that their appetite for information was personal and easily satisfied by oratory and gossip (105); consequently she resented the time spent with acquaintances "who regarded books as not only unnecessary in well-bred circles, but as an unwarranted extravagance. . . . 'You are too attractive to be strong-minded,' they would remark, reassuringly" (90). Glasgow's view has echoes of Mencken's "Sahara of the Bozart," but it should be observed that she does not exempt the North from similar charges; her home, the place she knows best, may be the South, but she moves beyond this region in her social critique. New York enjoyed its share of the second best, she claims; in this cultural center, as in Richmond, "social charm presided over intelligence" (139). As for the issue of race, Glasgow is peculiarly silent: African-Americans, when they do appear, are subsumed into that dispossessed group that includes animals, women, the inarticulate, the poor.

In *One Writer's Beginnings*, Welty is somewhat more pointed in not-ing the South's racial distinctions, and she even suggests what segre-gation meant to her as a southerner. She explains that her schooling at Mississippi State College for Women presented her the chance to ob-serve, for the first time, the diverse population of her home state— "what differences in background, persuasion of mind, and resources of character there were among Mississippians—at that, among only half of us, for we were all white. I missed the significance of both what was in, and what was out of, our well-enclosed but vibrantly alive society" (77). Welty's view of the South, as this passage indicates, is not a scold-ing view; her outlook is even less hostile than Glasgow's. What one glimpses in *One Writer's Beginnings* are images of Welty's section of the South in action. She moves from her educational background (where the school's honor roll would become an important item in the local newspaper) to the telling regional detail, such as the religious road sign with all its iconographic significance; from the ancestral mix that is most common in her part of the South to her mother's reaction— that of a transplanted insider—to that other section of the country: " 'Oh yes, we're in the North now,' said my mother after we'd crossed the state line from West Virginia into Ohio. 'The barns are all bigger than the houses. They care more about the horses and cows than they do about—' She forbore to say" (61). Welty dwells on none of these details, and though her view of the South is hardly Menckenesque, she never discounts its distinctiveness. One of the things she learns from her travels is the importance of regional borders: "you rode ready for them. Crossing a river, crossing a county line, crossing a state line— especially crossing the line you couldn't see but knew was there, be-tween the South and the North—you could draw a breath and feel the difference" (44).

As children Glasgow and Welty were both wanderers (see Manning), devoted readers, and keen observers. Though there were indeed differ-ences between Glasgow's Tidewater Virginia and Welty's Deep-South Mississippi, the two women found themselves observing and respond-ing to many of the same regional customs and events—to the popular and highly visible southern revival meeting, to cite only one example. If a chief purpose of autobiography is to reconcile what one may have seen or experienced with what one has become, then their re-creations of and reflections upon these modern-day prophets and their devoted followers might be compared for what they suggest about the identities both writers inscribe.

Glasgow speaks of her exposure to revival meetings as prompting a short-lived religious conversion. As a child she would attend the revivals with her Aunt Rebecca. To what Glasgow recalls as her "burning humiliation," she is one day "singled out for praise by the evangelist" and instructed by his "awful voice" to lead the audience in a hymn. With the help of her aunt, Glasgow complies and leads the worshippers in a chorus of "Rescue the Perishing." The experience was mortifying, and her conversion ended as quickly as it began: "The evangelist passed on to wider fields and to riper harvests, while I relapsed, permanently, into 'original corruption,' and was 'bound over to the wrath of God' " (*The Woman Within* 34–35). Glasgow's quote marks speak for themselves. She relates the incident for at least two reasons: it underscores her sense of singularity within a society drawn to both high and low forms of religious ritual, and it functions as a transition to the opening of the next chapter in which she recalls an entirely different sense of religious supplication—her personal prayer to God as a child that he let her become a writer of books (36–37).

Welty's reaction to the traveling evangelists is similar though, characteristically, more humorous. Though hers "was never a churchgoing family," Welty, like Glasgow, was sensitive to the fact that she grew up in a very "religious-minded society" (*One Writer's Beginnings* 31). Also like Glasgow, Welty was fascinated by the religious hymns, and particularly by the contradiction between their sprightly rhythms, derived as many of them were from old English rounds and dance tunes, and the more disturbing nature of their content. Always drawn to entertainers, Welty was fascinated by the evangelists who visited Jackson and who "seemed to be part of August" (32). One of these, Gypsy Smith, Welty describes as capable of leading even "the firebrand editor of the evening newspaper" to the altar of salvation. It was an experience that made the editor "lastingly righteous so that he knew just what to say in the *Jackson Daily News* when one of our fellow Mississippians had the unmitigated gall to publish, and expect other Mississippians to read, a book like *Sanctuary*" (32).

Welty did not go on to produce anything quite like *Sanctuary*, and, along with her father and mother, she resisted the call to be saved. She acknowledges her life-long susceptibility "to anyone on a stage," even circuit-riding evangelists, but she admits that the "secular longing" to provide pleasure—to assist the magician on stage at the Century Theatre—was a more compelling prompting, and the one she chose to follow. Like Glasgow, Welty relates the episode with the revivalists for clear reasons; as always, she looks to the larger and more important implication of the previous experience: "I painlessly came to realize that the reverence I felt for the holiness of life is not ever likely to be entirely at home in organized religion" (33). Following her mother's more personal example of reading the Bible for herself, of even quibbling with her Baptist preacher ancestors, Welty briefly considers what these earlier experiences have meant to her own sense of vocation, but this is one instance in which she does not emphasize her own singularity: "How many of us, the South's writers-to-be of my generation, were blessed in one way or another, if not blessed alike, in not having gone deprived of the King James Version of the Bible. Its cadence entered into our ears and our memories for good. The evidence, or the ghost of it, lingers in all our books." This evidence, she believes, is strong enough to speak of itself: " 'In the beginning was the Word' " (33–34).

Unlike Lillian Smith, who devoted a whole segment of *Killers of the Dream* to the psychological and ideological damage of the fundamentalist revivals on the mind of the South, neither Glasgow nor Welty considers anything but the significance of these events to her inner life and the work that evolves from this interior world. As Welty remarks in "Finding a Voice," the outside world—the world of events and persons that impress themselves on her consciousness—is "the vital component of my inner life. My work, in the terms in which I see it, is as dearly matched to the world as its secret sharer" (76). Neither Glasgow nor Welty goes as far as Smith in drawing the social implications of her distinctly southern experience, yet neither diminishes the reality of her region's complexity. It may not be necessary to isolate those regional elements that each writer omits in her life story; as William Andrews has suggested, the important thing to determine is the extent to which loyalty to a sense of home subverts intellectual honesty with oneself, the extent to which selfhood is defined, confined, or left unresolved at the end of the southern autobiographer's narrative. Neither Glasgow nor Welty sacrifices honesty for regional identification—or for regional brandishment. Despite their sheltered upbringing in a region that has valued a woman's ability to endure silently, Glasgow and Welty define selves that are "daring," "without surrender," and, perhaps most important, capable of creating and thus sustaining their deepest sense of identity.

As noted earlier, Lillian Smith, late in her career, articulated a criteria for autobiographical greatness that does not rely upon masculinist notions of achievement and influence; for Smith, greatness is a matter of capturing the fundamental mystery that is the human being, an emphasis that is germane to both Glasgow's and Welty's undertaking. Further, Smith took an important step in the movement away from assessing an autobiography's strength by its level of facticity. Like Patricia Meyer Spacks who followed her, Smith understood that autobiographies are not lives, but stories about lives (Spacks, "Selves in Hiding" 132). Her many different autobiographical works, including *A Journey* (1954) and *Memory of a Large Christmas* (1962), must have led Smith to see that the self is not an a priori existence that the autobiographer discovers along the way: "when a story teller—and every autobiographer is a story teller—starts out to tell his own story, he has to search deep and wide to know what that story really is. This is a spiritual and intellectual ordeal. It is more: it is a creative ordeal for he is actually creating his own Self and his own life as he writes, because he is giving it its meaning." Smith was not surprised that "most of us settle for smaller matters," or that "women for the most part have settled for notebooks and diaries and journals—as have some of our great male writers" (*Winner* 196).

Recent academic and popular interest in women's autobiographies has prompted feminist critics such as Spacks, Carolyn Heilbrun, and Estelle Jelinek to follow Smith's lead and explore those experiences and the shared secrets women have put into and omitted from their life-stories. Both Welty and Glasgow omit any reference to their sexual development and thus provide evidence for Spacks's claim that, as a topic of self-inquiry, sex becomes a "trap" for the female autobiographer ("Reflecting Women" 32); or, as Sidonie Smith more trenchantly remarked, the female autobiographer's authority to speak too often relies upon an "erasure" of her sexuality, for "the woman who would write autobiography must uphold her reputation for female goodness or risk her immortal reputation" (55–56). It is a dilemma or trap that becomes especially confounding for the southern woman whose goodness and sexual purity are only two elements of her traditional value as symbol of the South itself.

In addition to these omissions, both writers project onto their readers what Sidonie Smith calls "engendered cultural expectations" about the value of women's life stories (49–50). Glasgow understands that her quest for self-realization might be interpreted as narcissistic self-pity, and Welty reassures her readers that a sheltered life can in fact be daring without ever directly engaging the public sphere. What might be added here is that, in her own way, each writer echoes Anais Nin's understanding that our culture is suspicious of the sustained inward glance, of something it associates with the feminine but which one might assume is fundamental to the act of writing one's life. Each has given us an autobiography that proves the validity of Nin's response to this suspicion: "The personal life deeply lived takes you beyond the personal" (162).

The patterns and motifs that have been identified by feminist scholars are especially useful in locating and understanding the differences between *The Woman Within* and *One Writer's Beginnings*. It seems clear that Glasgow had a greater need than Welty to rectify what she deemed the public's misconception of her, a need that, according to Jelinek, has motivated a great many female autobiographers (*Tradition* 186). The smiling, ironic pose—itself a form of deception—may have functioned as a means of survival for Glasgow, but it was still a pose, and one she finally revealed without the personal risk of self-exposure during her lifetime. It is also clear that what Sidonie Smith calls the "tension between two competing self-representations"—"maternal self-effacement" and "paternal self-assertion" (61), a tension that Smith believes operates on a prominent or subconscious level in all autobiographies by women—is less pronounced in *One Writer's Beginnings*, where the maternal influence lacks no self-assertion and where the distinctions between maternal and paternal realms are just that, distinctions rather than binary oppositions. Glasgow came from a more traditionally structured southern home, with parents who embodied more clearly defined roles and expectations. She struggled against, but did not succeed in completely rejecting, the world of her father; and though she aligned herself with her mother—even signing her name as Ellen Anderson Gholson Glasgow in tribute to her mother and her maternal ancestors (McDowell 46)—she could not fulfill the expectation that she too would become submissive and self-effacing, content to suffer without articulating herself. While both writers stress their singularity, a sense of feeling other, of being separate, emerges from *The Woman Within*. One cannot resist the evidence that Glasgow's autobiography, written over a period of nine years, was, as Spacks might argue, a form of "psychic compensation" ("Reflecting Women" 38), a way of salvaging something from a world she found essentially hostile.

The various tensions that characterize women's autobiography are indeed more pronounced in *The Woman Within*, but one should also acknowledge that Glasgow covers terrain that many women autobiographers have attempted to avoid.[10] Glasgow may omit the subject of her sexuality, but she does not exclude romantic love, nor does she understate the crises and anger of girlhood. In this respect, she is a clear exception to Heilbrun's claim that only in the eighties has women's autobiographical writing "become an exploration of painful experience rather than a denial of pain and struggle" ("Women's Autobiographical Writings" 22). Welty may see anger as the emotion least responsible for her work, but the same cannot be said of Glasgow. Without questioning her love of craft, few would fail to see that anger is a chief ingredient of Glasgow's fiction and that it suffuses *The Woman Within* as well.

Despite these dissimilarities, it is necessary, in the end, to focus on what as autobiographers these two writers share. Again, a chief value of recent feminist theory is that it calls attention to those features that not only unite the two works but that also underscore their distinctiveness as examples of women's self-writing. Given the nature of a patriarchal culture, one can understand why women autobiographers have often downplayed their accomplishments, but, as Estelle Jelinek has found, even literary women who choose to write about themselves have often avoided mentioning their own writing—its genesis, qualities, failures, and importance to their sense of self (*Tradition* 166). In their autobiographies as well as in their essays and interviews, Glasgow and Welty never hesitate to stress their professional lives (indeed, Glasgow's *A Certain Measure* can be seen as an autobiographical work that takes as its chief goal the valorization of one woman's vocation), nor do they minimize or mask their commitment to the work that has brought them public attention. Each is a notable exception to Patricia Meyer Spacks's conclusion that women who produce autobiographies traditionally fail "to affirm their status as moral beings making conscious choices significant in relation to their development" ("Women's Stories" 40)—a conclusion that Spacks applies even to women like Eleanor Roosevelt and Golda Meir whose lives have had enormous influence on others ("Selves in Hiding" 113–14). Because Glasgow and Welty are able to conflate the personal and the professional in their self-narratives, neither, in the end, infers that she is somehow "unfinished" (see Jelinek, *Tradition* 187); rather, each seeks out and confirms the continuity and fulfillment of a life that has evolved from very deliberate choices. Finally, neither writer defines herself indirectly through a relationship with what Mary Mason calls "another consciousness . . . the identification of an 'other' " (210); their emphasis on "the woman within" requires, rather, a strategy that moves in an altogether different direction.[11]

In "Reflecting Women," Patricia Meyer Spacks observes that "women use the knowledge and tradition gained from the outer world as a way of shaping and comprehending their inner experience," an experience that then becomes the basis for "claiming the attention of the outer world" (27). These remarks undergird the present analysis of both *The Woman Within* and *One Writer's Beginnings*. Crucial, however, is the fact that when they move from memoirs, journals, and diaries to full-length autobiographies, women and men have often ignored the inner self—a fact that makes Glasgow's and Welty's autobiographical achievement all the more notable. Estelle Jelinek quotes William Matthews's explanation of why autobiographers so often omit the self that lies within: "Few autobiographers put into their books very much of that private, intimate knowledge of themselves that only they can have. Oftener than not, they shun their own inner peculiarities and fit themselves into patterns of behavior and character suggested by the ideas and ideals of their period and by the fashions in autobiography with which they associate themselves. The laws of literature and the human reluctance to stand individually naked combine to cheat the expectations of readers who hope to find in autobiographies many revelations of men's true selves" (*Women's Autobiography* 5).

Glasgow and Welty may not stand naked at the conclusions of their autobiographies (Lillian Smith, for one, would contend that self-definition rather than self-exposure is the desired goal), but they do—and this is the point that must be stressed—make the inner self the focus of their self-narratives. They are concerned with surface details only to the extent that these details in some way illuminate their sense of something more profound. The conscious, thinking, reflective, and creative inner self: this is the subject of both *The Woman Within* and *One Writer's Beginnings*.

In confronting self-writing by southern women, it becomes apparent that one cannot ignore an ideology—indigenous to no specific culture but particularly pernicious in the South—that maintains that women are creative only at a remove from their original procreative function and that, if they do choose to create, the less said about it the better. By making the creative, inner self the very basis of their autobiographical enterprise, Glasgow and Welty not only reveal their greatest affinity but also help to dismantle the illiberal ideology that holds that creativity and the ability to articulate the source and nature of one's creative impulse are ipso facto male prerogatives.

4.

LILLIAN HELLMAN AND KATHERINE ANNE PORTER

Memoirs from Outside the Shelter

Lillian Hellman and Katherine Anne Porter did not produce autobiographies on the order of *The Woman Within* or *One Writer's Beginnings*, though, like Lillian Smith, they did attempt to represent themselves within works that combine self-analysis and cultural critique.

As noted earlier, Smith, Hellman, and Porter were each drawn to one
important theme—the dangers of a passive collusion with evil—and
each has used her self-writing to explore her own motives while venting
scorn on those who, through passivity, ignorance, or their own refusal
to explore themselves, allow reactionary leaders and masses to perpetrate their own forms of evil. Neither Hellman nor Porter suffered
Smith's ostracism for their liberal commitments. Their acceptance by
a large number of readers should not suggest, however, that their memoirs, especially *Scoundrel Time* (1976) and *The Never-Ending Wrong*
(1977), have been read and interpreted in the most meaningful ways.
The memoir has suffered a peculiar fate: rarely has it failed to create
problems for readers and rarely has it been privileged by intellectual

historians in their attempts to chart the course of modern American (or southern) history and culture. Yet an understanding of the memoir as a distinctive genre of self-writing is germane to an understanding of *Scoundrel Time* and *The Never-Ending Wrong*, two remarkably similar works that provide the basis for a new look at how these two enigmatic southern writers chose to understand and represent themselves within a political framework.

Undoubtedly, the liberalism espoused by Lillian Hellman and Katherine Anne Porter owes something to their wide travels, though in this respect neither writer is unique. Most women writers of the Southern Renaissance traveled in Europe or other parts of the world. Glasgow said England was her second home; Gordon and McCullers lived for intervals in Paris (Gordon the agrarian regretted that she had to leave the Paris cafes); Lillian Smith traveled widely and taught for three years in China; Welty traveled in Europe and Ireland; and O'Connor, though more homebound than the others, spent a brief period in Lourdes. It is Hellman and Porter who traveled most extensively, however, and who produced works such as *Watch on the Rhine* (1941) and *Ship of Fools* (1962) that are decidedly international in focus (an unknowing reader might feel caught off-guard to discover that either work is the product of a writer with strong ties to her native region). It is not surprising that both women left memoirs that define selves within a community that is not circumscribed by regional borders.[1]

Published within a year of one another, the two memoirs take as their immediate subject the writer's reaction to an event that occurred in the past—an event with both personal and national implications. *Scoundrel Time* is Hellman's reflection on the McCarthy era and specifically her testimony on 21 May 1952 before the House Committee on Un-American Activities (HUAC); *The Never-Ending Wrong* is Porter's account of the Sacco-Vanzetti trial and execution and her limited involvement, under the direction of a Communist support group, as the translator of the two men's letters to friends in the outside world.[2] Hellman's memoir was published almost twenty-five years after her appearance before HUAC; she had attempted to produce a similar work on two previous occasions but was not pleased with the results. Porter's memoir was published for the fiftieth anniversary of Sacco's and Vanzetti's execution. She had attempted to produce her memoir for the twenty-fifth anniversary but, like Hellman, found that she needed even more time to synthesize and come to terms with her many reflections.

Both writers define themselves within the context of four predominant and overlapping themes: the betrayal of liberalism by liberals themselves; the role of the state and its power, and the failure of traditional ethics when power is abused and justice miscarried; the value of anger and personal heroism; and, perhaps most southern in emphasis—though with a distinctive twist—the necessity of both personal and national recollection. It is these connections that prompt an intertextual examination of the two works.

While critics have linked Porter's fictional techniques to those of Welty, McCullers, O'Connor, and Gordon, there is not only a greater thematic resemblance but a more pronounced affinity of life experiences between Hellman and Porter, each of whom projected images, written and pictorial, of herself as a grand dame. An extended comparison would have to include the following details. Both were able to use their art to make themselves very wealthy: Hellman's estate at the time of her death in 1984 was estimated at nearly four million dollars, and though Porter lived at times in near poverty, the film rights to *Ship of Fools* alone brought her close to one million dollars. Both women had many affairs: Hellman's paramours included Dashiell Hammett, theatrical agent Arthur Kober, magazine manager Ralph Ingersoll, and Third Secretary of the U.S. Embassy in Moscow, John Melby, one of the men whose reputations she tried to protect during the time of her hearing. Porter was married four times—to John Henry Koontz, Ernest Stock, Eugene Pressly, and Albert Erskine. "If all the men I'm supposed to have lived with were crammed into this room," she once remarked, "we couldn't turn around" (Givner, *Conversations* 157). As the photographic legacy reveals, both women were attracted to the world of glamour and high fashion: the huge emerald ring that Porter was at last able to purchase in the midsixties is one of the items on display in the Katherine Anne Porter Room in the McKelden Library at the University of Maryland; Hellman of course created a minor sensation when in the midseventies she posed for a Blackglama fur ad under the caption, "What Becomes a Legend Most?" Both women worked for a period of time in Los Angeles (each detested the West Coast and most of the work she did there), both became lecturers and campus celebrities, and both were candid about their experiments with marijuana, though Porter, for her part, was less willing to acknowledge her reputation as a hard drinker.

The careers of the two women overlap in other surprising ways as well. Each was strongly affected by her personal exposure to the Russian filmmaker Sergei Eisenstein (he is only thinly disguised as Andreyev in Porter's "Hacienda"); each wrote reviews for the *New York Herald-Tribune* at the start of her career; and each secured the same publisher, Little, Brown, and Company, a firm noted for its receptiveness to liberals and leftist writers. (Without making too much of the matter, one cannot fail to notice a similarity between even the dust jackets of *Scoundrel Time* and *The Never-Ending Wrong*, a pronounced red motif that functions, at least with *Scoundrel Time*, as a subliminal cue to any knowing reader's expectations.) The most significant similarity, however, is that these two women from the South could not accept the prevailing gender norms of their culture. Porter said in a 1974 interview that she left Texas because she did not "want to be regarded as a freak. That was how they regarded a woman who tried to write. I had to make a revolt, a rebellion . . . so you see, I am the great-grandmother of these bombers, and students beating each other up with bicycle chains" (Givner, *Conversations* 165). Neither Hellman nor Porter could remain detached and uninvolved—prerequisites for the traditional southern lady. Further, each had the knack of placing herself in positions in which she could observe and even participate in events that have marked the century. Hellman's dangerous 1944 flight across Siberia in a one-engine plane to observe, as a cultural emissary, the German attack on the Russian front is analogous to Porter's brief encounter with Hermann Goering in Berlin as the Nazis rose to power or her revolutionary activities in Mexico.[3]

Politically, however, Hellman and Porter took separate paths. Both were unmistakably liberal, but while Hellman continued to advance political causes—many of which had Communist backing—Porter became disillusioned with and shied away from politics altogether. Neither was ever a hard-nosed ideologue: Hellman regretted that she was not a radical in the truest sense (that is, her love of wealth and comfort did not always complement her political sympathies), and Porter, though she was drawn to the essential tenants of anarchism, could not embrace this philosophy anymore than she could accept the worst excesses of unchecked capitalism, or what she called in her memoir "the never-never-land of the theoretically classless society that could not take root" (24).

In *The Never-Ending Wrong*, Porter notes that she served for a short time as assistant to the editor of ROSTA (later TASS), the official Russian news agency and propaganda center in America. Her experiences in Mexico finally led her to distrust Communists, and she eventually accused them of the very behavior that Hellman would defend them against: their policy, as Porter saw it, to join in and take over, their eagerness to comply with whatever the party ordered (18–19). Still, though Porter came to disparage the behavior of Communists and their vision of society (see, for example, a letter to *The Nation*, 11 May 1947, that is included in her *Collected Essays*), she cannot be numbered among the passive liberal anti-Communists that Hellman attacks in *Scoundrel Time*. To the contrary, Porter once covered a political debate for a California newspaper—a confrontation between anti-Communists who claimed that Hollywood was a seething bed of Red activity (including the mother of Ginger Rogers and Senator Jack Tenney) and the men who countered their distorted charges (Emmet Lavery, president of the Screen Writers Guild, and Albert Dekker, an actor and former state assemblyman). Porter resented the staging of the event— it reminded her of Hitler's demand for compliance—and she was disturbed that Rogers and Tenney could so cavalierly dismiss the "piece of good American doctrine" that says it is not acceptable to discriminate on the basis of religious or political beliefs. This witty article, "On Communism in Hollywood," reveals that as early as 1947, even before the trial of the Hollywood Ten, Porter discerned the threat of what became known as McCarthyism. "I still don't know how many Communists there are in Hollywood, nor where they are," she concludes; "but I will trust Mr. Dekker and Mr. Lavery and that audience to fight them more effectively than any number of Anti-American Activities Committees, whose activities have seemed to me from the beginning the most un-American thing I know" (*Collected Essays* 205–8).

It is necessary to differentiate Porter from those liberal anti-Communists who did find astounding ways to defend the HUAC hearings and the anti-Communist sentiment (Red-baiting) that scarred this country during the midpoint of the century.[4] Any student of American history can see the connection between, say, the Palmer Raids of 1919, the Sacco-Vanzetti affair, motivated as it was by both xenophobia and an often irrational fear of radicalism, and the worst abuses of the Mc-Carthy era. In a review of *The Never-Ending Wrong*, John Deedy correctly notes that "Sacco and Vanzetti were the victims of a political hysteria that was no less real, only less sophisticated, than that of the McCarthy era thirty years later" (572). Not all liberals saw the blatant abuse of political power in Boston as evidence of an innately corrupt capitalist system, but few if any defended what took place there. Indeed, Sacco and Vanzetti initiated more single pieces of protest literature than did any other figures of what was a fundamentally conservative era. By contrast, while McCarthyism became the subtext of many works of the fifties—for example, Lillian Smith's *One Hour* (1959), Arthur Miller's *The Crucible* (1953), and Hellman's own translation of Jean Anouilh's *The Lark* (1955)—McCarthy did not spark a major protest literature against the abuse of basic civil liberties. The mood of the country had become so divided that even in 1978 Diana Trilling could make this amazing defense: "The actions of the HUAC and of McCarthy were plainly anti-liberal. But this is not to say that everyone who came under their attack was thereby redeemed of responsibility for his own acceptance of the destruction of liberty by Communism: it takes more than victimization by illiberalism to certify one's liberalism. And even in those dark years of violation of civil rights, the only punishment of these 'dissidents' was loss of very high-paid jobs or, at worst, which was indeed bad enough, a short jail term; no one was put to death for exercising his right of free speech" (*We Must March* 50).

As David Cook points out in a standard history of narrative film, many of these dissidents did lose their lives: "Philip Loeb, one of the stars of the popular television series *The Goldbergs*, committed suicide; the screen actors John Garfield, Canada Lee, J. Edward Bromberg, and Mady Christians died as a result of the stress they were subjected to" (409). Sadly, these are only a few of the names that such a list might include.

It is by no means insignificant that the largest group of people brought before HUAC were connected in one way or another to the highly visible entertainment industry; it was, in fact, a former Hollywood connection, Martin Berkeley, that led to Hellman's subpoena. Most of those summoned had abandoned their leftist ties by the time of their testimony and many had been only marginally connected with the Communist party in the first place. As Victor S. Navasky observes in *Naming Names* (1980), a work that examines a period in American history in which the traditionally despised informant achieved the dubious status of folk hero, many Hollywood people had joined the Communist party because it seemed to be the most liberal thing going. They were not people with access to atomic secrets, nor could they easily sway the nation's young. Diana Trilling and those who have upheld her argument tend to gloss over the uglier dimensions of the McCarthy era. Since most of the witnesses were not connected to the government, Navasky questions HUAC's role as an overseer: "The purpose of the hearings, although they were not trials, was clearly punitive, yet the procedural safeguards appropriate to tribunals in the business of meting out punishment were absent: there was no cross-examination, no impartial judge and jury, none of the exclusionary rules about hearsay or other evidence" (xiv). Those who acted on behalf of HUAC—not only McCarthy, but others like Senator Pat McCarran, whose power exceeded that of McCarthy himself—had at least one clear goal in mind. "The Committee's action was scandalous," David Cook writes, "but its meaning was crystal clear: HUAC wished to purge Hollywood and, if possible, the entire country of any and all liberal tendencies by creating and then exploiting anti-Communist hysteria" (408). The result, Cook adds, was a Hollywood that mirrored the "intellectual stagnation and moral paralysis" that came to characterize the nation as a whole (410).[5] In short, HUAC was a formidable opponent to a left that had divided itself since the time of Sacco and Vanzetti. It is against this backdrop of American leftism and its divisions that Hellman's and Porter's memoirs might best be read and judged.

Neither Hellman nor Porter produced the kind of autobiography that sets out to examine a life in its totality. *The Never-Ending Wrong* is, in fact, Porter's longest autobiographical work. At the age of eighty-five, Porter joked, "*I'm* not going to write my autobiography. Every book I pick up these days has something about me in it, right or wrong. So I don't have to bother" (Givner, *Conversations* 185). Her biographer, Joan Givner, takes another perspective; she argues that Porter must have known she could not produce a genuinely honest autobiography: "in the accounts given in autobiographical notes, essays, and interviews she resembles her own description of Mexico. She called it 'this sphinx of countries which for every fragment of authentic history yields two riddles' " (*A Life* 22). Hellman's biographers, William Wright and Carl E. Rollyson, would agree that the same could be said of her. While Porter shied away from a book-length autobiography, Hellman in her early sixties did not hesitate to write about her past; indeed, she set out to discover a form that would accommodate her particular sense of self.

In an interview with Nora Ephron, Hellman made this comment regarding her first book-length autobiography, *An Unfinished Woman* (1969): "It was *faute de mieux*, that book. I decided I didn't want to write for the theatre, so what was I to do? I didn't want to do an autobiography—that would have been too pretentious for me. I had a lot of magazine pieces I'd done that hadn't been reprinted, and I started to rewrite them. But I didn't like them. I thought, maybe now I can do better with the same memories" (134). In *An Unfinished Woman*, a short chapter sets the stage for a vivid period from Hellman's life which is then developed in the longer chapter that immediately follows. Hellman concludes the book with portraits of Dorothy Parker, her maid Helen, and Dashiell Hammett. It is the portrait—an indirect means of self-presentation—that Hellman perfected as a mode of self-representation in *Pentimento* (1973) and that critics agree will remain her most significant contribution to twentieth-century autobiographical writing. In an interview with Stephanie de Pue, Hellman accounts for her indirect approach: "I don't ordinarily talk about myself very much. That's why I try to write memoirs without being a central part of them." She added, "It seems to me that summation of what you feel, not what's happened but of what you *feel*, is a dangerous game to play. The words become too simple" (Bryer 201).[6] Unlike Porter, Hellman was not a writer of great psychological depth, though it may be that—like Porter—she understood her limitations. One cannot imagine Hellman producing an autobiography such as Ellen Glasgow's *The Woman Within*; in none of Hellman's memoirs does she speak at any length about her creative processes. Yet as Maureen Howard observed, Hellman did formulate an autobiographical style that relates "the emotionally charged moment to a wide cultural reference" ("Scoundrel Time" 134) and that, as Doris Falk remarked, allows "for unanswered questions, and for a certain mysterious quality that evoked a response from readers who knew that mystery for their own" (157).

Perhaps the chief problem that both Hellman and Porter pose as memorialists is that, as their biographers have made clear, neither writer was apparently capable of complete honesty about her own past; Porter, for instance, perpetrated stories about an aristocratic lineage that did not exist (see Jefferson). As much as they may have insisted upon truth in art (and from others), both writers produced a body of personal commentary that has required their biographers to become detectives who sift through the self-images each writer perpetrated at different times and for different reasons. It is possible to take a sympathetic view of either writer's misrepresentations; one might argue that their diverse accomplishments as artists outweigh their value as truth-bearers. Porter, for example, went so far in questioning the old order—the southern patriarchy with its cavalier myths—that her inability to be completely honest about herself is, as far as her art is concerned, a fairly moot point, but how is one to judge a memoir by a woman like Lillian Hellman whom a significant section of the reading public now identifies as a morally damaging prevaricator?[7] This question necessitates an analysis of the memoir as genre. Such an examination will clarify the modes of self-representation that this often misunderstood genre affords; it should also aid in understanding that facticity—as is true of autobiography—must not obscure the deeper level of self-definition the memoir inscribes.

In what may be the most complete assessment of the memoir as genre, Marcus Billson, writing in 1977, stated, "The current academic interest in forms of self-literature, such as autobiographies and diaries, has curiously excluded memoirs from serious critical attention. . . . Literary critics have faulted memoirs for being incomplete, superficial autobiographies; and, historiographers have criticized them for being inaccurate, overly personal histories" (259). Billson is concerned that so much misunderstanding has resulted from what appears to be an inability on the part of historians and critics to read the memoir on its own terms or to understand what it requires from both writer and reader. Hence Billson's definition, which sets out to valorize the memoir as a form of self-literature, works from a consideration of what the memoir is not.

After noting briefly, "The memoir recounts a story of the author's witnessing a real past which he considers to be of extraordinary interest and importance" and embodies "a moral vision" of that past (261), Billson goes on to insist that the artful memorialist never produces a mere document of reportage or a simple chronicle of fact. Nor can the memorialist be overly disturbed by the modern historian's demand for objectivity: "the memorialist accepts quite freely the subjectivity of his own perception as the *sine qua non* of his work; without it, his work would have little interest or meaning; it would not be a memoir" (264). It is for this reason that Hellman and Porter stress the subjective nature of their accounts. Porter calls *The Never-Ending Wrong* "my story" and admits in her Afterward that she refused to read other accounts of the Sacco-Vanzetti affair until she had revised her own notes (58). Hellman concludes the first section of *Scoundrel Time* with this remark: "I tell myself that this third time out, if I stick to what I know, what happened to me, and a few others, I have a chance to write my own history of the time" (43).[8] These remarks help to substantiate Billson's argument, "The memoir is never a presentation of history; it is a representation of history, sometimes an argument, always a personal interpretation" (264).

It would thus appear that as a genre the memoir is not particularly suited for self-scrutiny or self-definition, yet the focus of the memoir's narrative is not exclusively outward as some have argued. As with autobiography, the memoir's narrative can take a sustained inward turn, and at times the two genres appear to merge in a single work. Thus "what distinguishes the memoir from the autobiography is not the focus of the narration, but the interplay of two specific factors in a given work: the length of time of the narration, and the dynamic nature of the author's represented self" (Billson 265). The self a memoir inscribes may be no less whole than that of an autobiography: what is generally missing from the memoir is an attempt to trace the stages in the growth of the memorialist's sense of self. Billson displays an androcentric bias (aside from Gertrude Stein, he cites only works by male writers), but he correctly observes that a "lack of kinesis in the author's concept of himself as an ontological being separates the memoir from the autobiography" (265).

One additional feature of the memoir deserves attention. Because of its more compressed scope, "the Memoir as genre is closely associated with periods of crisis, both historical crises, such as wars and revolutions, and intellectual crises, as Ortega y Gasset defines them, such as periods of intellectual and spiritual transition" (Billson 280). In *Scoundrel Time* and *The Never-Ending Wrong*, Hellman and Porter confront individual crises that are part of what they perceive to be a larger national crisis—a crisis that, as far as the life of a nation is concerned, carries grave consequences. This notion of a self in confrontation with a crisis explains part of the memoir's distinctive appeal. Readers of Hellman and Porter not only get to glimpse two embarrassing eras in our nation's history, but they get to view these periods through the consciousness of two women whose fiction and drama and whose lives have exerted a real influence on the literary life of our time. It is not just a matter of the reader's living "vicariously the quality and essence of the memorialist's being there" (Billson 280); it is additionally a matter of the reader's knowledge that what the author conceals can be as revealing as what she gives. As Pauline Kael remarked of *Julia*, the 1977 film based on a chapter from *Pentimento*, Hellman's memoirs are "more exciting as drama than her plays are, since you can feel the tension between what she's giving you and what she's withholding" (308). Readers know that with *Scoundrel Time* they may not be getting a view of the past that is true in all its particulars, but as Victor Kramer remarked of Tennessee Williams's opposite attempt to be brutally honest in his *Memoirs* (1975)—to tell all—a "life" is a matter of self-perception and self-deception: it is more than the events that have come to comprise a "public" record (665).

In terms of direct self-presentation, Hellman provides more personal background than does Porter. Like the bulk of her generation of the late twenties and early thirties, Hellman was "a kind of aimless rebel" (43), but she says twice that she cannot define herself as a genuinely committed radical despite her sympathy with a great many radical goals. Hellman speaks of her own family's corruption (her mother's relatives made money by exploiting African-Americans but Hellman does not say how), and she acknowledges her guilt about the money she made in an era of mass poverty and suffering. Hellman does not downplay the importance of Dashiell Hammett's presence in her life, nor does she disavow the tag of "southerner"—in fact, this label figures prominently in her justification of her own value system. Finally, Hellman claims not to be a political person or to belong to any political group, but she undercuts such assertions by expressing a number of political views and by even detailing some of her contributions to various political groups, particularly her involvement with Henry Wallace and his Progressive party of 1948.

Porter also notes an affinity between herself and the generation of the late twenties; Hellman's phrase, "aimless rebel," applies equally well to Porter, a woman who emphasizes her own "lifelong sympathy" with those who devoted themselves to ameliorating "the anguish that human beings inflict on each other—the never-ending wrong, forever incurable" (62). What neither Hellman nor Porter say directly is that their rebellion became less aimless and their focus more clearly centered on its fundamental causes. Like Hellman, Porter claims to have been politically mistaken, but she knows that it would be pointless to claim that she had no real political leanings: "I was then, as now, a registered voting member of the Democratic Party, a convinced liberal—not then a word of contempt—and a sympathizer with the new (to me) doctrines brought out of Russia from 1919 to 1920 onward by enthusiastic, sentimental, misguided men and women who were looking for a New Religion of Humanity, as one of them expressed it, and were carrying the gospel that the New Jerusalem could be expected to rise any minute in Moscow or thereabouts" (14).

Porter defines her early political thinking as "the lamentable 'political illiteracy' of a liberal idealist—we might say, a species of Jeffersonian" (13). Unlike Hellman, what Porter does not provide is any direct reference to her southern upbringing (though certain values she expresses here might best be illuminated by comments she has made elsewhere on her southern past); nor does she allude to the many friends or companions in her life at the time. Porter does not even refer to her vocation as a writer since in 1927 she had been read by only a handful of people; her first collection of stories, *Flowering Judas*, did not appear until 1930.

Part of what prompts each writer to (re)construct her memories is her sense of victimization. Each depicts herself as having been duped— Hellman by Stalinism, Porter by Communists and the nasty "self-appointed world reformers" (38); but worse, from a later perspective, each feels betrayed—Hellman by the intellectuals she feels stood by and passively watched McCarthy, Nixon, and their cohorts damage the lives of others, Porter by those not concerned with a fair trial or with an honest enactment of justice. Hellman and Porter did not agree on the nature of communism—Porter says she "flew off Lenin's locomotive and his vision of history in a wide arc" just days before Sacco and Vanzetti were put to death (20)—but they were altogether alike in defining selves that, within the community of morally responsible men and women, sense a betrayal of their most deeply felt moral values and who, upon careful examination, see themselves as somehow separate and at least partially heroic.

Their shared anger accounts in part for a similarity of style—a hard-boiled edge that verges at times on cynicism. Here is Hellman describing some of the key participants in her story:

> The McCarthy group—a loose term for all the boys, lobbyists, Congressmen, State Department bureaucrats, CIA operators—chose the anti-Red scare with perhaps more cynicism than Hitler picked anti-Semitism. He, history can no longer deny, deeply believed in the impurity of the Jew. But it is impossible to remember the drunken face of McCarthy, merry often with a kind of worldly malice, as if he were mocking those who took him seriously, and believe that he himself could take seriously anything but his boozed-up nightmares. And if all the rumors were true the nightmares could have concerned more than the fear of a Red tank on Pennsylvania Avenue, although it is possible in his case a tank could have turned him on. (41)

Hellman denies that McCarthy, Whittaker Chambers, or Nixon—with his unfortunately justified "contempt for public intelligence" (42)—or any of the others ever bothered her on a serious level; rather, she was deeply grieved by the intellectuals she believed stood passively by "when McCarthy and the boys appeared! Almost all, either by what they did or did not do, contributed to McCarthyism, running after a bandwagon which hadn't bothered to stop to pick them up" (42).

Couched in the same hard-hitting prose is Porter's meditation on an earlier public's reaction to large-scale crime. She opens her memoir by noting that Sacco's and Vanzetti's offense was rather commonplace, the distinctive "feature being that these men were tried, convicted, and put to death"; she continues with a passage that sets the tone for the rest of her piece:

> Gangsters in those days, at any rate those who operated boldly enough on a large scale, while not so powerful or so securely entrenched as the Mafia today, enjoyed a curious immunity in society and under the law. We have only to remember the completely public career of Al Capone, who, as chief of the bloodiest gang ever known until that time in this country, lived as if a magic circle had been drawn around him. . . . When he died, there was a three-day sentimental wallow on the radio, a hys-

terical orgy of nostalgia for the good old times when a guy could really get away with it. I remember the tone of drooling bathos in which one of them said, "Ah, just the same, in spite of all, he was a great guy. They just don't make 'em like that anymore." Of course, time has proved since how wrong the announcer was—it is obvious they do make 'em like that nearly every day . . . like that but even more indescribably monstrous—and the world radio told us day by day that this was not just local stuff, it was pandemic. (3–4)

The similarity of tone is not accidental. Both writers wish to convey the impression that they have lived through and thought long about the events they will narrate; one can guess that the "wise-guy" attitude—so reminiscent of thirties protest literature—helped them to establish their authority to comment on the course of modern history. There are moments in each work, however, when the writer's tone becomes softer, more sympathetic, and at times even mournful. Porter was praised by several reviewers for the poetic nature of her images (and particularly for her re-creation of the death night), and even Hellman's relentless tone gives way to a lyrical description of the night, not long after her appearance before the committee, when she and Hammett observed the silent movement of a herd of deer across her farm. For the most part, though, the tone of the two works is harsh. Neither writer forgives those who perpetrate against others what Porter calls the never-ending wrong. Both feel isolated even from people who share their own feelings. The tone of the two memoirs underscores what Marcus Billson detects as the key irony of memoir writing: "the participant desires to define himself as in society, and yet paradoxically to see himself also as against it" (277).

Structurally, the two memoirs are also alike. Each progresses within a loose chronology, with each building to the climactic event: Hellman's presence before the committee (covered in roughly 13 of her 124 pages), and Porter's account of the night the execution took place (about 5 pages of her 63-page text). These sections are inherently dramatic, and neither writer downplays their intensity. Billson notes that the memorialist's art derives in part from his or her "exhilarating awareness of actual life as drama" (269). The distinguishing structural feature of the two works is not their dramatic build-up, however. Life may be fused with emotional intensity and a sense of dramatic movement, but rarely is it structured like a well-made play, and history itself is more than a linear pattern of intense moments. As Hellman remarks in a moment of introspection, "It is impossible to write about any part of the McCarthy period in a clear-dated, annotated form; much crossed with much else, nothing obeyed a neat plan" (80), and Porter remarks in a similar vein, "After more than half a long lifetime, I find that any recollection, however vivid and lasting, must unavoidably be mixed with many afterthoughts. It is hard to remember anything perfectly straight, accurate, no matter whether it was painful or pleasant at that time" (31–32). Porter adds a comment that would appear to typify Hellman as well: "I find that I remember best just what I felt and thought about this event in its own time, in its inalterable setting; my impressions of this occasion remain fast, no matter how many reviews or recollections or how many afterthoughts have added themselves with the years" (32). It is these afterthoughts, the many rearview glances and recollections—the evidence of a thinking, reflective self—that tend to structure the memoir and give it its nonlinear, often anecdotal, but not necessarily arbitrary form.

Scoundrel Time contains seventeen sections; *The Never-Ending Wrong* contains twenty sections and an Afterword. The sections vary greatly in length and are not numbered in either work. Few reviewers failed to note the elliptical quality of the two books. The form of the memoir itself seems to mandate the loose organizational scheme, for the memoir writer is not offering pure history but a confrontation of the self with history (which, in a sense, may be a more authentic way of writing history than the objective accounts that textbook writers set out to provide). Both writers rely heavily on diary notes, and even refer to their diaries in order to validate their memories. Each finds herself jumping ahead in time, and each work includes sections that are almost free-associational. In just one paragraph, Porter moves from the "terrible irony" of Mussolini's asking Governor Fuller of Massachusetts to grant clemency, to her own experience in Mexico with refugees from Mussolini's Italy, to "Voltaire's impassioned defense of an individual's right to say what he believed," to her conclusion that the Communists were in on the protests for their own benefit (40–41). Section ten of *Scoundrel Time* has the same free-associational quality. Hellman even transcribes diary notes that cover the week before her testimony, notes that include impressions of her dutiful cab driver in Washington, her desire "to go to bed with an orangutan" (100), and her revulsion at having J. Edgar Hoover pointed out to her during a luncheon. Her loosely joined reflections culminate in her displeasure over her lawyer Joseph Rauh's awareness that she might sink under the pressure once she is in the committee room: "It is impossible to think that a grown man, intelligent, doesn't have some sense of how he will act under pressure. It's all been decided so long ago, when you are very young, all mixed up with your childhood's definition of pride or dignity" (103).

Even in passages where she is not citing notes, Hellman's representation of history is anecdotal, occasionally gossipy, and characterized by sometimes abrupt shifts. After announcing to Rauh that she would not cite the articles in which certain Communists had denounced her and her work — "my use of their attacks on me would amount to my attacking them at a time when they were being persecuted and I would, therefore, be playing the enemy's game" (64) — Hellman turns her attention, with no transition, to Clifford Odets, a dramatist whose work she had admired, but with whom she had never been good friends (Hammett, she discloses, thought very little of Odets or his work). Though her shift of attention to Odets is abrupt, it is not without significance. Apparently Odets wanted to meet with Hellman to find out how she might act if subpoenaed by the committee, claiming that he himself would "show them the face of a radical man and tell them to go fuck themselves" (69). As it turns out, Odets became a friendly witness. This incident leads Hellman into a lengthy consideration of the paranoia that plagued the movie bosses who employed writers like her and Odets and what she saw as the willingness of these men "to act out the drama that the government committees preferred" (75). At this point, some of the previous and seemingly random impressions, trivia, and short anecdotes gel in the stringently stated moral she derives from the cowardly behavior of the men who controlled the studios: "It is well to remember what these very rich movie men were like, since I doubt they have changed. . . . Hollywood lived the way the Arabs are attempting to live now, and while there is nothing strange about people vying with each other for great landed estates, there is something odd about people vying with each other for better bathrooms. It is doubtful that such luxury has ever been associated with the normal acts of defecating or bathing oneself. It is even possible that feces are not pleased to be received in such grand style and thus prefer to settle in the soul" (73–74).

Hellman then illustrates her moral with an account of how she had to turn down Harry Cohn's offer of a lucrative and very attractive movie contract at Columbia Pictures because she could not agree to the terms of an agreement that, as she tells us in a parenthetical remark, made a "straight demand that nothing you believed, or acted upon, or contributed to, or associated with could be different from what the studio would allow" (77).

Hellman's brief portrait of Cohn, which culminates in an act of pettiness (he denies an employee the luxury of a simple chicken sandwich) is only one of many such essentially negative, even hostile portraits that are scattered throughout both *Scoundrel Time* and *The Never-Ending Wrong*. Hellman provides an especially scathing account of Henry Wallace, whose Progressive party she had supported and had hoped might make a small difference in the life of American liberalism and political reform. Not only does Hellman express her doubts about Wallace's "suspicious innocence" of Communist involvement in his party, but she also describes Wallace's miserliness; he never left adequate tips and had the gall to invite her to a measly dinner of eggs on shredded wheat. Porter's account of Rosa Barron, the woman who headed her outfit at the protest, is equally blistering; not once, but three times Porter repeats Barron's view that—all questions of their innocence aside—Sacco and Vanzetti could do the Communists no good alive. Her portrait of Lincoln Steffens is only slightly less caustic (16–17).

These miniportraits, which seem at times to emerge full-blown from nowhere, serve various purposes. Often they culminate in the author's realization of something about herself and her own motives. Hellman's description of Wallace, for example, leads her to reveal that she was misguided in her own assumption that "the Communist Party is dictated to by a few officials" (129). Similarly, Porter prepares the way for one of her own realizations as she describes a Mrs. Leon Henderson, another champion of the two accused men, a vegetarian who could not bear the thought of "eating blood" but who apparently had no reservations about wearing the skins of animals: "I could not avoid seeing her very handsome leather handbag, her suede shoes and belt, and a light summer fur of some species I was unable to identify lying across her shoulders. My mind would wander from our topic while, bewildered once more by the confusions in human feelings, above all my own, I gazed into the glass eyes of the small, unknown peaked-faced animal" (35). Invariably, these miniportraits, which rely upon the quick brush stroke—the telling detail—present Hellman and Porter as they perceive themselves in contrast to others whose personal characteristics or approaches to life and its problems they do not share. To what extent they intend to represent themselves so obliquely is open to question, but the often hostile portraits do figure in one's assessment of the self each writer deliberately or inadvertently defines. These sometimes intimate observations of other people—themselves a part of the flow of history—are the particulars of each writer's response to an era she is remembering; that they often end by highlighting the pettiness of human nature (a quality neither writer consciously perceives in herself) is itself a reflection of two historical periods that now evoke a loss of balance and a failure of moral responsibility.

Such sections, though they seem to meander, convey a sense of immediacy; readers share not only the author's sense of having been there, but also her impressions—filtered through the years—of what it meant to have been there. These two highly self-conscious women are always aware of their roles as participants or performers on the stage of twentieth-century history. Hellman must have known that she was giving a dramatic but fitting name to a whole era of American history, and though she may have seen herself as a fairly menial participant—a kitchen policeman—Porter nonetheless dramatized her own limited involvement. About halfway through her narrative, she even transcribes into dialogue her notes of the conversations she had with the blond policeman who escorted her to jail on each of the days she was sent out to picket. The dialogue takes on the character of a morality play as these two figures make contact:

Second day:

HE: (taking my elbow and drawing me out of the line; I go like a lamb): 'Well, what have you been doing since yesterday?'

I: 'Mostly copying Sacco's and Vanzetti's letters. I wish you could read them. You'd believe in them if you could read the letters.'

HE: 'Well, I don't have much time for reading.' (26–27)

Their conversations end after the last picket line forms and it is clear that the governor will not issue a reprieve. Porter gives their parting scene an almost conscious cinematic quality: "We did not speak or look at each other again, but as I followed the matron to a cell I saw him working his way slowly outward through the crowd" (28).

"Well, it was fifty years ago and I am not trying to bring anything up-to-date. I am trying to sink back into the past and recreate a certain series of events recorded in scraps at the time which have haunted me painfully for life" (46). This is a clear expression of Porter's self-reflexive goal, and perhaps the word that deserves emphasis is "scraps." Like Hellman, Porter relies upon her scraps—the contents of diaries and notes—as she structures her narrative. Notes that were taken as a record of previous impressions are reflected upon through the lens of the passing years; consequently, both of the memoirs exhibit a double reflexivity. While each writer attempts to be true to earlier impressions—Porter, for example, insists that her's is the story of what happened, not of what should have been—neither writer can resist the inclination to reconceptualize the past. Hellman, especially, is drawn to remarks about what she should have said or done. She says that what she would like to have told the committee would go something like this: " 'You are a bunch of headline seekers, using other people's lives for your own benefits. You know damn well that the people you've been calling before you never did much of anything, but you've browbeaten and bullied many of them into telling lies about sins they never committed. So go to hell and do what you want with me!' I didn't say any of that to [Abe] Fortas [the lawyer she first consulted and a subsequent Supreme Court Justice] because I knew I would never be able to say it at all" (57).

Such a comment reveals the complexity of defining one's true or deepest sense of self, for it shows that what never took place can figure as prominently in a sense of personal identity as what actually occurred. One observes the same complexity in Porter's self-representation. While Porter is generally reluctant to acknowledge an irritable streak in her nature (something that Hellman freely acknowledges), she too shows that what she would like to have done is not only part of the record of her impressions but that it weighs heavily in the way she perceives herself. One example in particular stands out. As she and other protestors were on the way to their "trial," she overheard one man—the stereotype of a "capitalist monster" that "no proletarian novelist of the time would have dared to use"—make the following comment: "It is very pleasant to know we may expect things to settle down properly again" (45). Porter's response is unlike anything else in her nonfiction prose: "To this day, I can feel again my violent desire just to slap his whole slick face all over at once, hard, with the flat of my hand, or better, some kind of washing pot or any useful domestic appliance being applied where it would really make an impression—a butter paddle—something he would feel through the smug layer of too-well-fed fat. . . . My conscience stirs as if, in my impulse to do violence to my enemy, I had assisted at his crime" (49–50).

As this passage indicates, an overheard remark can be the basis of a genuine self-revelation. Both Porter and Hellman refer often to what they hear in passing, and not infrequently these remarks lead to self-discovery and become central to the self-image each writer wishes to project. Moments before she is to be questioned, Hellman makes this observation: "I hadn't seen the Committee come in, don't think I had realized that they were to sit on a raised platform, the government having learned from the stage, or maybe the other way around. I was glad I hadn't seen them come in—they made a gloomy picture. Through the noise of the gavel I heard one of the ladies in the rear cough very loudly. She was to cough all through the hearing. Later I heard one of her friends say loudly, "Irma, take your good cough drops" (109).

Hellman says nothing else; she allows the overhead remark to speak for itself and to highlight the fact that her predicament is not hers alone, that she is a pawn in a public spectacle complete with a gallery of passive (and callous) bystanders. It is of course another overheard remark that has become almost legendary and that tends to figure prominently in any critical reaction to Hellman's personal history. After Judge John S. Wood agrees to enter a letter from Hellman into the official transcript of her hearing—a letter in which she proclaims her willingness to answer any questions about herself but not about others—Hellman overhears a comment from a member of the press: "Thank God," the voice exclaimed, "somebody finally had the guts to do it" (114).

Within the arena of the memoir, overheard remarks can assume as much significance as the formal documents—such as letters—that become part of the official historical record. Porter relies heavily on overheard remarks, but she also quotes generously from Sacco's and Vanzetti's letters, telling her policeman that he would believe in them if he could examine their correspondence. Hellman's letter to Judge Wood is so fundamental to her self-understanding that she reprints it in full, giving it a section to itself with only the sketchiest of prefacing remarks. After stating her willingness to answer anything about herself—"I have nothing to hide from your Committee and there is nothing in my life of which I am ashamed" (97)—she expresses her difficulty in understanding the legality that would require her to answer questions about others if she fails to plead the Fifth Amendment. Hellman then gets to the gist—to the punch—of her request:

> But there is one principle that I do understand: I am not willing, now or in the future, to bring bad trouble to people who, in my past association with them, were completely innocent of any talk or any action that was disloyal or subversive. I do not like subversion or disloyalty in any form and if I had ever seen any I would have considered it my duty to have reported it to the proper authorities. But to hurt innocent people whom I knew many years ago in order to save myself is, to me, inhuman and indecent and dishonorable. I cannot and will not cut my conscience to fit this year's fashions, even though I long ago came to the conclusion that I was not a political person and could have no comfortable place in any political group. (98)

Hellman makes one additional remark; she proclaims that her values are those that stem from "an old-fashioned American tradition" and that she does not believe Judge Wood would desire her "to violate the good American tradition from which they spring" (98).

On the most basic level, Hellman includes the entire letter because it covers succinctly her reasons for not wishing to plead the Fifth Amendment. Yet the letter is also a clear expression of the liberal values that underlie her deepest sense of self. Carl Rollyson, Hellman's most recent biographer, accurately observes that "the cunning" of her defense "resided in her letter to HUAC," a document that "made her seem entirely reasonable . . . a person of conviction and conscience who only wanted to do the right thing . . . a dissenter who respected authority" (327–28). Rollyson claims that the bulk of the letter is Rauh's but that "the ringing phrases" are indisputably Hellman's (319). Such phrases—especially the unexpected "bad trouble"—are brief indexes to the self Hellman is preserving for history, and built into these ringing phrases are indictments of those who would claim the same liberal and "old-fashioned American tradition" but whose very actions reveal that it is not in fact a tradition they can live up to. The sometimes radical playwright is out to save her own hide but not without a clear stab at the enemy. The historical circumstances require that Hellman define and defend her sense of self.

Significantly, Hellman presents her letter immediately before the long series of notes that dramatize her state of awareness in the days preceding the hearing itself, which is to suggest, once again, that she structures her memoir so that it builds dramatically. This is not to say that there is anything affected or artificial about her account. Marcus Billson explains that the memoir writer views "time as extraordinary" and writes with the "kind of consciousness that vitalizes all experience" (269). Though Hellman has been accused of overworking the dramatic element in her self-presentation, even Carl Rollyson, who takes every opportunity to note those instances in which her account is questionable, concedes that the centerpiece of *Scoundrel Time*, those few pages in which Hellman recounts her appearance before HUAC, stick close to the events that actually occurred, filtered though they were through the consciousness of a woman who was always attuned to the dramatic possibilities of a given situation. Rollyson quotes Joseph Rauh on the accuracy of Hellman's version of the hearing: "I would say it is Lillian's dramatization of it. I don't want to say anything that throws doubt on her veracity. . . . It was pretty exciting. Even if I had told the story in a pedestrian way, it would still be pretty exciting. But when she got done with it, it was better than a Babe Ruth home run" (330).

The same is in its own way true of Porter's evocative rendering of Sacco's and Vanzetti's execution night. The drama of the event was actual but, again, filtered through the consciousness of a woman attuned not only to the drama but to the whole nightmarish quality of the occasion—a consciousness that could perceive and render the event in precisely etched images such as the one of a dazed Lola Ridge as she stood beneath one of the mounted policemen. Porter's memoir is in fact structured as though it were a series of slides with each dramatic image carrying its own emotional weight. One reviewer made this observation: "Not always coherent, random and shifting as memory itself, it gains power and reveals some indelible pictures: of Luigia Vanzetti looking with horror into the faces in the crowd raging at a rally for her doomed brother; of the midnight vigil outside Charleston prison, where the men were being put to death; of a 'party' afterward, wake-like, desperate, and charged with guilt and anger" (Fludas 32).

In his review of *Scoundrel Time* for the *New York Review of Books*, Murray Kempton was more than mildly outraged over Hellman's description of Henry Wallace's parsimony. Even if such accounts are accurate, Kempton did not believe they have a rightful place in Hellman's memoir. On issues that were less impressionistic, that could be judged by a standard of accuracy, reviewers did not hesitate to charge both writers with technical inaccuracies and, in the case of Hellman, willful misrepresentation. When Porter's memoir first appeared as half of the June 1977 issue of *The Atlantic*, it contained errors that the subsequent issue took note of, but these were not corrected by the time the book appeared in August. The source of these errors—confused places, dates, and titles—is in all likelihood the fifty-year gap between occurrence and recollection; they do not stem from the same kind of biographical misrepresentation that characterizes some of Porter's more informal essays.[9]

Hellman's veracity is a more complex issue; while no one accused Porter of overplaying her role in the drama that unfolded before her, Hellman, in addition to factual errors, was accused of egoism and of overvaluing her importance as a key figure in the McCarthy era. Here again, her letter to Judge Wood becomes central to the charge. Though in *Scoundrel Time*, Hellman tends to downplay its significance for others who would testify after her, a remark she made in 1978 to Peter Adam clearly indicates her pride in the stand she and Rauh so carefully articulated: "That letter, as you, Mr. Adam, know, had a very beneficial effect in many ways. It gave other people a place to stand, a legal place to stand, and was the first of its kind. Of that I'm proud" (Bryer 226). Carl Rollyson, for one, refuses to see Hellman in the same light, noting that though she did in fact take a difficult stand, her approach was not as brave as that of Arthur Miller who based his defense on the First rather than the Fifth Amendment (329). Rollyson claims that Rauh's reaction was much the same, that he too refused to "accept the image of [Hellman] as a heroine, a leader of 'the moral forces' " (329). In order to prove his point, Rollyson questions the authenticity of the incident involving the press member who supposedly applauded Hellman's courage: "There is no question that this is what she wanted to hear," he notes; nor could Hellman "resist adding that when the press gallery voice was greeted by Chairman Wood's threat to remove the press from the room, the voice answered, 'You do that, Sir.' The polite but steely rejoinder sounds just like the way Hellman would write the scene for a play" (327).

If Rollyson does not come right out and say that Hellman invented the voice from the press gallery, he does offer evidence in other places to show that she did not always resist her inclination to alter or reshape certain facts that can be verified. On at least four occasions in *Scoundrel Time*, Hellman equates selling her Pleasantville farm with the pain she retained from the whole McCarthy experience; she even says at one point that "the sale of the farm was the most painful loss of my life" (120). Rollyson, however, gives this version: "Always one to make a story better, in *Scoundrel Time* she puts the selling of Hardscrabble Farm in 1952, after her testimony before HUAC. Actually, the farm was gone by the end of 1951. She knew her idyll in Pleasantville was over" (317). Perhaps a more important issue is Hellman's claim in her HUAC letter that she "was not a political person and could have no comfortable place in any political group"—the implication being that she could not have been a real Communist, an assertion she has upheld in subsequent interviews. "In any case, whether I signed a Party card or didn't was of little importance to me," Hellman writes in *Scoundrel Time*. "I couldn't have known then what importance would be attached to it a few years later" (47). Rollyson discovered that, in an early draft of her HUAC letter, Hellman had in fact admitted to membership in the party between 1938 and 1940; he adds that Rauh, the leader of the influential Americans for Democratic Action, had himself "forgotten her admission of Communist party membership and was surprised by it when he recently examined his papers, now on deposit with the Library of Congress" (319). Of course it was probably wise in 1952 for Hellman to refrain from so readily admitting to party membership, but in 1975 one could wonder why Hellman persisted in equivocating on her Communist connections, especially when, as Robert P. Newman makes clear in his recent *The Cold War Romance of Lillian Hellman and John Melby* (1989), her membership, if it ever existed, was brief and hardly synonymous with party enthusiasm. Finally, Rollyson argues that "her decision in *Scoundrel Time* to 'stick to what I know, what happened to me' is disabling. . . . Her account of the Hiss-Chambers case, for instance, is seriously in error and significantly compromises her personal Cold War history" (13).

"If," as Marcus Billson writes, "the memoir genre projects a personal vision of past life which may not be in all particulars factually true, one is led to ask what the reader looks for when he picks up a memoir" (280). Billson, who devotes a brief section of his essay to reception theory, answers his question by saying that the reader wants more than facts and that "if we are to understand the memoir as literature, we, as readers, must be willing to allow the memorialist his projection of what he hopes will be remembered as 'the way it was' " (280). Reviews of Hellman's and Porter's memoirs would appear to substantiate these claims, for even the negative reviews often single out these authors' abilities to evoke the mood—the zeitgeist—of a vanished era. Rollyson rejects Hellman as a historian but draws attention to "her extraordinary talent for projecting her personality on the times" (489). Billson's theory of the memoir reader's response is acceptable as far as it goes, but the many negative reviews—some of them charged with anger—reveal that many readers look for more than a sense of authentic experience, and this may be especially true with writers like Lillian Hellman and Katherine Anne Porter who have produced a large body of writing, much of it concerned with the self and its moral responsibilities, prior to the memoirs that appeared rather late in each author's life. Readers familiar with these two women's work would have been dismayed had they produced nothing but a record of their experience. To understand the many negative reviews, particularly those of *Scoundrel Time*, it is necessary to take another look at the memoir as genre, and here again Billson's seminal essay provides some useful grounding.

Billson sees the form of the memoir as consisting of "three rhetorical stances—the eyewitness, the participant, and the *histor*—employed by the memoir-writer to evoke the historicity of his past and to argue for the truth of his vision of history" (271). The first of these, the eyewitness, is the central means of asserting "one's authority to recall and to interpret the past" (273). Hence, in *The Never-Ending Wrong*, Katherine Anne Porter can declare that she knows what she knows because she heard and saw (11). This stance assumes what Billson calls the ideographic strategy: "The substance of life presents itself as scattered until the memorialist organizes it through analysis" (274), an analysis that relies heavily upon metaphor. The eyewitness stance often merges with that of the memorialist as a participant who "concentrates on himself and relates the course of his own role, however major or ancillary, in the story he has to tell" (275). Since the memorialist as participant can examine a role or performance that has ended, he or she can project a sense of closure that is not always characteristic of the autobiographer. Billson uses the term "egotistical" to characterize the strategy of the participant, a figure whose personal desires and social self-interests are always near at hand. These self-interests become a paramount concern of critics evaluating *Scoundrel Time* and *The Never-Ending Wrong* (though less so with Porter since, as she willingly admits, her role was ancillary). With Hellman, the crucial problem is the extent to which her egoism undermines the heroic self her memoir so carefully if at times obliquely defines.

Billson identifies one additional rhetorical stance, that of the memorialist as *histor*: "Whenever the narrative intention shifts noticeably toward providing information or establishing facts, the *histor* is raising his head" (279). Since the memoir-writer rarely accommodates "the rigorous standards expected in modern historiography," Billson warns against confusing the memorialist with the historian. The Romantic movement, with its valorization of subjectivity, may have enabled memoir writers to claim merit for their books on the basis of subjective truth alone, but few memoir writers can resist the need to contextualize, to move beyond the range of their own memories. Thus the "great digressions of the memoir genre—the editorializing and the generalizing—are all done from the *histor* stance with its concomitant contextualist strategy," a strategy that aims for integration and synthesis (279).

It is the interplay of these rhetorical stances and strategies—along with "various techniques customarily associated with artful narrative: characterization, dialogue, stream of consciousness, and landscape description" (262)—that make *Scoundrel Time* and *The Never-Ending Wrong* such intriguing works of self-literature. It is, however, the stance of *histor* that has caused the greatest difficulty for the critics of both works. Before assessing the critical response, it is necessary to look at those passages where the voice of the *histor* is most apparent. It is through their historical perspectives that Hellman and Porter exhibit what is probably their closest affinity.

Throughout their memoirs, both writers interrupt the narrative of events to make connections, to place a single event or thought within a larger framework. Thus, Porter speaks of her mistaken hopes that were rooted in the values she had been taught in ethics courses: "Based on these teachings, I never believed that this country would alienate China in the Boxer Rebellion of 1900; or that we would not help France chase Hitler out of the Ruhr . . . or that we would aid and abet Franco; or let Czechoslovakia, a republic we had helped to found, fall to Soviet Russia" (*The Never-Ending Wrong* 13). Porter, of course, is writing fifty years after the fact, and she is aware that, in her attempt to contextualize the Sacco-Vanzetti affair, she must define the big "isms" that are fundamental to an understanding of the era. Though xenophobia and American puritanism were most assuredly at the heart of the Sacco-Vanzetti trial (and Porter does not downplay the fear of things foreign—a fear that led to and indeed was fueled by McCarthyism three decades later), her most provocative explanation of the fear that defined the era centers on something more than human prejudice. In her synthesis, prejudice and ignorance are "in some deeply mysterious way" subsumed by a more fearful term: "Anarchy had been a word of fear in many countries for a long time, nowhere more so than in this one; nothing in that time, not even the word 'Communism,' struck such terror, anger, and hatred into the popular mind; and nobody seemed to understand exactly what Anarchy as a political idea meant any more than they understood Communism . . ." (6). What became evident to Porter is that

> the human mind can face better the most oppressive government, the most rigid restrictions, than the awful prospect of a lawless, frontierless world. Freedom is a dangerous intoxicant and very few people can tolerate it in any quantity; it brings out the old raiding, oppressing, murderous instincts; the rage for revenge, for power, the lust for bloodshed. The longing for freedom takes the form of crushing the enemy—there is always the enemy!—into the earth; and where and who is the enemy if there is no visible establishment to attack, to destroy with blood and fire? Remember all that outcry when freedom is threatened again. Freedom, remember, is not the same as liberty. (7)

From Porter's point of view, human beings are deeply flawed; they retain ideals that interfere with their ability to understand themselves or to form workable governments. In a sense it becomes an act of heroism even to acknowledge the deceptions and to admit one's complicity with a social order that could not exist without deception. It is a cynical view but one that is in keeping with a predominant theme in Porter's non-fiction, a theme that she stresses in her self-reflective essay, "Saint Augustine and the Bullfight" (1955). It could be argued that Porter becomes the *histor* with a vengeance; a writer with a strong polemical sense, she cannot resist the urge to sermonize or to reduce her fifty-year reflections to a series of what she calls "truisms" (*The Never-Ending Wrong* 46).

It might appear that Gary Wills's Introduction to the American edition of *Scoundrel Time* provides needed historical background and a necessary revisioning of events that led to McCarthy and his era. Actually, Hellman's revisionary perspective stands on its own; she needed no introductory apparatus and subsequently omitted the piece by Wills when she collected her three memoirs in 1979. Hellman says that after World War II "the time was ripe for a new wave in America" and that McCarthy and his aids and representatives merely seized their chance as political opportunists (40). In a key paragraph that follows, Hellman provides her own historical synthesis; she argues that the new wave was not in fact new:

> It began with the Russian Revolution of 1917. The victory of the revolution, and thus its menace, had haunted us through the years that followed, then twisted the tail of history when Russia was our ally in the Second World War, and, just because that had been such an unnatural connection, the fears came back in fuller force after the war when it looked to many people as if Russia would overrun Western Europe. Then the revolution in China caused an enormous convulsion in capitalist societies and somewhere along the line gave us the conviction that we could have prevented it if only. If only was never explained with any sense, but the times had very little need of sense. (39–40)

Hellman may say that historical conclusions are not her game, but she does not refrain from making them; thus: "It was not the first time in history that the confusions of honest people were picked up in space by cheap baddies who, hearing a few bars of popular notes, made them into an opera of public disorder, staged and sung, as much of the Congressional testimony shows, in the wards of an insane asylum" (40). If Hellman's liberalism is not absolutely clear by this point, she adds, "A theme is always necessary, a plain, simple, unadorned theme to confuse the ignorant. The anti-Red theme was easily chosen from the grab bag, not alone because we were frightened of socialism, but chiefly, I think, to destroy the remains of Roosevelt and his sometimes advanced work" (40–41).

Put briefly, Hellman and Porter leave us with a vision of history that can be defined as follows: people are fickle, confused, and become, as Porter tersely writes, "intoxicated with the vanity of power," the kind of power that manifested itself in Judge Webster Thayer's boastful remark during a game of golf: "Did you see what I did to those anarchistic bastards?" (5). People cause one another great harm and are willing, even eager, to forget the evils of the past. To prove this point, Hellman notes that if it were true that "when the bell tolls it tolls for thee," then Americans could not have elected Richard Nixon so soon after the McCarthy debacle (159). Towards the conclusion of *Scoundrel Time*, she makes this frequently quoted assertion: "We are a people who do not want to keep much of the past in our heads. It is considered unhealthy in America to remember mistakes, neurotic to think about them, psychotic to dwell on them" (159). Porter does not limit this problem to Americans; in "Notes on Writing," she says, "One of the most disturbing habits of the human mind is its willful and destructive forgetting of whatever in its past does not flatter or confirm its present point of view" (*Collected Essays* 449). That she and Hellman share the same view on the nature of a nation's collective memory is clear from the brief Foreword that Porter attached to her memoir when it appeared in book form. To a newspaper reporter's response to hearing that Sacco and Vanzetti were the subjects of her new work — "Well, I don't really know anything about them . . . for me it's just history" — Porter rejoins with, "It is my conviction that when events are forgotten, buried in the cellar of the page—they are no longer even history" (*The Never-Ending Wrong* vii). In their attempts to establish the historical significance of the events they narrate, both writers come to the same conclusions: for Hellman, McCarthyism was one step on the road to subsequent abuses of individual privacy, a step on the road to the nation's acceptance of Nixon, Watergate, and Vietnam; for Porter, the Sacco-Vanzetti trial was even more grave; it was a turning point in "the long death of the civilization made by Europeans in the Western world" (31). "The evils prophesied by that crisis," she adds, "have all come true and are enormous in weight and variety" (32).

Though both writers take note of the historical fact that masses of people often behave as a herd and succumb to fallacies that appear valid if only because they have been repeated often enough (anarchists pose a threat that must be destroyed; Communists are a menace set out to penetrate the pluralistic fabric of American life), they nonetheless believe that certain groups of people can be expected to behave more responsibly than the herd and its leaders. Hence, Hellman feels betrayed by the intellectuals and liberals who stood passively by, or who did not remain passive but who nonetheless allowed their fear of communism to lead them into complicity with what should have been their mortal enemy. She is not naive enough to ignore why many liberals feared radicals and those with radical leanings: "Not alone because the radical's intellectual reasons were suspect, but because his convictions would lead to a world that deprived the rest of us of what we had." Yet she also says that "radicalism or anti-radicalism should have had nothing to do with the sly, miserable methods of McCarthy, Nixon and colleagues, as they flailed at Communists, near Communists, and nowhere-near-Communists. Lives were being ruined and few hands were raised to help. Since when do you have to agree with people to defend them from injustice?" (*Scoundrel Time* 89).[10]

Porter's sense of betrayal is equally great and, like Hellman's, it too is rooted in the problem of justice. The case of Sacco and Vanzetti led Porter to see that liberalism itself is subject to human frailty; highly conscious of the gulf between her status as an intellectual-cum-artist and that of the proletarians she set out to defend, Porter feels betrayed by the angry bystanders and the power-hungry men who can so cavalierly dismiss the necessity of a fair system of justice. The group she most resents and defines herself as being against, however, are the nasty "self-appointed world re-formers" (38), those like Rosa Barron whom she had expected to behave differently if only because she, again like Hellman, had wanted to believe in the existence of a small coterie of people whose sense of social responsibility did not exist at the expense of others.

Hellman and Porter become *histors* in order to define the state of affairs that forced them to rely upon their own inner resources and to substitute more personal values for those they believed had been abused. Hellman says that for liberalism she has substituted "something private called, for want of something that should be more accurate, decency" (118). Porter is not alone in insisting that Judeo-Greek-

Christian ethics could not adequately prepare one for the mixed motives and outright malice that characterize human behavior. Both writers use the memoir to test beliefs they were brought up with; Porter contrasts her observation of the various factions of policemen—the well-behaved Pink Tea Squad as well as those menacing figures mounted on horses—with her belief, formed in childhood, that the police existed for her protection. Hellman, comparing herself to Hammett, asserts that her own nature and upbringing would not tolerate any notion of easy compliance: "It was not only my right, it was my duty to speak or act against what I thought was wrong or dangerous. It is comically late to admit that I did not even consider the fierce, sweeping, violent nonsense-tragedies that break out in America from time to time, one of which was well on its way after World War II" (51–52). Had Hellman provided an itemized list of such nonsense-tragedies, she would surely have included the deaths of Sacco and Vanzetti.

In addition to the stance of *histor*, such statements may suggest the presence of a rhetorical stance that Marcus Billson does not identify, that of the memorialist as confessor, or, rather, the memoir writer whose meditations on the self in confrontation with history prompt revelations of a frankly personal nature. Fully conscious observers of their pasts, Hellman and Porter use the memoir to acknowledge and confront the pain that accompanied their self-realization.

If both writers admit to personal failings and to a previous lack of sophistication about the way of the world, both also indicate that they would have had no right to produce these memoirs had they not behaved properly. To be sure, knowing how to act is not easy in a time when wrongs are blatantly perpetrated against others—a scoundrel time. Nonetheless, underlying their shared moral vision is a belief held by both writers that a modest personal heroism can and must exist, even in a time of scoundrels. Porter downplays the threat to her own security, but as others have pointed out, one could not have participated in the demonstrations without courage and a real sense of danger. In *Writers on the Left* (1961), Daniel Aaron cites Michael Gold's description of a city " 'in the lynching mood.' It was dangerous for anyone to walk through the police-cordoned streets if he wore a beard, had 'dark foreign hair or eyes,' or acted in any way like a man who had not graduated from Harvard" (170). Hellman, by contrast, does not underplay the possible consequences of behaving honorably; nor does she hesitate to identify those features of her personality that qualify as heroic—her refusal, for example, to use articles that Communists had written against her since in her "thin morality book it is plain not cricket to clear yourself by jumping on people who are themselves in trouble" (*Scoundrel Time* 93–94). Hellman's method of self-representation may be oblique, but it is nonetheless clear where she stands. She may even insist that she does not much like what she did before the committee, but her indirect method of self-representation—her tendency to characterize herself through the remarks of others—leaves little doubt about how she wishes to be perceived. In addition to the voice from the press about someone finally having "the guts to do it," she quotes the comment of another lawyer to Joseph Rauh—"You and [Abe] Fortas are making a martyr of this woman" (106)—and she paraphrases a remark from Rauh himself to the effect that "everybody had a right to make themselves a little more heroic, maybe I would do it, too" (102). When Ruth Shipley, head of the State Department's Passport Division, issues Hellman a passport in spite of the accusations that had been brought against her, Hellman submits to Hammett's explanation of why she was perhaps the only unfriendly witness to have received one: "one Puritan lady in power recognized another Puritan lady in trouble. Puritan ladies have to believe that other Puritan ladies don't lie" (86–87).[11]

It is not, however, their status as women memorialists that has elicited the negative critical commentary; it is when they assume the rhetorical stance of *histor* that Hellman's and Porter's memoirs appear to antagonize the greatest number of readers. *The Never-Ending Wrong*, though it did not pass by unnoticed, solicited nothing like the sometimes violent response that was accorded *Scoundrel Time* and its author. Still, readers were puzzled by a number of Porter's historical conclusions. All of the letters to the editor that appeared in the August 1977 issue of *The Atlantic*, two months after it published Porter's memoir, were harshly critical of her historical position. One writer noted that she failed "to establish her main thesis; namely, that the deaths of two impoverished immigrants, one a shoemaker, the other a fishmonger, constituted a grave miscarriage of justice which can never be effaced." Another asked: "What was the 'wrong' that brought forth all those words?" Still another was disturbed by Porter's conclusion that authorities must not place the law "above the judgment of the people," meaning of course "some people" (28–29). It was also noted that since Porter acknowledges in her Afterword the possibility that Sacco may have in fact been guilty, a possible miscarriage of justice becomes even more problematic.

Many of these observations were developed at greater length in the reviews that appeared in the following months. In *Commonweal*, John Deedy argued that Porter became too entrenched in "the fair-trial issue" and that her "interest in the case turns out to have been, and remains still, more institutional than individual" (571). In the *Times Literary Supplement*, Julian Symons took note of Porter's "customary brilliant clarity" but claimed that her argument is "distinctly confused." He pointed specifically to her conclusion that the trial and execution were symptomatic of a frighteningly new public willingness to accept as commonplace the abuse of power—a change so sinister that Porter claims it evades her powers of analysis. Symons took exception to this assertion and to Porter's suggestion that more recent protest movements have not been characterized by the same "selfless innocence" that typified her motives and those of the men and women who joined her in Boston. Symons's response is that people have not changed. "The mistake made by unreconstructed liberals like Miss Porter," he argues, "is not to understand that the motives of practical politicians are never pure, as are those with a single fixed end like banning nuclear weapons, or preserving the countryside, or reducing aeroplane noise" (198).

Since Porter's memoir did not generate the kind of response that would prompt reviewers and critics to challenge one another's observations, no one has yet addressed these criticisms of her historical conclusions, and though her memoir can surely stand on its own, it seems necessary to counter some of the objections that have been brought forth. Unlike Dos Passos, Porter never renounced her liberalism, and her work, especially her nonfiction, retained its polemical edge. She did, however, become distrustful of all political groups and much less prone to play the part of activist. The trial of Sacco and Vanzetti came at a point in Porter's life when she was beginning to realize her creative potential; her goals became more clearly focused, and she subsequently devoted most of her energy to her writing, interrupted though it always was. The Sacco-Vanzetti affair appears to have functioned as

a catalyst to her self-understanding. In what may be the most self-reflexive passage in her memoir, Porter writes:

> I was not an inexperienced girl, I was thirty-seven years old; I knew a
> good deal about the evils and abuses and cruelties of the world; I had
> known victims of injustice, of crime. I was not ignorant of history, nor of
> literature; I had witnessed a revolution in Mexico, had in a way taken
> part in it, had seen it follow the classic trials of all revolutions. Besides
> all the moral force and irreproachable motives of so many, I knew the
> deviousness and wickedness of both sides, on all sides, and the mixed
> motives—plain love of making mischief, love of irresponsible power, un-
> scrupulous ambition of many men who never stopped short of murder,
> if murder would advance their careers an inch. But this was something
> very different, unfamiliar. (56)

What Porter saw at first hand was something that another southern
writer, Walker Percy, would later articulate as the most distinguishing
characteristic of evil in our century: its sheer banality (156). It is not
insignificant that Porter finally defines the event as a "tragic farce," for
gathered in Boston were the finest writers of a generation, all come to
protest not merely the thinly veiled assault on American leftism but the
glaring abuse of human rights guaranteed by our constitution. It was
an event that did in fact foreshadow the public's acceptance of larger
abuses of power, of even more banal wrongs to come. Though it may
have received less attention than any of her other works, *The Never-
Ending Wrong* is one of the essential fragments of the larger plan that
Porter mentioned in her famous 1940 Preface to *Flowering Judas and
Other Stories*. It is, in effect, the culminating expression of a moral
vision that was brought into focus by Porter's minimal participation in
an event that occurred half a century earlier.

Porter's work is not the "plain, full record" she claims it to be in her
Foreword, but she does not fail to prove her thesis. Nor is it really logical to argue that her speculation regarding the innocence or possible
guilt of the two accused men undermines her claim that justice was
miscarried. As Roger Starr remarked in his *Commentary* review, the
mystery of Sacco's and Vanzetti's innocence has dogged liberals from
the late twenties on: "The questions multiply even if they never erase
the implacable fact that the two men were put to death on findings of
guilt which satisfied almost no educated American under fifty" (95).
Starr shows that Porter's memoir has a historical value that lies beyond

its specific historical conclusions, for in one brief work, Porter managed to emphasize the mystery of the affair; she highlighted the socioeconomic threats that emigrants posed for the country's upper and lower classes; she drew attention to the presence and importance of American Communists; and through her own presence in Boston, she signaled a "periodic emergence in America of a social protest led by members of the ruling class, or what would elsewhere be called the ruling class" (96).[12] It is not incidental that the last three of these concerns also play a major role in the critical reaction to Hellman's historical synthesis.

It is safe to say that Hellman's attempt to define herself and her role within the course of twentieth-century political history set off a reaction that has had few parallels in the last several decades. Anyone who had a stake in defining himself or herself as a liberal anti-Communist felt compelled to respond to *Scoundrel Time*, a book that received an initial set of highly favorable reactions before the more negative and, some would say, more text-centered appraisals began to appear. Almost without fail, critics centered their responses on one or more of four issues: Hellman's charge that magazines that were in the position to denounce McCarthy and his tactics failed to do so; her theory about the children of immigrants and their cultural assimilation; her contention that liberal anti-Communists played into the hands of the men who led the nation to Vietnam, Watergate, and beyond; and what was frequently taken to be her ignorance about the real nature of communism. It goes without saying that Hellman's decision to point a finger at people who were still living—at Diana Trilling, for instance—assured the notoriety of her self-presentation, for it is largely by means of contrast to Trilling and others that Hellman characterizes herself.

"*Partisan Review*, although through the years it has published many, many pieces protesting the punishment of dissidents in Eastern Europe, made no protest when people in this country were jailed or ruined. . . . *Commentary* didn't do anything. No editor or contributor ever protested against McCarthy" (90). William Phillips, editor of *Partisan Review*, responded to this charge by noting that Richard Rovere, Arthur Schlesinger, Dwight McDonald, and Philip Rahv, among others, made several anti-McCarthy statements; he added, "I suppose if we were the ideal, selfless human beings we sometimes pretended to be, we would have . . . come to the defense of people we thought to be the instruments, whether conscious or not, of a new barbarism" (338–39). Irving Howe takes note of his own violently anti-McCarthy article for *Partisan Review*, a piece that Hellman herself singled out for praise even though it appeared at the rather late date of 1954, only shortly before the Army-McCarthy hearings would begin to silence McCarthy and help curb the nation's hysteria. Though Hellman did not single out *The Nation*, editor Carey McWilliams felt the need (in the same issue that included a highly favorable review of *Scoundrel Time*) to clear the magazine of any guilt by association; he pointed specifically to a 28 June 1952 special issue, "How Free Is Free?" These pieces aside, it seems clear that Hellman has not distorted the historical picture on this point. Thus it is not surprising that her opponents would sidetrack the issue and fall victim to a common fallacy of argument. Sidney Hook (whose invective is rivalled only by that of William Buckley) maintains that Hellman had no right to charge others with negligence when she herself never protested the abuses of human rights under Stalin, and Howe protested what he saw as the timidness and rather late date of Hellman's own realization of Stalin's "sins." Nathan Glazer takes perhaps a more subtle tack when he says that Hellman, a respected and talented writer with many readers, was in the position to offer a better understanding of communism but failed in her own intellectual responsibilities: "Perhaps *Communism* in the world was a threat but *Communists* at home were not? Very well, let us hear about it" (38). Glazer has a point, but he seems to have forgotten the Red-baiting and generally hostile atmosphere of the postwar era.

Since they rest on generalities that cannot be substantiated by something as neat as a date of publication, the other charges brought against Hellman's historical conclusions are less easy to prove or disprove. Hellman contends that "thoughtful and distinguished men and women" who failed to speak out against McCarthy have not yet found it "a part of conscience to admit that their cold-war anti-Communism was perverted, possibly against their wishes, into the Vietnam War and then into the reign of Nixon, their unwanted but inevitable leader" (*Scoundrel Time* 90–91). This is a broad generalization, as Howe observed in what is the most spirited attack on this feature of Hellman's argument (378–79), but it is not so broad that it loses all credence. In effect, Hellman is saying that silence itself gave tacit approval to greater and even more dangerous government abuses and intrusions. Her account of the CIA agent who trailed her in Europe during the months after her hearing pales by comparison to the revelations about CIA and FBI surveillance of private citizens which emerged during Watergate and its aftermath. Hellman aligns herself with the revisionist view that the hysterical fear (and silence) that characterized the fifties played into the hands of an emerging military-industrial complex that, even now, continues to find ways to sanction its intrusions and imperialistic missions (Hellman did not live to see the appalling Iran-Contra scandal of the mid-1980s). Yet while she makes the connection between then and now, Hellman does not offer enough evidence to convince the skeptical; as Doris Falk rightly notes, such facts "were plentifully available in the publications of her own Committee for Public Justice, and might have strengthened her position" (152).

Nothing about Hellman's historical stance seems to have ignited more ire than this assertion: "Many [American intellectuals] found in the sins of Stalin Communism—and there were plenty that for a long time I mistakenly denied—the excuse to join those who should have been their hereditary enemies. Perhaps that, in part, was the penalty of a nineteenth-century immigration. The children of timid immigrants are often remarkable people: energetic, intelligent, hardworking; and often they make it so good that they are determined to keep it at any cost" (*Scoundrel Time* 43).

Hellman may have thought she was referring primarily to the many immigrants who had made their fortunes in Hollywood, but her critics still charged that this statement undermined her liberalism through its implication that she herself was in some way fully American and not subject to the same fear or weaknesses (see Kazin, "Legend of Lillian Hellman" 34; Marcus 97; Glazer 38; Kempton 22; Hook 85–86). Here the generality of Hellman's historical conclusion is less offensive than its glaring arrogance. Only Victor Navasky was willing to look past Hellman's condescension in order to concede her point. In what is arguably the most provocative examination of Cold-War Hollywood, Navasky implies that Hellman may not have taken her historical observation far enough: "For some, the very act of denouncing was a form of assimilation, of status elevation . . . the truth was that by denouncing fellow immigrants (or children of immigrants) before HUAC, one consolidated one's identification with the dominant society. The practice came with the prestige of the state conferred upon it; it legitimated betrayal" (322).

The fourth charge—that Hellman was naive about Communists and their real intentions—rests upon her belief that there was never a Communist menace in this country. It is a charge that holds up as badly as the other three. While Nathan Glazer believes that Hellman failed in her obligation to explain why she saw no Communist threat, in Hollywood or the country at large, Irving Howe focuses on what he sees as an even greater failure: "Those who supported Stalinism and its political enterprises, either here or abroad, helped befoul the cultural atmosphere . . . helped destroy whatever possibilities there might have been for a resurgence of serious radicalism in America" (382). Howe and Sidney Hook are not alone in calling Hellman a hardnosed Communist; Paul Johnson makes the same conclusion in his book on the moral credentials of intellectuals to position themselves as advisers to others. All of these claims have been successfully countered by Robert P. Newman in *The Cold War Romance of Lillian Hellman and John Melby* (1989), the most sustained examination of Hellman's leftist involvements to date. Anyone interested in an undistorted picture of Hellman's politics can do no better than to begin with Newman's carefully researched biography.

Taking an unbiased approach to his topic, Newman concludes that there is no evidence to suggest that Hellman was ever anything other than a fellow traveler. Any careful reader of her plays will admit that she was more interested in character and personality than in political theory; in *Scoundrel Time*, Hellman remarks that one of her central complaints against Communists is their obsession with theory. Newman shows that it is absurd to suggest that Hellman ever kowtowed to the Communist position on anything. *Watch on the Rhine*, the antifascist play that figures prominently in her FBI file, was actually an outcry against the Soviet Union's decision to form a pact with Hitler; it was denounced by both the *Daily Worker* and the *New Masses*. When Hitler broke the pact and invaded Russia, it was the party line that followed Hellman. Still, Newman argues, "To the extent that Communist Russia was for most of the Hitler period the chief force opposed to fascism, her support of Russia was understandable" (299). Hellman may have overestimated the Communist commitment to peace, especially during the postwar years, but at the heart of her many leftist involvements was an intense desire for world peace. Hellman had, after all, observed from close range the devastation of World War II; it was this first-hand experience that prompted her to make this remark at the 1949 Waldorf Conference: "It no longer matters whose fault it was. It matters that the game be stopped. Only four years ago millions upon millions of people died, yet today men talk of death and war as they talk of going to dinner" (quoted in Newman 300).

After returning from Russia in 1945, Hellman held a New York press conference in which she noted, "I wouldn't want to see Communism here. We're never going to have it. It is no problem with us. I see no signs of it here." As Newman discovered, the FBI deleted these remarks from the file it "later passed out to right-wing columnists, congressional committees, and the Passport Office" (54). Such deception does not surprise Newman, who claims that the FBI's methods are amateurish and unquestionably biased against radicals and others identified with liberal-left causes. Hellman had friends that "ranged across the ideological spectrum" (298), yet the FBI interviewed only sources that were hostile to her, who would confirm their suspicions or who would remain quiet about the investigation. Newman discredits most of the accusations in Hellman's file (including those of key informant Louis Francis Budenz), but perhaps his most valuable service has been to show how meaningless it is to continue calling Hellman a Stalinist: "As to the Stalinist label, since she was pro-Communist but not a Trotskyite during the 1930's, it might have been appropriate then. In the 1980's it is ludicrous. What could it mean now? She has fully repudiated the purges and Stalin, their instigator, as well as Vishinsky, their prosecutor. There is no possible meaning of the term that could now be applied to her. In this era, Stalinism is simply a swear word applied by fanatical anti-Communists to people whom they dislike" (304).

Hellman's critics have faulted her for, one, not seeing quickly enough and, two, for understating the "sins" of Stalin only when they became publicly apparent. What these critics want from her is something akin to the degradation ceremonies carried out by the committee: a simple acknowledgement of human frailty is not enough. Yet Hellman was too cagey, too scrappy, to concede anything more; she was too knowing to play into the hands of Cold-War sentiment and give reactionaries or even anti-Communist liberals any further reasons to rail against the blindness of American radicals. Newman concludes his appendix—"Was Lillian Hellman a Communist?"—with this defense: "In the final judgment, one is forced to conclude that Ruth Shipley, hard-nosed anti-Communist that she was, using the FBI files as she did, solicitous as she was of the good name of the United States to the nth degree, was right: Lillian Hellman was not a Communist in any significant sense, certainly not in the 1950's. It is simple nonsense to call her this; sheer polemics to call her a Stalinist; and plain insanity to believe, as J. Edgar Hoover did at one time, that she was in any way disloyal to the United States of America" (329).

When the various objections to the historical conclusions of both writers have been countered or at least acknowledged, there still remains a puzzling, at times even ambivalent, edge to the selves they define within the given historical context. At the heart of both memoirs is a tension that neither writer seems to acknowledge: a desire, on the one hand, to demonstrate that she is a responsible, thinking, political human being and a reticence, on the other hand, to provoke the charge that her politics have in any way diminished her value as an artist. Richard King has recently analyzed a reluctance on the part of southern writers, both male and female, to explore "the essential arrangements of the political order, including of course power-relationships" and "what it means to lead a political life," this despite the fact that, as King puts it, "being political and acting politically are as clearly part of our experience as falling in love, making money, having a religious experience, finding satisfaction in the life of the mind, or in 'mere' everydayness" ("Politics and Literature" 190–91). King points specifically to Eudora Welty's contention that fiction, at least, must keep a "private address" and that the artist must reject any intrusion, political or otherwise, into her inward space. Part of the reluctance King observes can be traced to the bias of the southern New Critics against works that were blatantly political—their tendency, as King remarks, "to locate the field of significant action in artistic expression itself" (197). Another part of this reluctance may be traced to the southern writer's often-noted fear of abstraction. In an essay on E. M. Forster, Porter declared that human relationships must be formed "not in the mass, not between nations, nonsense!—but between one person and another" (*Collected Essays* 74). In this context it is necessary to remember that, because they ardently rejected any system of thought that placed man as a political being at its center, some of the men who contributed essays to *I'll Take My Stand* (1930) had wanted to call their Agrarian manifesto *Tracts against Communism*. King's analysis focuses almost exclusively on fiction, but it bears upon the fact that Hellman and Porter, two southern writers, have produced memoirs that engage the political sphere but that define selves with only the broadest of political terms. The piecemeal nature of their political definition has forced others to clarify what they themselves might have made more explicit.

There is a surprising coyness of tone in *Scoundrel Time* whenever Hellman alludes to her political thinking and involvements, and her pronouncements do not always coincide with the facts her biographers have uncovered. Hellman claims not to fit into any party and even tells Judge Wood in her letter that she is not a political person, yet she admits to having had easy access to high-ranking Communist party members, to having had very specific plans for the Progressive party (she hoped to secure a modest future for the new organization by avoiding Wallace's plan to mount a major presidential campaign), and she boldly decries what she perceived to be a political vacuum in "the American creative world" (119). Moreover, towards the conclusion of her memoir, she asserts, "In every civilized country people have always come forward to defend those in political trouble" (161), which is itself a political act. One can accept Hellman's claim in *An Unfinished Woman* that "rebels seldom make good revolutionaries, perhaps because organized action, even union with other people, is not possible for them" (118), but it is disconcerting to turn from this work in which Hellman details her extensive reading of the great political theorists of our time, to her apology in *Scoundrel Time* for making her political history "too simple" (49). A reader might justifiably ask why Lillian Hellman, a woman who helped to form the Committee for Public Justice, who was one of four to initiate a law suit that pressured Richard Nixon to release the Watergate tapes—why she of all people would find it necessary or desirable to simplify her political history, as indeed one might wonder why upon two occasions in *Scoundrel Time* alone she would understate her radicalism, perhaps the one inherently political term that encompasses the woman and her worldview as it emerges from the pages of *Scoundrel Time*.[13]

In 1979 Hellman collected her three memoirs and supplied new commentaries on each work. While she acknowledged the charges that were brought against *Scoundrel Time*, she did not take this opportunity to address any of the issues that had been raised. Instead, her remarks indicate that precise political self-definition was never her goal in the first place. Again, she focuses on those early anti-Communists whose "view from one window, grown dusty with time, has blurred the world and who do not intend ever to move to another window." The curious thing about this commentary is that Hellman seems unaware that most of her angry critics had faulted her for the very thing she says she tried to get around in *Scoundrel Time*—for moralizing rather than clarifying herself. She writes: "I tried to avoid, when I wrote this book, what is called a moral stand. I'd like to take that stand now. I never want to live again to watch people turn into liars and cowards and others into frightened, silent collaborators. And to hell with the fancy reasons they give for what they did" (*Three* 722–26). Hellman's commentary does little more than reify her earlier stand.

Katherine Anne Porter was as reluctant as Lillian Hellman to describe her political beliefs and commitments. It was in her Introduction to Eudora Welty's *A Curtain of Green* (1941) that Porter gave a mini-sermon on the artist and her necessary disengagement from the world of politics. Porter says that Welty escaped "a militant socialist consciousness" and "has not expressed, except implicitly, any attitude at all on the state of politics or the condition of society." For Porter, Welty's work is grounded rather in "an ancient system of ethics," in "an unanswerable, indispensable moral law." The absence of politics in Welty's writing does not disturb Porter, who believes that when the artist abandons such laws "in favor of a set of political, which is to say, inhuman rules, he cuts himself away from his proper society—living men" (*Collected Essays* 287).[14] Porter wrote this piece in 1941; the international political mess at that time helps to account for a tone that becomes even more indignant as she continues: "There exist documents of political and social theory which belong, if not to poetry, certainly to the department of humane letters. They are reassuring statements of the great hopes and dearest faiths of mankind and they are acts of high imagination. But all working, practical political systems, even those professing to originate in moral grandeur, are based upon and operate by contempt of human life and individual fate; in accepting any one of them and shaping his mind and work to that mold, the artist dehumanizes himself, unfits himself for the practice of any art" (287).

As unyielding as these comments may seem, they provide the necessary focus for a complete understanding of Porter's enduring attachment to the Sacco-Vanzetti affair. It is reductive to argue that her long-evolving interest in the two men resulted primarily from her nagging belief that they had not been given a fair trial or that she wrote *The Never-Ending Wrong* to express her fifty-year outrage over having been a pawn for a Communist organization. Though Porter does not make the connection for her readers (and perhaps she did not fully see the connection herself), the two men and their trial grew to embody her suspicion that government and politics, unlike art or religion, could never serve as a genuinely effective means of ordering lives. Her Introduction to Welty's stories strongly indicates that Porter accepted anarchism as a philosophy or vision of society that, though it has taken many forms, hinges on one necessary but seemingly impossible goal: the liquidation of all state authority. Porter quotes Nietzsche—"The State is the coldest of all cold monsters"—and then adds her own belief that "the revolutions which destroy or weaken at least one monster bring to birth and growth another" (61).

At the conclusion of her memoir, Porter recounts a conversation with one of the best-known anarchists of the age:

> In 1935 in Paris, living in that thin upper surface of comfort and joy and freedom in a limited way, I met this most touching and interesting person, Emma Goldman, sitting at a table reserved for her at the Select, where she could receive her friends and carry on her conversations and sociabilities over an occasional refreshing drink. . . . She finally came to admit sadly that the human race in its weakness demanded government and all government was evil because human nature was basically weak and weakness is evil. She was a wise, sweet old thing, grandmotherly, or like a great-aunt. I said to her, "It's a pity you had to spend your whole life in such unhappiness when you could have had such a nice life in a good government, with a home and children."
>
> She turned on me and said severely: "What have I just said? There is no such thing as a good government. There never was. There can't be."
>
> I closed my eyes and watched Nietzsche's skull nodding. (62–63)

Porter does not call herself an anarchist, but this passage makes it unquestionably clear that she was drawn to the anarchistic critique of society. As a social force, anarchism may have failed for reasons Irving L. Horowitz explains in his still useful introduction to the major anarchists and their writings. Though theoretically sound, anarchism tended to focus on "the world of what ought to be" (60); further, it never got beyond primary group associations and "never admitted of a strategy and theory for the *maintenance* of power" (61). Yet as the conversation with Emma Goldman reveals, anarchists, and intellectuals like Porter who were drawn to their critique, saw that they could survive on what Horowitz calls "the unmasking tradition" (61)—on what Porter has identified elsewhere as her own position: "the great tradition of dissent."[15]

In short, Hellman and Porter may shy away from political definition, but their disclaimers do not hold up under careful scrutiny. Though Porter remained a liberal idealist, she came to believe that no government or political philosophy could protect the human rights of those without power or property. The first object of the United States Constitution is, according to James Madison, the protection of an unequal distribution of both property and power. Porter and Hellman would accept what Irving Horowitz calls the anarchist's only true morality: the belief that there must be no distinction between what is done for self and what is done for others. Yet after her experiences in Mexico, Porter could not accept the "never-never-land" of a "theoretically classless society" (24). It does not appear that Hellman, on the other hand, ever lost faith in the power of the state to eradicate inequality; she thus became, if somewhat unwittingly, an apologist for the Soviet Union: "I thought that in the end Russia, having achieved a state socialism, would stop its infringements on personal liberty. I was wrong" (*Scoundrel Time* 49). The difference between the two women is in some respects the difference between an anarchistic and a socialistic critique of society, the difference between two competing visions that are for the most part submerged but surface intermittently in the two memoirs.

The ambivalence each writer expresses regarding her political identity extends to the way she does (and does not) confront her southern past. Hellman draws upon her southern upbringing to account for, even to justify her independent and rebellious nature: "Whatever is wrong with white Southerners—redneck or better—we were all brought up to believe we had a right to think as we pleased, go our own, possibly strange ways" (47). The paradox is that these "strange ways" resulted in the degradation and subordination of a whole race of people. Hellman does not take note of the irony when she recalls that it was a black woman—her nurse Sophronia—who instructed her in the value of anger. For her part, Porter never mentions her southern background in *The Never-Ending Wrong* except to say that after the executions she felt far from home. There may be a reason for this omission other than the fact that most readers would have been familiar with her status as an important southern author. In those pieces in which Porter does confront her southern past—"Noon Wine: The Sources" and "Portrait: Old South"—she falsifies the record in order to identify with a class of aristocratic southerners she did not in fact belong to. Whatever prompted her need to have descended from the wealthy slave-owning plantation owners, it remains that such an identification, real or imaginary, would have been at odds with her assertion in *The Never-Ending Wrong* that she had lived the span of nearly a century in sympathy with those who had devoted their lives to ameliorating "the anguish that human beings inflict on one another" (62). "The Never-Ending Wrong" is in fact a title Porter had originally intended for another work: an unpublished story about a southern lynching.

Though in interviews both writers have adopted a somewhat less somber tone regarding the same events and experiences they narrate in their memoirs,[16] the worldview that unites *Scoundrel Time* and *The Never-Ending Wrong*—the titles are almost interchangeable—is pessimistic, even at times grim. "There are not many places or periods or scenes," Hellman writes, "that you can think back upon with no rip in the pleasure" (132); Porter goes one step further and denounces "the whole evil trend toward reducing everything human to the mud of the lowest common denominator" (12). Both attack the gullibility of Americans—their willingness to believe almost any assertion that is repeated often enough, as well as their willingness to forget sections of the historical past that do not please or flatter. Both have been guilty of the same forgetfulness, but memorialists see themselves as separate from others even while they acknowledge their own frailty and their own mixed motives. This isolationist posture cannot fail to raise problems (and pleasures) for the reader who must accept or reject the subjectivity that undergirds the memoir as a genre that blends history with self-reflexivity.

Writing for the *Miami Herald*, one reviewer said that *Scoundrel Time* "could have been a spectacular book" but that it falls short: "We have come to expect more of this decent, gracious, undeniably courageous woman" (Hartt 7); the reviewer for *Commonweal*, John Deedy, made a similar comment regarding *The Never-Ending Wrong*: "As the last of keen eyewitnesses, [Porter] could have left behind an important historical document. Instead she wills the world a thin and garbled memoir, beautifully expressed and deeply felt, but so much less than we might expect of anything from Katherine Anne Porter" (572). These reviews are not atypical of a certain response that each book received, but they are faulty on at least two accounts: the reviewers apparently fail to understand or at least appreciate those elliptical features that tend to characterize the memoir genre, and they do not provide evidence that these works are something less than readers might have expected. On the contrary, these memoirs are precisely what a reader familiar with Hellman's drama or Porter's fiction might have anticipated. Both works extend themes their authors had explored in earlier works—themes that are very much the same for both writers.

Even in the earliest published work of each writer, one can see the threads that would be more pronounced in the subsequent memoirs. Hellman's first play, *The Children's Hour* (1934), is a searing depiction of scandalmongering; it concludes with the ruin of two school teachers' lives as the result of unchecked hysteria (the charge brought against the two teachers: lesbianism). Hellman's antifascist plays, *Watch on the Rhine* (1941) and *The Searching Wind* (1944), are forceful denunciations of people who remain passive in the face of social and political threats. In what is probably her most popular play, *The Little Foxes* (1939), the family servant, Addie, makes an observation that solidifies one of Hellman's central themes: "Well, there are the people who eat the earth and eat all the people on it like in the Bible with the Locusts. Then there are the people who stand around and watch them eat it. Sometimes I think it ain't right to stand and watch them do it" (*Collected Plays* 182). Hellman has acknowledged her attraction to innately evil characters; in an interview with Stephanie de Pue, she admitted, "I've long been fascinated by villains who very well know they were villains, who didn't give a damn" (Bryer 190). Her most pressing concern, however, is the danger of a passive collusion with such villains, a theme that obsessed Porter as well. Doris Falk has highlighted a pattern of evil or villainy that emerges from Hellman's sustained glance at her own past and from her observation of the world at large. This pattern, which characterizes so much of her drama, finds one of its most stringent embodiments in Hellman's memoir: "The 'scoundrels' of the title resembled the characters of Hellman's plays: they included not only the active villains, the 'despoilers,' like Senator McCarthy himself, but those whom Hellman accused of being *his* fellow-travell- ers—the 'bystanders' who supported the 'witch-hunt' by failing to at- tack McCarthy or to defend or rescue those like herself whose reputa- tions and fortunes had been damaged. In fact, Hellman is harder on these than she is on the senator and the various committees" (147–48).

Fortunately, Hellman's moral vision does not stop with a duality of active and passive doers of evil; in her adaptations she has been drawn especially to characters who discover a measure of personal dignity— even a degree of heroism—by finding and remaining true to moral commitments, who become radicals in the best sense of the word. In *Montserrat* (1949), taken from a French play by Emmanuel Robles, the central character refuses to say where a South American liberator is hiding during the Spanish occupation of Venezuela in 1812; because he remains faithful to his own values and refuses to speak, he is forced to watch six innocent men and women put to death and then suffers the same fate himself. It could have been no surprise to viewers of her work, and to those familiar with her public life, that Hellman was drawn to the historical figure of Joan of Arc. Three years after her hear- ing, Hellman adapted Jean Anouilh's *The Lark* (1955) with a Joan that freely sacrifices her life for a political ideal. In 1956 Hellman collabo- rated with Leonard Bernstein and Richard Wilbur on a musical adap- tation of Voltaire's *Candide*. Hellman translates Candide's final remark to Cunegonde as "We will not live in beautiful harmony, because there is no such thing in this world, nor should there be. We promise only to do our best and live our lives" (*Collected Plays* 678). A reader familiar with Hellman's adaptations can see that Montserrat, Joan, and even Candide merge in the pivotal character of *Scoundrel Time*: Lillian Hellman herself.

Katherine Anne Porter's fascination with villainy and the inquisito- rial spirit was germane to her uncompleted biography of Cotton Mather and dates as far back as her first newspaper reviews for the *Rocky Mountain News*. Joan Givner has discovered that these early pieces contain an embryonic expression of a moral vision that lies at the heart of Porter's subsequent fiction and that is fundamental to her long-standing interest in the case of Sacco and Vanzetti. Givner quotes a 1919 review in which, like Hellman, Porter admits her "longstanding fascination with the psychology of villainy," adding that "it takes imagination and real nerve to become a first class sinner" (quoted in Givner, *A Life* 134). Givner also points out that after she recognized the "positive qualities" of the villain, Porter turned her pen to "the virtuous, passive heroine, and it was on this figure that she eventually focused all her scorn and contempt" (134–35). The figures that most incensed Porter are those who through their complacency or passivity allow evil to occur.

Givner sees this philosophy at work in an early story, "Magic," in the more famous "Flowering Judas" with its triangular cast of characters— Braggioni, a pure unmitigated villain; Eugenio, the victim; and Laura, the indifferent heroine—and in *Ship of Fools* where it is given one of its fullest and perhaps most explicit expressions. Here Dr. Schumann, in agreement with the ship's captain, claims that "it takes a strong character to be really evil. Most of us are too slack, half-hearted or cowardly—luckily, I suppose. Our collusion with evil is only negative, consent by default you might say" (quoted in Givner, *A Life* 136). Incidentally, when Porter singles out various twentieth-century villains she does not exclude the key figure in America's Red-baiting: "the collusion in evil that allows creatures like Mussolini, or Hitler, or Huey Long, or McCarthy—you can make your own list, petty and great—to gain hold of things, who permits it? Oh, we're convinced we're not evil. We don't believe in that sort of thing, do we? And the strange thing is that if these agents of evil are all clowns, why do we put up with them? God knows, such men are evil, without sense—forces of pure ambition and will—but they enjoy our tacit consent" (quoted in Givner, *A Life* 316).

With *The Never-Ending Wrong*, the victims are clearly identifiable as those who suffer at the hands of callous, complacent, and power-hungry men like Governor Fuller, Judge Thayer, and the judges who sentence the protestors to their small and demeaning fines. The victims are the two men who did not receive a fair trail, their families, and the many well-wishers from the community of artists and intellectuals who demonstrated on their behalf. The bystanders in this work are not entirely passive, however; their collusion with the villains becomes blatant to Porter if not to themselves; hence her repetitive emphasis on Rosa Barron's terse remark that the two foreign men could do "us" nothing good as long as they were alive.

Eudora Welty was the first reviewer who knew Porter's writing well enough to make the connection between *The Never-Ending Wrong* and the thematic concerns of Porter's fiction. In her piece for the *New York Times Book Review*, Welty writes: "Elements of guilt, the abandonment of responsibilities in human relationships, the betrayal of good faith and the taking away of trust and love are what her tragic stories are made of. Betrayal of justice is not very different from the betrayal of love" (29).

It seems somehow right that Welty would produce one of the most perceptive pieces on Porter's last book; it was, after all, Porter who had helped to launch Welty's career by writing an enthusiastic and discerning introduction to *A Curtain of Green*, Welty's first collection of stories. There is, however, one connection between *The Never-Ending Wrong* and Porter's fiction that neither Givner, Welty, nor any other reviewer took note of. Like Hellman, Porter was adept at creating believable male characters. Elizabeth Hardwick, in her Introduction to Virago's edition of Porter's *Collected Stories*, notes, "A hard knowledge of the world in extreme, masculine dilemmas was part of the knowledge [Porter] brought to fiction. So it was her good luck after all not to be quite as she would have wished—a Southern lady" (xi). Taken as a whole, however, most of Porter's heroes are not men but women like Granny Weatherall whose life has been blighted by her rage and sense of powerlessness at having been jilted; or Sophia Jane Rhea whose sense of herself as a commanding matriarch does not deflect the reader's awareness of her subordinate status in the southern patriarchal order; or most important because she was Porter's fictional stand-in, Miranda Gay, who embarks on a quest for self-authenticity in "Old Mortality" but who, in "Pale Horse, Pale Rider," sinks into a listless depression as she looks squarely into the war-ravaged world of men. Porter may have disclaimed the feminist label, but what she presents is in essence a feminist critique of a world in which women, even when they refuse to cooperate with their oppressors, are still often stupefied by their lack of power. She may acknowledge her own propensity for evil, but in *The Never-Ending Wrong*, she is neither villain nor passive bystander; the memoir is rather a record of her defiance. Yet it is also a record of her own sense of victimization and powerlessness in the face of an event that had become a "tragic farce" (54). She explains her feelings after the execution: "In my whole life I have never felt such a weight of pure bitterness, helpless anger in utter defeat, outraged love and hope" (48). In the briefest section of her memoir—and consequently emphatic in its brevity and position near the end—Porter attempts to crystallize the most intense images she has retained since that date: "Now, through all this distance of time, I remember most vividly Mrs. Harriman's horsehair lace and flower garden party hats; Lola Ridge standing in the half darkness before Charleston Prison under the rearing horse's hoofs; the gentle young girl striding and drinking gin from the bottle and singing her wake-dirges; Luigia Vanzetti's face as she stared in horror down into the crowd howling like beasts; and Rosa Barron's little pinpoints of eyes glittering through her spectacles at me and her shrill, accusing voice: 'Saved? Who wants them saved? What earthly good would they do us alive?' " (56–57).

It is neither accidental nor insignificant that Porter's memories focus entirely on the women participants, two of whom are dazed or bewildered, all of whom, even Rosa Barron, were like Porter herself—ultimately powerless to effect change.

What is implicit regarding gender and its restrictions in Porter's memoir is neither explicit nor implicit in *Scoundrel Time*. Hellman clearly sees herself as a woman who can compete and stand on her own in a man's world, and indeed, her account has led a great many readers to believe that hold her own she did. When asked to explain the nature of her victory, Hellman quotes her lawyer Joseph Rhau: " '[The committee] had sense enough to see that they were in a bad spot. We beat them, that's all" (117). This explanation may be valid; and by reducing it to a note, Hellman is again underplaying her own heroism. Valid or not, it is important to see this explanation in light of one that appeared in *Time* a week after Hellman's hearing. In a patronizing tone that seemed built into all Luce publications of the time, a nameless reporter says, "Playwright Hellman, who once described herself as 'the greatest meeting-goer in the country,' went last week to meet the House Un-American Activities Committee." After insinuating strongly that Hellman, "an expert at smooth dialogue," used her dramatic skills on her own behalf—that she performed rather than cooperated—the *Time* reporter clinches his piece: "After she had been excused, Chairman Wood said gallantly: 'Why cite her for contempt? After all, she's a woman' " (74).

Hellman and Porter were each drawn to classical women heroes, a further connection between the two women that seems appropriate in concluding this examination. Like Hellman, Porter was particularly intrigued by the historical figure of Joan of Arc—by her sense of divine mission and her prominence as a victim of the capriciousness of human nature. In 1955, the same year that Hellman's translation of Jean Anouilh's *The Lark* opened to perceptive and appreciative notices (it ran for 229 performances), Regine Pernoud published *The Retrial of Joan of Arc* with a Foreword by Katherine Anne Porter. Pernoud's book is a selection of the proceedings of the rehabilitation trials that took place at the request of Charles VII twenty years after Joan's death. Fifteen hundred witnesses gathered throughout France to clear Joan of heretical charges; she was declared innocent at Rouen in 1456, six years after the rehabilitation began. The witnesses highlighted the deceptive nature of Joan's trial, her humiliating prison experiences, her essential goodness and chastity. The trial of Joan of Arc had merged for Porter with that of Sacco and Vanzetti, and even with that of Christ, all of them trials in which the accused were assumed guilty from the outset. Porter's Foreword was well received, and her interest in Joan as a victim of a predetermined verdict was not lost on the book's reviewers, one of whom summarized the sham of Joan's original trial: "Testimony was suppressed or altered before it got into the record. Witnesses were bribed or frightened; the questioning was organized so as to confuse rather than elicit fact, legal counsel was denied. . . . All of which—and more—has a terrifyingly familiar ring today and makes Miss Pernoud's book doubly fascinating" (Chubb 50).

Likewise, Hellman's translation of Anouilh's *The Lark*, which appeared three years after her hearing, is as much about the mood of the McCarthy era as it is about a medieval French peasant hero. Though Hellman is working with Anouilh's material, the play is undeniably self-referential; Joan's inquisitors merge with the "Inquisitor priests" Hellman denounces in *Scoundrel Time* (83). The play opens with the Earl of Warwick's question: "Everybody here? Good. Let the trial begin at once. The quicker the judgment and the burning, the better for all of us" (*Collected Plays* 551). Joan's inquisitors are petty, small-minded men, intolerant even of one another's differences. They embody the fear of genuine liberalism in Hellman's own era. Warwick says, for example, that "as a man of politics, I cannot afford the doctrine of man's individual magnificence. I might meet another man who felt the same way. And he might express his individual magnificence by cutting off *my* head" (567). It is Cauchon who claims that "the time will come when our names will be known only for what we did to her; when men, forgiving their own sins, but angry with ours, will speak our names in a curse" (568). It is a remark that seems less pointed at McCarthy, Roy Cohn, Wood, and the other "cheap baddies" than at those who yielded to them, who for whatever reason chose to play their game and "name names."

Beyond her value as victim, Hellman and Porter were even more intrigued by Joan's importance as a female hero with a fiercely independent nature. Joan makes it clear that, regardless of the consequences, intelligent and morally responsible behavior is not only sexless but inseparable from self-realization. To Cauchon's question, "Are you in a State of Grace?" she replies: "When I lost my faith, when I recanted, or when, at the very last minute, I gave myself back to myself? When—" (556). In Hellman's translation, Beaudricourt tells Joan, "A horse costs more than a woman. You're a country girl. You ought to know that" (561); but Warwick, ironically, understands and articulates Joan's true value: "The girl was a lark in the skies of France, high over the heads of her soldiers, singing a wild, crazy song of courage" (580). Do Hellman and Porter see themselves as Joan's descendants? The answer would seem to be a guarded yes. When Jane Fonda played Hellman in *Julia*, the 1977 film taken from *Pentimento*, she told an interviewer that the story centers on "a woman who is a real heroine. It is very important to make movies about women who grow and become ideological human beings and totally committed people. We have to begin to put that image into the mass culture" (Weintraub 17). One can see Hellman and Porter nodding in agreement.

5.

ZORA NEALE HURSTON

The Ethics of Self-Representation

"The tune is the unity of the thing. And you have to know what you are doing when you begin to pass on that, because Negroes can fit in more words and leave out more and still keep the tune better than anyone I can think of."

Zora Neale Hurston made this remark regarding the songs she had collected in her native Florida, the Bahamas, and elsewhere; she was warning the potential listener to beware of the singer's "over-enthusiasm." "For instance," she writes, "if a song was going good, and the material ran out, the singer was apt to interpolate pieces of other songs into it. The only way you can know when that happens, is to know your material so well that you can sense the violation. Even if you do not know the song that is being used for padding, you can tell the change in rhythm and tempo" (*Dust Tracks* 197–98). These comments would appear to bear on Hurston's own autobiographical enterprise, for many readers have sensed what they perceive to be too much art, too many "changes in rhythm and tempo," and too many "violations" in Hurston's one book-length attempt to define herself. In her Foreword to Robert Hemenway's biography of Hurston, Alice Walker says, "For me, the most unfortunate thing Zora ever wrote is her autobiography. After the first several chapters, it rings false" (xvii); Hemenway renders what, with a few important exceptions, has become a consensus view: "Her total career, not her autobiography, is the proof of her achievement and the best index to her life and art. Only when considered in the total context can the book be properly assessed, for it is an autobiography at war with itself" (277–78).

Hurston's lifelong concern with the self and its limitations (those imposed from without and from within) is, of course, the natural, perhaps even the proper subject of an autobiography. As Janie tells her story to Pheoby in Hurston's most celebrated novel, *Their Eyes Were Watching God* (1937), the narrator observes that "Pheoby [is] eager to feel and do through Janie . . . and Janie [is] full of that oldest human longing—self-revelation" (18).

Hurston knew that self-definition, though an insuppressible human need, is still a problematic undertaking. Sprinkled throughout *Dust Tracks* are remarks that, taken together, clarify many of the perils of autobiographical writing. In one frequently cited passage, Hurston notes that as a child she had not yet learned that "people are prone to build a statue of the kind of person that it pleases them to be. And few people want to be forced to ask themselves, 'What if there is no me like my statue?' " (34). She also notes that people seldom see themselves as they change. Later, after recounting her two marriages (one of which, like Katherine Anne Porter, she had tried to suppress from the public record), Hurston tells the reader to pay no attention to her advice about love, for "anybody whose mouth is cut cross-ways is given to lying, unconsciously as well as knowingly" (265). Earlier in the same discussion, Hurston makes this humorous but revealing comment: "Life poses questions and that two-headed spirit that rules the beginning and end of things called Death, has all the answers. And even if I did know all, I am supposed to have some private business to myself. Whatever I do know, I have no intention of putting but so much in the public ears" (261).

As the writer of her own life, Hurston's problems were compounded by the fact that she refused to produce the kind of text described by Stephen Butterfield in his commonly accepted definition of African-

American autobiography. According to Butterfield, "The 'self' of black autobiography . . . is conceived as a member of an oppressed social group, with ties and responsibilities to the other members. It is a conscious political identity, drawing sustenance from the past experience of the group, giving back the iron of its endurance fashioned into armor and weapons for the use of the next generation of fighters" (2–3). As indicated earlier, the brand of liberalism that runs throughout Hurston's autobiography is the radical individualistic strain (as opposed to the reform impulse associated with a white liberal such as Lillian Smith), and in her insistence on her own individuality—her desire to tell her own unique story—Hurston's autobiography bears more resemblance to *The Woman Within* or *One Writer's Beginnings* than to the autobiographies of African-American men such as Frederick Douglass or Richard Wright. A paradigm such as Butterfield's, which privileges texts by African-American men, can have only limited value for the Hurston scholar or the reader of *Dust Tracks on a Road*.[1]

With apparently good reason, Hurston was reluctant to take her publisher's suggestion that her fifth book be a work of self-writing; though it is clear from current perspective that she had published her best fiction by the early forties, her career was still not over. Hemenway cites a letter from 1943, a year after *Dust Tracks* appeared, in which Hurston claims that she "did not want to write it at all, because it is too hard to reveal one's inner self" (278), a remark that recalls Ellen Glasgow's insistence that only a revelation of the inner self can justify an intimate autobiographical undertaking. In his 1984 Introduction to *Dust Tracks*, Hemenway cites another statement in which Hurston expresses her "feeling of disappointment" about the autobiography: "I don't think that I achieved all that I set out to do. I thought that in this book I would achieve my ideal, but it seems that I have not yet reached it . . . it still doesn't say all that I want to say" (xxxviii).

This remark, intriguing as it is—and in keeping with Hemenway's view of the book—should be seen in the context of a statement Hurston makes in *Dust Tracks* itself. In the chapter she devotes to her publications, Hurston claims that she wrote *Their Eyes Were Watching God* "under internal pressure in seven weeks." Though now considered her fictional "masterpiece," Hurston says the book was "dammed up" inside her and that she would like the chance to rewrite it. "In fact," she adds, "I regret all of my books. It is one of the tragedies of life that one

cannot have all the wisdom one is ever to possess in the beginning"
(212).

Hurston must have known that her autobiography would arouse critical controversy, as had her previous novels. Her views on race were by
no means those expected of an African-American writer who had
achieved prominence during the depression. Unlike Ellen Glasgow,
she does not claim to write in order to shed light on the psychological
complexities of human behavior, but as the opening of *Dust Tracks* reveals, Hurston is very much aware that her revelations would be
greeted by readers she, through her art, could manipulate only so far:
"Like the dead-seeming, cold rocks, I have memories within that came
out of the material that went to make me. . . . So you will have to know
something about the time and place where I came from, in order that
you may interpret the incidents and directions of my life" (3). The critical controversy that surrounds Hurston's autobiography—with Robert
Hemenway, Alice Walker, Elizabeth Fox-Genovese, and Claudine Raynaud as the leading nay-sayers, now balanced in part by the yeas from
Henry Louis Gates, Nellie McKay, and Francois Lionnet—is itself evidence of Hurston's awareness that a "life" emerges only from a dialogue between speaker/writer on one hand and listener/reader on the
other.

Though it provides a useful context for an understanding of Hurston's role as a black southern woman of letters and her position, or
lack of one, in the Southern Renaissance, *Dust Tracks*, like Hurston's
subsequent essays, is a text that may never please those readers or critics who seem secretly to wish that Hurston had produced another kind
of book, one more in line with their political perspectives or with their
ideas about what constitutes African-American autobiography. Even
so, the goal here is to show that Hurston's autobiography is less a text
"at war with itself" than Hemenway contends and that—at its conclusion—Hurston is less a woman "half in shadow" than Helen Washington would suggest. This goal necessitates a new look at the many complex dimensions of Hurston's sense of self, her techniques of self-
revelation (some of which are direct while others are carefully encoded), and her sometimes ambiguous relation to the South, the nation, and its divided culture.

As Hurston's most extended piece of self-writing, *Dust Tracks* war-
rants further investigation or, as Hurston would have it, further inter-

pretation. Not only does it reveal Hurston's grappling with many of the same problems of region, identity, and personal ethics that preoccupied Glasgow, Welty, Porter, Hellman, and, particularly, Smith, but it also illuminates a number of tensions and constraints that are less central to one's understanding of the autobiographical prose of Hurston's white southern contemporaries—none of whom had to depend upon a patron who placed significant restrictions on what the artist might do with her work and none of whom confronted a publisher who was also a political censor. The manuscript Hurston submitted to J. B. Lippincott in 1942 was significantly edited; only with the appearance in 1984 of some of the deleted material is the picture more complete of what Hurston was aiming for. As a student at Yale's Beinecke Library, which holds the various versions of *Dust Tracks*, is said to have remarked, "You have to read the chapters Zora left out of her autobiography" (quoted in Dance 329).

In form *Dust Tracks* is not unlike Ellen Glasgow's *The Woman Within*; it is not rigidly chronological. The first half follows Hurston's life from childhood through middle age while the later chapters are, in effect, informal essays that resemble the journalism Hurston began to produce in the early forties. Still one has the feeling that Hurston was very deliberate about the topics she engaged and the disclosures she chose to make. Hurston's self-revelation works on at least four primary levels: through direct statements of goals and emotions; through a series of interlocking motifs and myths; through stories—about herself or others—that reflect or suggest her thoughts and ethics; and through the informal essays, or, better, the meditations that conclude the book.

In the midst of a depressing world at war, Hurston made one of her most self-revealing comments in a letter to folklorist Ben Botkin. "These do be times that take all you have to scrape up a decent laugh or so. I do not refer to the battlefields, but to this enormous pest of hate that is rotting men's souls. When will people learn that you cannot quarantine hate? . . . The world smells like an abbatoir. It makes me very unhappy. I am all wrong in this vengeful world. I will to love" (quoted in Hemenway 300–301). Though she made this revelation to a friend in late 1944, it contains the essence of the picture Hurston paints of herself in her autobiography.

Harold Bloom is correct in calling Hurston a "vitalist," a word meant to convey energy, vigor, animation—everything that distinguishes the living from the nonliving. Like Whitman, another vitalist, Hurston rarely shies away from the sentence that begins with "I."[2] The bulk of her direct statements of self-revelation depict a woman whose egoism (rather than egotism) cannot accommodate itself to what she denounces early on as the pigeonhole way of life. These statements are indicative: "I do not choose to admit weakness" (*Dust Tracks* 278); "I take no refuge from myself in bitterness. . . . I have no urge to make any concessions like that to the world as yet" (280); "Being an idealist, I too wish that the world was better than I am. My inner fineness is continually outraged at finding that the world is a whole family of Hurstons" (281–82). In the chapter "Seeing the World as It Is"—one of the deleted chapters Hemenway included in his Appendix to the 1984 edition—Hurston writes, "I do not wish to close the frontiers of life upon my own self. I do not wish to deny myself the expansion of seeking into individual capabilities and depths by living in a space whose boundaries are race and nation. Lord, give my poor stammering tongue at least one taste of the whole round world, if you please, Sir" (330–31). Perhaps most evocative—because of its boldness—is Hurston's expression of her self-worth: "Such as I am, I am a precious gift, as the unlettered Negro would say it. Stripped to my skin, that is just what I am" (308).

Such is the self Hurston reveals through direct statement—defiantly individualistic, unwilling to concede constraints, but eager to connect with others—"I am a precious gift." If Hurston expresses contradictions—and most of her critics insist that she does, more in fact than can be easily reconciled—one must concede that Hurston's idea of selfhood is expansive—or "cosmic," to use her term—and admits contradictions, paradoxes, ironies, all the various polarities of human experience. As she writes in "Looking Things Over," the concluding chapter of the manuscript that Lippincott originally published: "I can look back and see sharp shadows, high lights, and smudgy inbetweens. I have been in Sorrow's kitchen and licked out all the pots. Then I have stood on the peaky mountain wrappen in rainbows, with a harp and a sword in my hands" (280).

Hurston's memories of the past tend to become little dramas within themselves. She does not merely describe the revival meetings of her youth, for example; she re-creates them, with all their appealing absurdity. The same is true when Hurston adapts many of her fictional techniques in order to recount her fieldwork. She begins the chapter on collecting African-American folklore with a personal definition—"Research is formalized curiosity . . . It is a seeking that he who wishes may know the cosmic secrets of the world and they that dwell therein" (174)—but soon the chapter becomes a vivid re-creation of, among other places, Polk County, Florida, and its primitive inhabitants—a re-creation that relies heavily upon a series of rhetorical techniques (repetition and montage in particular) that convey Hurston's sense of having experienced this exotic place.

Despite her recent popularity, complete with stage and screen adaptations of her life, Hurston was not a Cinderella figure. The waif of the all-black town of Eatonville, Hurston refused to sever her connection with the community that nourished her early determination and confidence, nor did she see her central Florida environment as in any way inferior to the world of Harlem, in whose literary renaissance she became a major figure. Nor did Eatonville compare unfavorably with the academic world of Franz Boas, with whom she studied anthropology as Barnard's "sacred black cow." Born in 1891 to a large black southern family, by the midtwenties Hurston had traveled far beyond the security of her childhood world, much further, in fact, than the boundaries of her race and class would normally permit. Though she left the village shortly after her mother's death "never to return to it as a real part of the town" (94), in a very real sense Hurston never left Eatonville at all: it remained one major mark against which other experiences might be evaluated.

The centrality of her Eatonville childhood is evident in the attention Hurston gives it in *Dust Tracks*; roughly the first third of her autobiography is devoted to memories of Eatonville, its folk culture, her family, and the convergence of these elements in molding her sense of separateness—not from the community, but as someone within the community whose sense of quest, whose need to journey to the horizon, necessitates a movement beyond the community's borders.

Hurston is less given to an analysis of her life than she is to suggesting and conveying the nature of its emotional sources, and the account she provides of her formative years is full of divergent emotions, one of which she refuses to downplay: her anger. She was "of the word-changing kind" (27) and her forward behavior was cause of great alarm for her maternal grandmother—"She had known slavery and to her my brazenness was unthinkable" (46). In the classroom Hurston could not resist the urge to talk back to established authority, knowing "that established authority hated backtalk worse than barbed-wire pie" (95). After the death of her mother, she found that people resented her refusal, even in the face of homelessness, to be humble. Alone and poverty-stricken at an early age, Hurston says that she walked by her own corpse: "I smelt it and felt it. I smelt the corpses of those among whom I must live, though they did not. They were as much at home with theirs as death in a tomb" (117).

These remarks point to one of the primary tensions of Hurston's self-revelations. Though until the time of her mother's death she felt a sense of kinship within the community, she admits that her desire for action also drove her inward, as did her thirst for knowledge (fed in part by her exposure to books and myths), and these needs left her with a strong sense of separateness, an undeniable feeling of difference. From her adult perspective, Hurston admits that her continual questions made her "a crow in a pigeon's nest" and that this "was hard on my family and surroundings, and they in turn were hard on me" (33–34).

Like Eudora Welty, Hurston makes an honest attempt to isolate those features of her personality that she took from her parents, and in the first third of her autobiography perhaps no direct statement of self-revelation is so fraught with psychological implications as "I was Mama's child." Hurston makes this assertion as she wonders about her father's feelings the night of her mother's death—an event that leaves her with a profound sense of failure since she had not been able to defeat the force of Eatonville's rituals (and superstitions) and carry out her mother's last wishes.

Hurston offers a number of reasons for, near the age of fifty, identifying herself as Mama's child, not the least of which is the tolerance her mother expressed toward her creative ambitions and her earliest "lies"—the time for instance when she told her mother that the lake had talked with her and invited her "to walk all over it" (71).[3] It was Hurston's mother who "exhorted her children at every opportunity to 'jump at de sun.' " "We might not land on the sun," Hurston reflects, "but at least we would get off the ground" (21). Hurston's father— despite his own achievements as a successful minister and a prominent member of the town (he wrote the local laws of Eatonville and was elected mayor)—could not foresee the same success for his children. Hurston recalls his injunctions: "It did not do for Negroes to have too much spirit. He was always threatening to break mine or kill me in the attempt. My mother was always standing between us" (21). Hurston acknowledges that part of her father's fear was racially motivated but that the difference between his reticence and her mother's defiance and ability to dare stemmed from a larger philosophical difference— one that she captures in a single metaphor: "Rome, the eternal city, meant two different things to my parents. To Mama, it meant, you must build it today so it could last through eternity. To Papa, it meant that you could plan to lay some bricks today and you have the rest of eternity to finish it" (92).

Hurston returns to this essential conflict at various points throughout *Dust Tracks*. It colors her presentation of her father's second marriage to a woman she could not abide and finally his death as a wasted man only seven years later. "In reality," she writes, "my father was the baby of the family. With my mother gone and nobody to guide him, life had not hurt him but it had turned him loose to hurt himself" (172). While she does not dwell on the issue, Hurston shows that the differences between her father and mother, and the resulting dilemma for her father, are the consequences of gender-marked conflicts: "My mother took her over-the-creek man and bare-knuckled him from brogans to broadcloth, and I am certain that he was proud of the change, in public. But in the house, he might always have felt over-the-creek, and because that was not the statue he had made for himself to look at, he resented it" (92–93). Like Glasgow, Hurston resolves her conflict by rejecting the father's values—no matter how grounded in the social realities of the time—and aligning herself with those of her mother.

The narration works on two levels here; in addition to the immediate familial context, Hurston is providing the conflict of self that would germinate in her consciousness until it became the basis of her first novel, *Jonah's Gourd Vine* (1934). Hurston says the idea of writing a book came to her while she was doing research in 1929, but she found the idea presented problems: "For one thing, it seemed off-key. What I wanted to tell [in *Jonah's Gourd Vine*] was a story about a man, and from what I had read and heard, Negroes were supposed to write about the Race Problem. I was and am thoroughly sick of the subject. My interest lies in what makes a man or a woman do such-and-so regardless of his color" (207). It is her reverence for art and her need to transcribe what is on the inside—along with her sense of what constitutes the authentic—that forced Hurston to flaunt the generally accepted prescriptions for a writer of her era and race. Her remarks here prefigure Eudora Welty's "Must the Novelist Crusade?" In one interview, Welty tells about receiving calls from irate men and women who reminded her that people were dying in the South because of racial injustice and just what did she plan to do about it? (Prenshaw, *Conversations* 100) Both writers guard their need to follow the inner voice and both are equally reluctant to evaluate their success (or the extent of their originality) apart from the inner need their work fulfills. Perhaps nowhere is this reluctance more apparent than in the self-reflective comment Hurston makes regarding her attempt to "embalm all the tenderness" of her passion for one man into *Their Eyes Were Watching God*, a novel she wrote under intense emotional pressure in Jamaica. That the novel does in fact confront problems of racism (and sexism) seems less important for Hurston than the impulse that prompted her to write it in the first place.[4]

Hurston's heightened sense of self as revealed through direct statement is reinforced by the motifs that undergird the autobiography from the beginning chapter on. She represents herself as someone singled out because of her special awareness—her inner need and refinement (which, admittedly, she could not always reconcile with the outer reality). It is not insignificant that Hurston begins her self-story with an account of the three white frontier seekers who founded her town, for she clearly perceives herself—a wanderer if not a frontier woman—as sharing their spirit. The white man who accidentally (or providentially?) brings Hurston into the world personifies this frontier spirit. He employs Hurston not to be a coward and not to be a "nigger"—a word she defines (in a footnote) as "a weak, contemptible person of any race" (41). Hurston re-creates this man so that he embodies her own desire for action, her own individualistic values: "He was an accumulating man, a good provider, paid his debts and told the truth. Those were all the virtues the community expected" (43).

Though blatantly romanticized, Hurston's depiction of her childhood community is not lacking in either personal or cultural truth. In his book on black and white relations in the South, David R. Goldfield reminds us, "The South was a predominantly rural region well into the twentieth century, and its people lived in isolation, sometimes from each other, often from the outside world. They were frontiersmen long after the passing of the frontier, and the codes they lived by were private and local rather than public and national" (1). From her point of view, Hurston was fortunate enough to have her values shaped not only by the white man who assisted at her birth (the first of her many patrons), but also by an all-black community—a new kind of frontier, one whose mode of life was brilliantly realized for her in the town's central gathering place: "There were no discreet nuances of life on Joe Clarke's porch. There was open kindness, anger, hate, love, envy and its kinfolks, but all emotions were naked, and nakedly arrived at. . . . This was the spirit of that whole new part of the state at that time, as it always is where men settle new lands" (*Dust Tracks* 62).

Related to the frontier motif is the image Hurston creates of herself as a "wanderer." She credits an angry sow with initially prompting her to get off her feet and go. The young black southern woman who failed to internalize her father's injunctions that she learn her place, would, like the frontiersmen, "wander off in the woods all alone, following some inside urge to go places" (32). This behavior distressed her mother, who believed that an enemy "had sprinkled 'travel dust' around the door the day I was born" and who failed to see that for all their differences Hurston still resembled her father, the man "who didn't have a thing on his mind but this town and the next one" (32). Hurston's travels begin on a larger scale after the death of her mother. "That day began my wanderings," she writes. "Not so much in geography, but in time. Then not so much in time as in spirit" (89). These wanderings encompass her life from the time she realizes she is African-American, through her various attempts to find employment, through her travels with an operetta touring troop, and on to her enrollment at Howard University.

Wandering implies a certain aimlessness but also a challenging of the social constrictions of both gender and race. As a motif it must be seen in conjunction with the series of visions Hurston claims to have had as a child, beginning when she was seven years old: "Like clearcut stereopticon slides, I saw twelve scenes flash before me, each one held until I had seen it well in every detail. . . . I knew that they were all true, a preview of things to come, and my soul writhed in agony and shrunk away. But I knew that there was no shrinking. These things had to be" (57). The visions are never clearly itemized, and though Hurston refers to them intermittently, the reader will find it difficult to match their subsequent appearances with their first descriptions. Still, as a motif the visions are central to the self that Hurston defines. A relic of the more conventional spiritual autobiography, they punctuate her belief that she is someone extraordinary, and they provide a mythic, larger-than-life structure for her wanderings—for her quest. They also present a self-image that is far removed from most of the public accounts of Hurston by her contemporaries. In the passage in which she describes their initial appearance, Hurston presents a self that would appear to have more in common with the Ellen Glasgow of *The Woman Within* than with the carefree Zora Neale Hurston of, say, Langston Hughes's *The Big Sea* (1940). In an unusually somber tone Hurston writes: "I consider that my real childhood ended with the coming of the pronouncements. True, I played, fought and studied with other children, but always I stood apart within. . . . It is one of the blessings of this world that few people see visions and dream dreams" (60).

Some critics have argued that the visions do not shape the book. It might be more accurate to assume that Hurston intended them to structure or punctuate only part of the book, the years between her mother's death—and hence her exile from family and community— and the time she arrives at the home of the woman she would call her godmother, Mrs. R. Osgood Mason. More important than the visions as a way of giving shape to her autobiography are the various images and patterns of feminine power. "Ultimately," Claudine Raynaud observes, "the unifying motif of female friendship and rivalry, of female strength and courage, is much more powerful as a structuring device than the superimposed twelve prophetic visions" (127). Raynaud notes that the episode with Big Sweet, a woman who defends Hurston when she is threatened by the jealous wife of one of her Polk County informants, "calls to mind the other tales of female fighting which constitute a powerful thread running through Hurston's text" (126). Raynaud does not question the spiritual intent of Hurston's visions; what she underscores is Hurston's sense of herself as a female warrior, and what she brings to our attention is the fusion of religious and martial metaphors that culminate in one of Hurston's final and most powerful self-images: "I have stood on a peaky mountain wrappen in rainbows, with a harp and a sword in my hands" (*Dust Tracks* 280).

Hurston undergirds this sense of feminine power with the myths of Isis and Persephone. In her book on race, gender, and self-portraiture, Francois Lionnet offers a provocative analysis of Hurston's appropriation and cultural braiding of these mythic figures. Working on the theories of Michel Beaujour, Lionnet asserts that self-writing "is engendered primarily by the *impossibility* of self-presence, by the realization that realist narratives are functionally distorting and that myths are more appropriately evocative and suggestive of a subject's liminal position in the world of discursive representation" (122). As a "fictional alter-ego," Hurston chooses Isis, an Egyptian goddess who wanders the earth in search of Osiris, her dismembered brother, but Hurston is also drawn to the Eleusinian myth of Demeter searching for Persephone; it is her reading of this myth as a school girl that brings her to the attention of her first benefactors, two white women who reward her ability to read with gifts. Hurston/Isis wanders the land and "remembers the scattered body of folk material so that siblings can again 'touch each other' "; Hurston/Persephone is "not a rescuer but rather a lost daughter whose mother searches for her with passion" (119). Through her identification with Persephone, Hurston provides a distinctly feminist African-American variation on a Greco-Roman text. She travels "back to the underworld, to the 'dark realm' of her own people, to the friendship with Big Sweet, in order to learn to say what her dying mother could not, in order to name the chain of legendary female figures who can teach her to re-member and to speak the past" (128–29).

The stories—the narratives and mininarratives—that Hurston includes in her autobiography also function, like the fused myths of Persephone and Isis, through indirection. On the most basic level, they display Hurston's love of storytelling. It is not insignificant that she cites as her "first publication" an allegory she produced on the assembly hall blackboard at Morgan Academy, a comic and transparent series of tales that used faculty members as characters. Hurston's pleasure in recalling this antic is defined, to a large measure, by the pleasure it brought others. More often than not, the stories—many of which recount incidents that formed the folklore of her childhood—are carefully interwoven components of Hurston's self-representation. This is true even when the tales would appear to serve no larger purpose than to convey Hurston's delight in the process of memory itself. The marital exploits of her Aunt Caroline—this woman's affinity with Hurston's mother, who could deflate her husband's ego with just one well chosen word—suggest a great deal about the men of Eatonville, their sexual attitudes, and the inefficiency of these attitudes in subduing the spirit of Eatonville's women. They are stories that resonate and become even more suggestive of the processes that formed Hurston's values when, in subsequent chapters, she deals with her own relationships with men.

The complexity and multidimensionality of Hurston's self-representation is clearly evident in the concluding segment of her chapter on research as she tells the story of Cudjo Lewis, perhaps the only then living survivor of the last load of slaves to arrive in the United States. Cudjo Lewis, whose African name was Kossola-O-Lo-Loo-Ay, was living in the West African nation of Takkoi when "a whooping horde of the famed Dahoman women warriors burst through the main gate, seized people as they fled from their houses and beheaded victims with one stroke of their big swords" (201). These Amazons were warriors for the powerful king of Dohomey, who, as Cudjo Lewis told Hurston, had found the slave trade so lucrative that he "abandoned farming, hunting, and all else to capture slaves to stock the barracoons on the beach at Dmydah to sell to the slavers who came from across the ocean" (199). One of the captured who survived, Cudjo Lewis arrived in Mobile on the *Chlotilde* in 1859, lived as a slave for four years, became part of the black settlement of Plateau, Alabama, near Mobile, and died at ninety-five in 1935.

Like other parts of *Dust Tracks*, Hurston had presented some of this material in a previous essay, in this case "Cudjo's Own Story of the Last African Slaver" (1927), a dark point in her career, for as Robert Hemenway establishes, "Of the sixty-seven paragraphs in Hurston's essay, only eighteen are exclusively her own prose" (98). The rest is taken from Emma Langdon Koche's *Historic Sketches of the Old South* (1914). Hemenway makes no attempt to apologize for Hurston's fairly blatant theft. He speculates, however, that she was feeling the pressure of Franz Boas's scholarly expectations as well as the financial grip of historian Carter Woodson, under whose financial supervision she was employed as an investigator by the Association for the Study of Negro Life and History. Further, and for a wide variety of reasons, Hurston had found Lewis a difficult man to interview, though she would return to interview him again and eventually produce a still unpublished book-length study, a work that Hemenway identifies as a more honest handling of the scholarship and of Hurston's own interviews. Obviously the story of Cudjo Lewis had a profound impact on Hurston, for she would return to it in her own autobiography in 1942 and then again in 1944 with "The Last Slave Ship," a piece that she published in the *American Mercury* and that was condensed the same year in *Negro Digest* with the more richly suggestive title, "Black Ivory Finale." A brief comparison of the *Dust Tracks* and *American Mercury* versions shows how Hurston used Cudjo's story to suggest different elements of her own self-perceived identity.

In the *American Mercury* piece, Hurston describes the stockades the King of Dahomey "built for holding supplies of 'black ivory' until sold." She explains that the "captured tribes were each held in a separate barracoon, to prevent fighting. 'Do for do bring black man here from Guinea,' says the Jamaican proverb—which means that fighting among themselves caused black folks to be in slavery" (354–55). A reader of the *American Mercury* could not have missed Hurston's point: Africans mistreated other Africans. Hurston does not include the proverb in *Dust Tracks* (nor does she dwell as heavily on the fact that the men who sailed to West Africa in order to purchase the slaves were all northerners). In her autobiography, however, Hurston is much more forthright in drawing the moral for her readers and in linking it to her own radical individualism:

> One thing impressed me strongly from these three months of association with Cudjo Lewis. The white people had held my people in slavery here in America. They had bought us, it is true and exploited us. But the inescapable fact that stuck in my craw, was: My people had *sold* me and the white people had bought me. That did away with the folklore I had been brought up on—that the white people had gone to Africa, waved a red handkerchief at the Africans and lured them aboard ship and sailed away. I know that civilized money stirred up African greed. That wars between tribes were often stirred up by white traders to provide more slaves in the barracoons and all that. But, if the African princes had been as pure and as innocent as I would like to think, it could not have happened. No, my own people had butchered and killed, exterminated whole nations, and torn families apart, for a profit before the strangers got their chance at a cut. It was a sobering thought. (200)

There is even a hint of the disgust with her country's hypocritical and sanctimonious imperialism that Hurston presented in "Seeing the World As It Is," one of the chapters her publisher suggested that she omit. Cudjo Lewis's story sensitized Hurston to "the universal nature of greed and glory" and to the fact that "lack of power and opportunity passes off too often for virtue." This realization enables Hurston to question her own motives and impulses: "If I were King . . . would I put the cloak of Justice on my ambition and send her out a-whoring after conquests? It is something to ponder over with fear" (200).

In another passage that does not appear in the *American Mercury* version, Hurston describes the care and respect with which the King of Takkoi's skull was treated by the King of Dahomey, who would have expected the same respect had he fallen in battle. Hurston's contention that West Africans respected one another as both victors and victims precedes her deflation of another racial myth: that Africans of royal blood were sold as slaves rather than killed. According to Hurston, "The Negroes who claim that they are descendants of royal African blood have taken a leaf out of the book of the white ancestor-hounds in America, whose folks went to England with William the Conqueror, got restless and caught the *Mayflower* for Boston, then feeling a romantic lack, rushed down the coast and descended from Pocahontas" (202). With her supreme self-confidence and her unshakable sense of individualism, Hurston feels no such "romantic lack."

The account of Cudjo Lewis, near the end of her chapter on research, is representative of Hurston's early fieldwork—up to a point. The difference is that, through her editorial-like glosses on Cudjo's narrative, Hurston here assumes the voice of the cultural critic rather than the objective ethnographer. What Hurston extrapolates from the Cudjo Lewis experience should not, however, obscure what may be a less immediately apparent reason for her continuing involvement with his story. As Francois Lionnet observes, the parallels between Cudjo Lewis, who was abruptly separated from his family, and Hurston, whose childhood idyll ended when she too was separated from those she loved, highlight one of the most significant dimensions of Hurston's self-story, as she implies in her final image of Lewis: "After seventy-five years, he still had that tragic sense of loss. That yearning for blood and cultural ties. That sense of mutilation. It gave me something to *feel* about" (204, emphasis added).

Hurston does not linger with this somber emotion. In the last third of *Dust Tracks*, she turns her attention to particular topics—among them religion and religious opinion—and her tone, though it never loses its humor, becomes more meditative and more polemically focused. This shift has caused problems for a number of readers. Claudine Raynaud argues that the shift creates a rupture and thus jars our expectations. Francois Lionnet claims (with greater persuasiveness) that there is no such rupture, that, in fact, Hurston deliberately frames her personal experiences by more general assessments of, on one hand, her region and "folks" and, on the other, her adult views on general topics like love, religion, race, and—now that her original conclusion is available—nationalism. Robert Hemenway recognizes that Hurston is aiming for a holistic perspective with her closing chapters, but he believes, along with Raynaud, that the divided emphasis detracts from the book's effectiveness. Clearly these chapters deserve more attention—both for what they do or do not accomplish.

Hurston's table of contents in *Dust Tracks* suggests what may be an order of importance. She moves from race—"My People, My People"—to friendship, to love, to religion, to her final global perspective—"Looking Things Over." Though she leads us to believe that she thinks race consciousness is less significant than love between friends and less significant than one's relationship with the cosmos, Hurston nonetheless returns to the problem of race, particularly the problem of racial difference, in the final paragraphs of her autobiography. Critics seem willing to forgive or forebear any of Hurston's idiosyncracies and contradictions save those regarding her pronouncements on race. As Hurston might have anticipated, some readers have consequently regarded the other chapter-essays as less germane to her self-representation as an African-American woman artist in midtwentieth-century America. Yet any understanding of Hurston's racial consciousness as a black southern American must acknowledge the total self she attempts to delineate in each of these discursive chapters (including those that did not initially appear), beginning with her remarks about the nature of friendship.

" 'I will visit you with my love,' says the sun. That is why the hills endure" (307). Hurston has had many such visitations—that is, many enduring friends: "I am just sort of assembled up together out of friendship and put together by time" (314). These comments appear in the manuscript chapter "The Inside Light—Being a Salute to Friendship" that Hemenway includes in the Appendix to the 1984 *Dust Tracks* (a chapter written just before the book went to Hurston's publisher). The chapter in fact reads like a catalog; Hurston singles out, among many others, Mrs. R. Osgood Mason, Carl Van Vechten, Fannie Hurst, Miguel and Rose Covarrubias, James Weldon Johnson, Edna St. Vincent Millay, *Story* editor Whit Burnett, and her friend Katharane Edson Mershon who supported her while she completed *Dust Tracks* in California. The problem this chapter poses is that most of the names Hurston mentions are white; moreover, most have in some way helped to advance her career. Hence, the chapter can be construed (by a cynical reader) as not a tribute to friends but a salute to patrons—as Hurston's compilation of memories and debts owed. The flaw with this view is that it presumes friendships are one-sided or that Hurston got better than she gave.

Hemenway does not explain why this chapter was not included, though one can guess that, again, it was a matter of the publishers' preference (perhaps they found it boring). In the chapter on friendship that did initially appear, "Two Women in Particular," Hurston includes only Fannie Hurst (for whom she served as a hired companion) and Ethel Waters. "Two women, among the number whom I have known intimately force me to keep them well in mind," Hurston writes, and yet for some readers this dual scheme has fared no better than the inventory of the manuscript chapter. It has been suggested that what the chapter on Hurst and Waters really reveals is Hurston's careful balancing of one white friend with one black—her desire not to alienate her presumed white reader—but again, this view seems unnecessarily reductive; there is no real reason to doubt the sincerity of either portrait.

Because she was not a writer or an employer/patron, Hurston's friendship with Ethel Waters has received less attention than the friendship with Hurst. Yet of all the friends and acquaintances she mentions in *Dust Tracks*, only in the case of Waters does Hurston make a comment such as this one: "I am due to have this friendship with Ethel Waters, because I worked for it" (243). In 1942, eight years before the huge broadway success of *The Member of the Wedding*, Waters had established herself as a major African-American performer, but

Waters's fame does not weigh heavily in Hurston's reminiscence. Instead Hurston is drawn to Waters the artist and person: "I sensed a great humanness and depth about her; I wanted to know someone like that" (243). In no specific order, Hurston recounts some of the highlights of Waters's career along with a few incidents from the friendship that finally emerged between them. As her reminiscence unfolds, it becomes apparent that Waters's "struggle for adequate expression" (245) is Hurston's struggle as well; her portrait of Waters is ridden with references to "words" as an adequate or often inadequate mode of communication. Perhaps most provocative is Hurston's way of conveying her affinity with the legendary singer: "I am her friend, and her tongue is in my mouth. I can speak her sentiments for her, though Ethel Waters can do very well indeed in speaking for herself . . . she has words to fit when she speaks" (245).

Such a closeness may have fed the speculation that Hurston was a lesbian, a charge Alice Walker counters in her Introduction to Hemenway's biography (xv). Of the women Hurston knew intimately, Waters emerges from her brief portrait as one of the maternal figures. One recalls that Hurston describes her own mother as a woman who had a similar way with language—as someone who could consciously appropriate and thus empower herself through the use of "words." There is even a submerged link between Hurston's mother, Waters, and Big Sweet, Hurston's protectress in Polk County, a woman with remarkable physical strength who is also a powerful word-warrior. In a much discussed passage, Hurston recalls hearing Big Sweet "with her foot up on somebody" in the act of "specifying" (186–87). Her mother, Ethel Waters, and Big Sweet, for all their differences, represent feminine strength for Hurston.

What does one make of the friendship between Hurston and Hurst? Aside from the fact that they each produced their most widely read fiction in the thirties, it would be difficult to imagine two more different writers. Hurst was the author of such very popular melodramatic potboilers as *Back Street* (1931) and *Imitation of Life* (1933). One need only compare either work with *Their Eyes Were Watching God*, Hurston's feminist celebration of a woman who refuses to sacrifice herself for a man and who discovers for herself what love should be, to discern the fundamental difference between the two authors.

It is generally known that Hurston, while an undergraduate, served

as a secretary for Hurst. A poor typist, Hurston was fired as "amanuensis" but retained as a chauffeur. The element of Hurst's personality
that Hurston emphasizes in *Dust Tracks* is her unpredictable impish-
ness, which Hurston illustrates with several intriguing incidents, including the time she observed Hurst "invite" herself to tea and pretend
that "she had company with her for an hour or more" before returning
to her office and her work (239). Hurston claims to be thankful for the
friendship of both Hurst and Waters, but while she concludes the section on Waters with praise for her ability to live with both "great success and terrible personal tragedy" (248), she concludes the section on
Hurst with praise for what Hurst does with her appearance: "She
knows exactly what goes with her very white skin, black hair and sloe
eyes, and she wears it. . . . She will never be jailed for uglying up a
town" (243).

One of Hemenway's reasons for including the manuscript chapter on
friendship is that its "characterization of Hurst differs somewhat from
the published version" (288). The paragraphs on Hurst in the previously unpublished chapter contain two suggestive details. Again noting
Hurst's unexpected "transitions," Hurston writes: "I have watched her
under all kinds of conditions, and she never ceases to amaze me. Be-
hold her phoning to a swanky hotel for reservations for herself and the
Princess Zora *and* parading me in there all dressed up as an Asiatic
person of royal blood and keeping a straight face while the attendants
goggled at me and bowed low! Like a little girl, I have known her in the
joy of a compelling new gown to take me to a tea in some exclusive spot
in New York. I would be the press agent for her dress, for everybody
was sure to look if *they* saw somebody like me strolling into the Astor
or the Biltmore" (310).

Did Hurston resent becoming the "press agent" for a dress, or did
she merely accept such a status as the price of patronage? What about
the episode with "Princess Zora," which can be read as Hurst the liberal poking fun at and subverting an intolerant social system or, again,
as Hurston willingly accepting the role of toy. It is apparent that Hurston was drawn to the eccentricity of Fannie Hurst, but Hurston with-
holds her own reactions as the other player in these scenarios. Hurst
may have hinted at Hurston's private feelings when she recalls one
oblique yet pungent comment on their dinner together. After the meal
and what Hurst calls "some levity," Hurston "revealed for an instant

her mental innards: 'Who would think,' she soliloquized as we re-
sumed driving, 'that a good meal could be so bitter?' " ("Personality
Sketch" 20)

The account of Hurst in *Dust Tracks* is taken primarily from a longer
piece on Hurst that Hurston published in the *Saturday Review of Literature* in 1936. The earlier piece, written almost entirely in the second
person, is in some ways more satisfying than the sketch in *Dust Tracks*.
In part because it is lengthier and more carefully sustained, Hurst
comes off as less schizophrenic, and Hurston (at least viewed from the
vantage point of hindsight) reveals more about herself, but most important, Hurston does not neglect the subject of vocation in this piece:
"[Hurst] is a writer because she had to be one. . . . If everything she
writes is not a 'Humoresque,' a 'Backstreet,' a 'Lummox,' or a 'Vertical
City,' it is not a play to the gallery. It is because the gods have failed her
for the moment" (15). The early chapters of *Dust Tracks* make it clear
that Hurston perceived her own writing as the expression of an inner
need that cannot always articulate itself in any other way. If Hurston
becomes an apologist for Hurst's eccentricity, it is because her own
sense of self accommodates mood swings, contradictions, unpredicta-
bility. Hurston's apologetics merge with or at least embody her own
self-defense: "What the gods within her direct today may be absolutely
repudiated by what they dictate tomorrow, and *that is as it should be*.
So it is ridiculous to go and get your *mob-size measure* and attempt to
take her size" (15, emphasis added).

Virginia M. Burke has provided one of the most satisfying explorations of the Hurst-Hurston relationship, constructed from *Dust Tracks*,
the *Saturday Review* piece, Hurst's autobiography, *Anatomy of Me*
(which does not mention Hurston), her short introduction to *Jonah's
Gourd Vine*, and her "Personality Sketch" of Hurston that appeared in
the *Yale University Library Gazette* the year after Hurston's death.
Burke's conclusion is that, while Hurston "penetrated several dimensions of the Hurst mystique better than many who tried to do so during
Hurst's lifetime" (445), Hurst, in her characterization of her former
amanuensis, "ran afoul of stereotypes, in particular the classic stereotype created by whites during the Harlem Renaissance—the exotic
primitive—which prevented her from seeing very far beyond the surfaces of the Hurston personality" (446).

The most significant feature of Burke's essay, however, is her understanding of a submerged affinity between the two writers who could see one another as, simultaneously, woman, writer, and child. It is no accident that Hurston lingers so approvingly on the little girl image, especially in *Dust Tracks* where the focus is always—by implication or otherwise—her own self-awareness. The little girl is emblematic of the two women's shared refusal to mold themselves according to norms outside their own choosing. Their affinity is, finally, more important than their differences. As Burke observes, "The common factors here are that both women were eccentrics at heart, dramatizing themselves for their pleasure, caring little what others thought . . . they were both born to be themselves, they knew it, and they wanted it that way" (446).[5]

Burke's remarks serve as an interesting transition to the chapter on love that follows the one on Hurst and Waters, for Hurston's much-touted independence was the source of her romantic problems with men. More specifically, Hurston's career and the importance she gave to it stood in the way of any apparently workable or lasting relationship—at least from the man's point of view. If Hurston appears to find her relationships with women less complicated than those with men, it is not difficult to understand why. The Eatonville waif who defied gender norms by fighting with boys and torturing her dolls, who from her position on the gatepost solicited rides from strangers, could not accept the prevailing social constructions of "manliness" when she became an adult.

Hurston recounts the time, for instance, when she offered to loan a quarter to one of her lovers, Albert Price III, the man she identifies as A.W.P. Through indirect speech, she conveys her impression of his reaction: "What kind of coward did I take him for? How could he deserve my respect if he behaved like a cream puff? . . . *Please* let him be a man!"[6] Hurston concludes, "That very manliness, sweet as it was, made us both suffer. My career balked the completeness of his ideal" (253).

Despite her misgivings, Hurston calls this relationship with Price the real love of her life; he was a man who could beat her "to the draw mentally" (252), a man "who had nothing to offer but what it takes—a bright soul, a fine body, and courage" (255). This relationship lasted on and off for several years. Since the affair was still on as Hurston was writing *Dust Tracks*, she does not attempt to predict its end. Rather, she leaves the reader with a reflection that recalls Glasgow's summation of her affair with Henry Anderson. Whatever the outcome, Hurston writes, "I have the satisfaction of knowing that I have loved and been loved by the perfect man. If I never hear of love again, I have known the real thing" (262). The marriage ended in divorce in November of 1943.

Hurston's chapter on love is for many readers one of the thorns in her autobiography. She does not say that she married Price and she does not provide the name (or even the initials) of her first husband, Herbert Sheen. Hurston managed to conceal both marriages from patrons, fellow artists, and many of her friends. Like Katherine Anne Porter, Hurston jealously guarded her privacy, even to the point of distorting the public record. In this chapter she tells her reader, "Don't look for me to call a string of names and point out chapter and verse. Ladies do not kiss and tell any more than gentlemen do" (249).

The flippancy of Hurston's attitude is not without its point. It is, in fact, her sense of satire—which informs her understanding of sexual politics—that makes her self-portrait distinctive. Hurston's chapter on love has much in common with the attitudes that Edna St. Vincent Millay presented in the poems that made her an icon of the Greenwich Village scene and an embodiment of the "new woman" in the early twenties. Hurston, whose work Millay admired, suggested something of the same free-spiritedness for commentators on the Harlem Renaissance. (It is important to remember that there was a great deal of cultural crossover between the two Manhattan locales.) Like Millay—another "vitalist"—Hurston was apprehensive about the durability of relationships. Regarding her first marriage, she says, "The day and the occasion did not underscore any features of nature or circumstance, and I wondered why. Who had canceled the well-advertised tour of the moon?" (251). Also like Millay, Hurston could not resist the opportunity to dismantle the male ego or the sexual double standard: "a man may lose interest in me and go where his fancy leads him, and we can still meet as friends. But if I get tired and let on about it, he is certain to become an enemy of mine. That forces me to lie like the cross-ties from New York to Key West" (263). When the "ex-sharer of a mood" reminds Hurston of "every silly thing" she has said, her rejoinder is one that Millay might have given; Hurston simply denies any inconsistency: "I was sincere for the moment in which I said the things. It is

strictly a matter of time. It was true for the moment . . . the great difficulty lies in trying to transform last night's moment to a day which has
no knowledge of it" (204).

Has Hurston created a disguise to hide her more genuine and perhaps less easily articulated feelings, or has she constructed an image of
herself that is true to the reality and confusion of relationships as she
perceives them? Hurston is content to leave any final interpretation to
her reader, but the concluding paragraph of her lesson on love suggests
that balanced against her romanticism is a fundamentally skeptical nature: "So pay my few scattering remarks no mind as to love in general.
I know only my part. Anyway, it seems to be the unknown country from
which no traveler ever returns. What seems to be a returning pilgrim is
another person born in the strange country with the same-looking ears
and hands. He is a stranger to the person who fared forth, and a
stranger to family and old friends. He is clothed in mystery henceforth
and forever" (265).

In its suggestion that love inevitably confounds, it is a passage that
anticipates Carson McCullers's thesis on the lover and the beloved in
The Ballad of the Sad Cafe (1943). Hurston concludes by citing an "old
Negro folk rhyme" that may tell "all there is to know": "Love is a funny
thing; love is a blossom; if you want your finger bit, poke it at a pos-
sum" (265).

Hurston's skepticism extends to the discussion on religion that follows in which she defines herself as having been a quester from as early
as she can recall. If the spirit of Millay hovers over her chapter on love,
the presence of H. L. Mencken can be felt here. Right off, Hurston
establishes herself as a debunker, and this in spite of her religious upbringing: "You wouldn't think that a person who was born with God in
the house would ever have any questions on the subject" (267). But
Hurston the individualist is full of questions that lead her through a
demystification process and on to a quasi-pantheistic view of her place
within the cosmos. Her earlier mystical visions do not lead to any sort
of spiritual awareness and are, in fact, incidental to the essentially ra-
tionalistic approach she takes to religion in this chapter.

Hurston's perspectives on religious belief come as little surprise to
the reader who, by this point in *Dust Tracks*, has learned that the adolescent Hurston had no use for stories about little girls who gave their
hearts to Christ, who instead preferred the action stories of the Old

Testament. Hurston the adult skeptic is also the child who pitted Joe Clark's store against Eatonville's two churches, who opposed the disturbing force of religious ritual at the moment of her mother's death, and who held that voodoo is as valid as any other mode of worship. In her essay on religion, Hurston develops in detail the stance she hints at earlier in her narrative.

Her debunking of religion works from two directions: from what she observed as a child and from what she has come to understand as an adult. Thus Hurston recalls the "great protestations of love and friendship" that would precede the day of communion in her childhood church: "Come 'Love Feast' some of the congregation told of getting close enough to peep into God's sitting-room windows. Some went further. They had been inside the place and looked all around" (266–67). The problem for Hurston is that these chosen people failed to look or act any differently than they had prior to these encounters. "It mystified me," she writes: "There were so many things they neglected to look after while they were right there in the presence of All-Power. I made up my mind to do better than that if ever I made the trip" (267). Hurston could not reconcile herself to the many contradictions she observed, nor could she understand how people could declare love for "a being" they could not see—"Your family, your puppy and the new bull-calf, yes. But a spirit way off who found fault with everybody all the time, that was more that I could fathom" (268). If asked if she loved God, Hurston—like Lillian Smith—would say "yes" in fear of both authority and rejection. Unlike Smith, however, Hurston did not find the frequent revival meetings to be a source of anxiety; rather, she enjoyed them for much the same reason as did Eudora Welty; with their music, their testimonials, shouting, altar calls, and visions, they were the source of high drama and as entertaining as the baptisms and funerals. "But of the *inner* thing," she concludes, "I was right where I was when I first began to seek answers" (274, emphasis added).

This inner need or struggle stays with Hurston even as her subsequent surveys of philosophy convince her that God is a creation of man and the story of Christianity is synonymous with the history of violence and repression: "In Rome where Christians had been looked upon as rather indifferent lion-bait, and among other things as keepers of the virgins in their homes for no real good to the virgins, Christianity mounted" (276). The crusades of Constantine marked only the beginning: "Military power was to be called in time and time again to carry forward the gospel of peace. There is not apt to be any difference of opinion between you and a dead man" (276). Observing the same power play in "all the other great religions," Hurston vows to continue thinking and questing for herself—yet another manifestation of her individualism. "I have achieved a certain peace within myself," she adds, "but perhaps the seeking after the inner heart of truth will never cease in me. All sorts of interesting speculations arise" (277).

With the possible exception of Ellen Glasgow, Hurston goes further than any other southern woman writer of her generation in formulating for others the nature of her own unorthodox perspective. The last two paragraphs of her chapter-essay on religion contain the essence of her "belief":

> But certain things have seemed to me to be true as I heard the tongues of those who had speech, and listened at the lips of books. It seems to me to be true that heavens are placed in the sky because it is the unreachable. The unreachable and the unknowable always seems divine— hence, religion. People need religion because the great masses fear life and its consequences. Its responsibilities weigh heavy. Feeling a weakness in the face of great forces, men seek an alliance with omnipotence to bolster up their feeling of weakness, even though the omnipotence they rely upon is a creature of their own minds. It gives them a feeling of security. Strong, self-determining men are notorious for their lack of reverence. (277–78).

Hurston points again to Constantine, who, despite his own crusades, "refused the consolation of Christ until his last hour. Some say not even then" (278).

Having studied the great religions "by word of mouth and then as they fit into great rigid forms," Hurston claims to know "a great deal about form, but little or nothing about the mysteries I sought as a child" (277). Like Welty, she draws attention to her own reverence for the unknowable and her willingness to ponder rather than solve or rigidly codify life's inexplicability. Hurston defines her role as that of the celebratory participant within the great mystery: "Life, as it is, does not frighten me, since I have made my peace with the universe as I find it, and bow to its laws" (279).

As the conclusion of her "meditation" on religion makes clear, Hurston's belief fuses intellectual skepticism with romantic pantheism:

When the consciousness we know as life ceases, I know that I shall still be part and parcel of the world. I was a part before the sun rolled into shape and burst forth in the glory of change. I was, when the earth was hurled out from its fiery rim. I shall return with the earth to Father Sun, and still exist in substance when the sun has lost its fire, and disintegrated in infinity to perhaps become a being in matter, ever changing, ever moving, but never lost; so what need of denominations and creeds to deny myself the comfort of all my fellow men? The wide belt of the universe has no need for finger-rings. I am one with the infinite and need no other assurance. (279)

This statement of her immanent residence within the earth may recall Whitman and D. H. Lawrence, and particularly Lawrence's *Apocalypse* (1931), but it probably owes less to Eurocentric sources than at first may be apparent. Patricia Hill Collins defines what she calls an "ethic of caring" that is rooted in "a tradition of African humanism" and that, one could argue, captures the essence of Hurston's belief. In this ethic "each individual is thought to be a unique expression of a common spirit, power, or energy expressed by all life." Collins observes that the African "belief in individual uniqueness is illustrated by the value placed on personal expressiveness in African-American communities"; she cites a remark by an inner-city resident who says, "No matter how hard we try, I don't think black people will ever develop much of a herd instinct. We are profound individualists with a passion for self-expression" (766).

Given her sense of both individualism and cosmic residence, one can see why, near the conclusion of *Dust Tracks*, Hurston mentions her desire to read Spinoza and the mysticism of the East in her old age. Her system of belief is consistent with that of the Spanish Jew whose chief work, the *Ethics*, holds that everything in the universe is related and that recognizing this interconnectedness leads to "intellectual love of God." Spinoza distinguishes emotions from egoistic passions, which keep men and women from understanding the wholeness of Nature/God. As Bertrand Russell explains, "Spinoza's outlook is intended to liberate men from the tyranny of fear" (574); Spinoza, Russell writes, "is concerned to show how it is possible to live nobly even when we recognize the limits of human power. . . . Take, for instance, death: nothing that a man can do will make him immortal, and it is therefore futile to spend time in fears and lamentations over the fact that we must die. To be obsessed by the fear of death is a kind of slavery; Spinoza is right in saying that 'the free man thinks of nothing less than of death' "(578).

Russell also believes that Spinoza is right to insist that "a life dominated by a single passion is a narrow life, incompatible with every kind of wisdom" (575). Spinoza's *Ethics* may be useful not only to our understanding of Hurston's position on religion but to her position vis-à-vis the whole issue of racial consciousness—another "single passion" that has through the centuries dominated too many lives.

In "Looking Things Over," the closing chapter of *Dust Tracks* and the final synthesis of her self-perceived place within the cosmos, Hurston brings to the fore something that has been apparent all along—her understanding and appreciation of life's absurdities: "My sense of humor will always stand in the way of my seeing myself, my family, my race or my nation as the whole intent of the universe. When I see what we really are like, I know that God is too great an artist for we folks on my side of the creek to be all of His best works" (287). Like Lillian Hellman and Katherine Anne Porter, Hurston does not deny her idealistic aspirations, her own yearnings for "universal justice" (287), but she cannot conceive of a world without her own imperfections. Still, she refuses to be demoralized by a past she did not help to shape. Nor does she predict the future. Rather, she expresses her desire for more work and she highlights those goals that are achievable—"I want a busy life, a just mind, and a timely death" (285).

Nellie McKay provides a sound assessment of Hurston's autobiographical achievement. "If *Dust Tracks on a Road* is Hurston's statue," McKay asserts, "it celebrates a black woman who wanted us to know that very early in her life she decided to ride to the horizon on the finest black riding horse with the shiniest bridle and saddle she could secure" (188). While McKay rightly concludes that "*Dust Tracks* presents a view of black female identity that justifies its existence," it is still important to ponder the extent to which Hurston's racial politics undercut or diminish the force of her self-representation. Readers and critics seem to agree that one can accept all of Hurston's eccentricities save those regarding race. In her nexus of gender, family, region, nation, and race, it is race that remains the most problematic issue for Hurston's readers, if not for Hurston herself.

Hurston's position on race can be summed up in four sentences: "What the world is crying and dying for at this moment is less race consciousness. The human race would blot itself out entirely if it had any more. It is a deadly explosive on the tongues of men. I choose to forget it" (326). This statement, which did not make it into the original 1942 volume, is nonetheless consistent with the position Hurston takes throughout *Dust Tracks*. Perhaps her chief problem is that she cannot forget it; as she notes in the chapter devoted solely to the issue of race, "No Negro in America is apt to forget his race" (218). Hurston cannot get away with making herself "just folks." A few incidents recorded in *Dust Tracks* serve to show why this stance is, at best, a precarious one for her to maintain so persistently, but it seems necessary first to understand why Hurston takes the stand she does.

Her refusal to make race a cornerstone in what McKay calls her "self-in-writing" (188) is rooted in Hurston's abhorrence of abstractionism: "I maintain that I have been a Negro three times—a Negro baby, a Negro girl, and a Negro woman. Still, if you have received no clear cut impression of what the Negro in America is like, then you are in the same place with me" (237). This disdain for generality—grounded in Hurston's strong sense of individualism—encompasses whites who would peg an entire race as one thing or another, but it is also a reaction to the same reductive tendency on the part of her own people.

As an adolescent, Hurston could not understand how African-Americans could simultaneously extol their race as the most progressive, most beautiful, and bravest race on earth—"facing every danger like lions, and fighting with demons" (220)—and then denounce one another's behavior as typical of "niggers," who, like monkeys, must mimic the white man and "make a great big old mess" (221). The laughter at monkey stories puzzled Hurston, and despite the grand schoolhouse orations about the perfection of her race, she still observed "a general acceptance of the monkey as kinfolks" (224). Equally puzzling was her discovery that "always the blackest Negro" was "made the butt of all jokes,—particularly black women" (225). Just as she learns to question the great religious myths, Hurston questions myths about racial pride, prejudice, and solidarity. Perhaps most important—again in terms of the author Hurston became—is her inability to accept the faulty logic of those who "considered themselves Race Champions" but "wanted nothing to do with anything Negroid. . . . The spirituals, the Blues, *any* definitely Negro thing was just not done" (233). The contradictions lead Hurston to claim that "being black was not enough," that it takes "more than a community of skin color to make your love come down on you" (234–35). Once again she reifies her belief in individualism: "Light came to me when I realized that I did not have to consider any racial group as a whole. God made them duck by duck and that was the only way I could see them" (235).

It is for all of these reasons that Hurston refuses to provide an idealized depiction of African-American life in her autobiography. Her conception of Eatonville seems undeniably romanticized—"White Maitland and Negro Eatonville have lived side by side for fifty-six years without a single instance of enmity" (10–11)—but her depiction of intraracial affairs within this all-black community is untouched by sentimentality. This holds true even with her own family members—with her grandmother or stepmother for example. There is love and respect for one another, but there is also disharmony, blatant sexism, and jealousy of one another's economic status. When Hurston moves beyond the environment of Eatonville, her characterizations of African-Americans and their interactions are equally realistic. She mentions a time when she worked as a maid for a woman with two small children who formed an immediate attachment to their new source of entertainment. Hurston's popularity did not sit well with the "president of the kitchen," a "black old woman who had nursed the master of the house and was a fixture." Hurston learned that "nobody is so powerful in a Southern family as one of these family fixtures. No matter who hires you, the fixture can fire you" (119).

It is because she treats other African-Americans with such honesty that the reader wants to question Hurston's characterizations of whites. Hurston's claim to forget about racial consciousness is, finally, a hollow pose. Such consciousness is at the heart of the relationship she attempts to mold with her white reader. Her aim is to establish a harmonious exchange; hence, she downplays what one might justifiably suspect is resentment of a bifurcated social system, as when she dismisses the condescension of the operetta company's tenor to her request to borrow his books. Hurston is not beneath using subtle flattery to cater to the white reader's presumed sense of racial superiority. One passage from *Dust Tracks* that might well have been omitted would be the one in which she explains why her editor at J. B. Lippincott will always remain a Colonel to her: "When the Negroes in the South name a white man a colonel, it means CLASS. Somebody like a monarch, only bigger and better. And when the colored population in the South confer a title, the white people recognize it because the Negroes are never wrong" (212).

Unlike her white contemporaries, Hurston cannot forget about race because in the process of writing about herself she must continually explain or interpret patronizing and racially marked behavior. These explanations, which often delimit the cultural distance between herself, her reader, and other participants in her story, can take the form of simple appositives, as when she explains the assistance that Big Sweet provided in her research: "We held two lying contests, storytelling contests to *you*, and Big Sweet passed on who rated the prizes" (189, emphasis added). Throughout *Dust Tracks*, but especially in the chapters on her "folks" and her "people," Hurston identifies the presence of a reader whose range of cultural experience is clearly not that of her own. When, in reference to her father, she says, "A little of my sugar used to sweeten his coffee right now," the comment is followed by an explanation: "That is a Negro way of saying his patience was short with me" (27). The racially defined relationship between writer and reader is nowhere more visible than when the young Hurston expresses her desire to own a black riding horse, a wish that causes her father to lose his temper: " 'A saddle horse!' Papa exploded. 'It's a sin and a shame! Lemme tell you something right now, my young lady; you ain't white' " (30). In a footnote Hurston supplies yet another explanation: " 'You ain't white' is a Negro saying that means 'Don't be too ambitious. You are a Negro and they are not meant to have but so much' " (38). In this case the explanation seems less a needed gloss on a regional expression than a sly indictment of a social system that would necessitate such injunctions. Given that Hurston's publishers wanted a nonconfrontational autobiography, one can guess that she is using the footnote in this instance to provide a careful reader with a perspective that might not be immediately apparent.

It is, of course, one of Hurston's tactics in *Dust Tracks*, as in her fiction and folk collections, to reveal more than might be at once apparent. When she defines her region, rather than her town, Hurston does not at first appear to distinguish between black and white southerners. Here is how she describes the reaction of the Gilbert and Sullivan troop to their new "play pretty":

> I was a Southerner, and had the map of Dixie on my tongue. They were all Northerners except the orchestra leader, who came from Pensacola. It was not my grammar was bad, it was the idioms. They did not know of the way an average Southern child, white or black, is raised on simile and invective. They know how to call names. It is an everyday affair to hear somebody called a mullet-headed, mule-eared, hog-nosed, 'gator-faced' . . . unmated so-and-so! . . . Since that stratum of the Southern population is not given to book-reading, they take their comparisons right out of the barnyard and the woods. When they get through with you, you and your whole family look like an acre of totem-poles. (135–36)

One of the intriguing features of this passage is that, while Hurston displays her "southerness" and her enjoyment of the barnyard epithets, she herself is addicted to book reading and consequently her identification with this aspect of regionalism shifts along with her pronouns. "They" in this passage has two distinct antecedents: the acting troop and Hurston's fellow southerners. In a provocative discussion of voice in *Dust Tracks*, Susan Willis notes that her frequent "ungrammatical use of pronouns" is evidence of "the contradictory nature of Hurston's project as a black woman writer and intellectual attempting to mediate two deeply polarized worlds, whose terms include: South/North, black/white, rural/urban, folk tradition/intellectual scholarship" (27). Hurston's ploys or tricks enable her, as Willis observes, to dodge the charge that she assumes "a Northern, white identity" while she also removes herself "out of any possible inscription in the stigmatized view of Southern blackness" (28).

Any assessment of her identification with the South must take into consideration Hurston's description of the central Florida terrain itself. Here there is no subtle shift of pronouns, just Hurston's expression of love for certain features of her native state. Yet because she offers so few upfront indictments of the South and its divided way of life, Hurston's representation of the South will likely remain a vexing issue for readers of *Dust Tracks*. What Hurston does not include in her imagined tour for the Florida Chamber of Commerce are the segregated theaters, the separate fountains, and the most recent sites of mob lynchings. In other words, her tour would be much like the one she provides in

Dust Tracks—a tour that refuses to align itself with any further racial stigmatization.[7]

This is not to say that Hurston completely disguises the brutality that was and at times still is a very real part of the southern fabric. To cite one example, she describes the time when the body of her cousin Jimmie—her mother's favorite nephew—is found headless near her mother's childhood home in Alabama. While the circumstances of his death were never fully revealed, Hurston notes that the rumors claimed that Jimmie, light of skin, had been "shot in the head by a white man unintentionally, and then beheaded to hide the wound. . . . There was never any move to prove the charge, for *obvious* reasons (85, emphasis added). Hurston lets the obvious speak for itself; she also leaves it to the reader to make the connection between this death, her mother's sorrow, and the similar grief of Cudjo Lewis, whose son was beheaded in a train accident.

In the chapter on race, Hurston tells another, perhaps even more revealing story about racial tensions in the South, this time in her own home town. "One night just after dark, we heard terrible cries back in the woods behind Park Lake. Sam Mosely, his brother Elijah, and Ike Clarke, hurried up to our gate and they were armed." Hurston's account of what follows is genuinely frightening: "The howls of pain kept up. Old fears and memories must have stirred inside the grown folks. Many people closed and barred their doors" (227). The victim of the beating turns out to be white rather than black, and the men, including her father, return to their homes. For all its potential horror, Hurston concludes this story with an affirmative image of the community together again, the crisis averted, the men teasing one another, relieved that in this instance they had lived up to what the black "orators" had expected of them.

This memory is pivotal to the way in which Hurston writes the South; she acknowledges what could have been a tragedy, but her central focus is not the social system that could encourage such violence and fear; rather, it is the communal interaction of the Eatonville inhabitants— their self-doubts and heroic gestures. As she acknowledges earlier, "Nothing had ever happened before in our vicinity to create such tension. But people had memories and told tales of what happened back there in Georgia and Alabama and West Florida that made the skin of the young crawl with transmitted memory, and reminded the old heads that they were still flinchy" (229).

Hurston might easily have said that nothing like that had ever happened in "our protected vicinity," for the Eatonville she depicts for the reader of *Dust Tracks* is clearly not typical of the region as a whole. In his study of black and white relationships in the South, David Goldfield draws attention to the system of etiquette and the variety of coping mechanisms that southern African-Americans devised "to relieve the tension and assert their dignity," devices that range from an internalization "of white images" (Uncle Toms, Sambos), to violence (generally "black-on-black" violence since it was not feasible to attack whites), to leaving the South for the northern cities, to often petty and ultimately ineffectual attempts at revenge, and, most notably, to theft (9). It was an exploitative system that hurt both races, for "with blacks removed from political participation de jure, [poor] whites effected their own withdrawal de facto" (14).

For all of their relevance to a full understanding of southern culture, these coping mechanisms and defensive postures are never central to Hurston's representation of the South, but again, this does not mean that she was blind to the cultural and political implications of her emphasis on the all-black Eatonville. Hurston had a valid reason for making Eatonville the locus of her attempt to write the South and her goal may be more political than one might first suspect. In a seminal essay on Hurston and Wright, June Jordan noted what she believes is a dangerous form of binary thinking—a critical tendency to separate black protest literature, the prototypical embodiment of which is Richard Wright, from the literature of black affirmation, perhaps best represented by Hurston. To this dualistic paradigm, Jordan responds: "The functions of protest and affirmation are not, ultimately, distinct . . . affirmation of Black values and lifestyle within the American context is, indeed, an act of protest." In this sense, "Hurston's affirmative work is profoundly defiant, just as Wright's protest unmistakably asserts our need for an alternative, benign environment. We have been misled to discount the one in order to revere the other" (5). In short, Jordan explains how an essentially "affirmative" vision such as Hurston's can also be innately "political."

It seems reasonably clear, at least regarding her nonfiction pieces, that Hurston wrote with fewer constraints when she was addressing a predominantly black audience. Critics have pointed specifically to "My Most Humiliating Jim Crow Experience," an essay that appeared in the *Negro Digest* in June 1944. When in 1931 Hurston developed a stomach ailment, her white patron, Mrs. R. Osgood Mason, arranged at her own expense for Hurston to see a white specialist. When she arrived for her appointment, Hurston was glared at and finally ushered into a laundry closet where the doctor quickly assessed her symptoms. Hurston stayed with the doctor as long as she could in order "to see just what would happen, and further to torture him more." The note of protest—with its implicit denunciation of existing power relations—is nowhere muted in this piece; Hurston claims that "anything with such a false foundation [as segregation] cannot last" and that "whom the gods would destroy they first made mad" (*I Love Myself* 163–64). The piece is as strong, in fact, as anything excised from *Dust Tracks*. Significantly, Hurston does not see this experience as indigenous only to the South; she stresses that it took place in Brooklyn, and she concludes the piece by emphasizing the pathos of Anglo-Saxon civilization itself.

One might wish that Hurston had included this incident in *Dust Tracks*, but she obviously had more in mind for her autobiography than a series of social or cultural indictments. Not enough has been made of the fact that throughout *Dust Tracks* one can see Hurston constructing a personal scheme of ethics—her own system of what constitutes proper behavior between human beings as family members, friends, lovers, and separate races. (Her attachment to the author of the *Ethics* is rooted in something more than his metaphysics.) Hurston delineates her system of ethics when, for example, she denounces her maternal grandmother's unreasonable expectations and her refusal to allow Hurston's mother a rightful share of the family estate. On the other hand, Hurston's ethics do not condone self-repression solely for the sake of family or romantic ties. When her brother offers her what appears to be a temporary end to her wanderings, Hurston is overjoyed; when he reneges on the offer and provides her only a place to stay in return for her help around the house and her care for her sister-in-law's children, Hurston is forced to define the limits of her ethical/familial responsibility. In her chapter on love, Hurston articulates what might best be called her own ethic of relationships: "I have a strong suspicion, but I can't be sure, that much that passes for constant love is a golded-up moment walking in its sleep. Some people know that it is the walk of the dead, but in desperation and desolation, they have staked everything on life after death and the resurrection, so they haunt the graveyard. They build an altar on the tomb and wait there like Mary for the stone to roll away. So *the moment has authority over all of their lives.* They pray constantly for the miracle of the moment to burst its bonds and spread out over time" (264–65, emphasis added).

It is difficult to say just how much of her ethics Hurston took from Spinoza, but it should be remembered that a fundamental principle of the *Ethics* is the need to see life in something resembling its totality (in this sense, Hurston and Spinoza were both precursors of the gestalt therapists). The words of Bertrand Russell again seem appropriate: "When it is your lot to have to endure something that is (or seems to you) worse than the ordinary lot of mankind, Spinoza's principle of thinking about the whole, or at any rate about larger matters than your own grief, is a useful one. There are times when it is comforting to reflect that human life, with all that it contains of evil and suffering, is an infinitesimal part of the life of the universe" (580).

The parallels with Spinoza (via Russell) are cited in order to provide a context for Hurston's personal philosophy; these comparisons are not intended to suggest that the scheme of ethics encoded in *Dust Tracks* is always foolproof or that Hurston has outlined a code of behavior that can always account for the complexity of human motives, least of all her own. Hurston reveals at least one instance in which one might question her ethics. While a student at Howard, she worked as a manicurist in a Washington salon where she received the confidences of bankers, congressmen, and members of the press (confidences she refused to betray even when she was bribed with tantalizing payoffs). The salon was owned and staffed by African-Americans but served an all-white clientele. When, in a gesture of protest, a black man walked in one day and demanded to be served, arguing that it was his right to be waited on wherever he pleased, he was thrown out. Though she did not "participate in the melee," Hurston admits that she too wanted the potential martyr removed—"My business was threatened" (*Dust Tracks* 163–64). Later, Hurston realizes that she was tacitly sanctioning Jim Crow, which theoretically she felt obligated to resist. Neither she nor her fellow employees could think through the implications of the scene as it took place; rather, they acted instinctively. It might have been a "beautiful thing" to have stood in solidarity, Hurston concedes, but such a gesture would have resulted in their loss of employment and for her the return to wandering. She does not disguise what she believes would have been the consequences had the man been served: "Wrecking George Robinson [the salon's owner] like that on a 'race' angle would have been an ironic tragedy. He always helped out any Negro who was trying to do anything progressive as far as he was able" (165).

From the perspective of the years following the civil rights era, the complexity and perhaps even the flaw (however human) in Hurston's position is apparent. It was, after all, individual acts of protest such as the one described here that fueled the civil rights movement and led ultimately to collective action and improved social conditions for women and individuals of all minorities and races. Hurston admits her failure to decide who was ultimately right—the shop's employees or the "militant Negro" (165). Three years later, she would appear to be on the side of the militant protestors. In "Crazy for This Democracy," a piece she published in the *Negro Digest* in December 1945, Hurston speaks as a militant herself. She denounces the hypocrisy of her country's disheveled democracy. Like Lillian Smith, she says that the Jim Crow laws are not without an ideological or psychological purpose; their goal is "to promote in the mind of the smallest white child the conviction of First by Birth, eternal and irrevocable like the place assigned to the Levities by Moses over the other tribes of the Hebrews." Comparing the United States to a smallpox patient, Hurston calls for an immediate injection of serum: "I see no point in the picking of a bump. Others can erupt too easily. That same one can burst out again. Witness the easy scrapping of FEPC [Fair Employment Practices Committee, the federal government's first foray into programs designed to improve the economic and social standing of African-Americans]. No, I give my hand, my heart and my head to the total struggle. I am for complete repeal of all Jim Crow laws in the United States once and for all, and right now, for the benefit of this nation and as a precedent to the world." (*I Love Myself* 168).

Whatever the difference between the tone of this piece and Hurston's memory of the scene in the G Street salon (a difference that may owe something to publisher's restraints, or perhaps to a development in Hurston's perspective as World War II came to an end), her belief that segregation is the manifestation of a deeper sickness is nonetheless consistent with the ethics she outlines in *Dust Tracks*. In "Looking

Things Over," she claims, "Real slavery is couched in the desire and the efforts of any man or community to live and advance their interests at the expense of the lives and interests of others. All the outward signs come out of that" (*Dust Tracks* 283). To illustrate her belief that a workable system of ethics must subsume rather than be defined by the issue of race, she puts the aforementioned words into the mouth of a white man who, in an imaginary conversation, rejects the accusation that, as the grandson of a slave owner, he is responsible for his grandparents' behavior or that he detests the institution of slavery any less than does the actual descendant of a slave.

Hurston's ethics embody an ideal, the inherent limitations of which she fully understood and made clear in the manuscript chapter, "Seeing the World As It Is," her original conclusion. Marion Kilson has argued that after Hurston published *Dust Tracks*—which he classifies as one of her "fictions" (114)—she relinquished her role as "ethnographic artist" to become a "critical ethnographer" (112). Kilson points to the fact that the number of essays and nonfiction pieces far exceeds the number of fictional works following the appearance of *Dust Tracks*. Kilson's thesis is correct, though "Seeing the World As It Is," along with the essay-chapters on race and religion, suggests that Hurston had actually made the transition to critical ethnographer at least by the time she wrote her autobiography. This transition would have been more apparent had "Seeing the World As It Is"—her most devastating critique of the failures of Western civilization—appeared in 1942 rather than 1984.

Though this chapter contains some of the material that did in fact appear with the book's initial publication (Hurston's deconstruction of various race labels, for example), on the whole it is apparent that Hurston is fully speaking her mind here, with no constraints and sparing no one's feelings in the process. Hurston's remarks on pride in one's gender or race—at best a debased kind of gratification—are even more trenchant than those already mentioned. The same holds true for her discussion of the link between religious opinion and political power and, again, the gap between such opinion and her own system of ethics. The chief problem with Christianity, for instance, is that it calls for meekness, a quality that forever alludes the Westerner's grasp. Consequently, "we have turned the Gospel of peace into a wrestle. . . . We can give up neither our platitudes nor our profits. The platitudes sound beautiful, and the profits feel like silk" (335). Naturally, a man like Mahatma Gandhi, who gives more than lip service to Christian principles, is deemed "a bad thing for business" (336).

In "Looking Things Over," Hurston observes the link between national power and colonialism; in "Seeing the World As It Is," she issues a forthright exposure and condemnation of imperialism with all its sanctimonious disguises. "Being human and a part of humanity," she writes, "I like to think that my own nation is more just than any other in spite of the facts on hand" (337). Hurston then gives her reader a tour of the facts as she sees them, complete with an outline of major imperialistic abuses. While slavery no longer exists in the United States (it is considered bad form to allow it on one's home turf), Hurston claims that "the principle of human bondage" has not died out; instead of domestic chattel slavery, we have the exploitation of "raw material" within a market economy (338). To concretize these generalizations, she notes that Americans "consider machine gun bullets good laxatives for heathens who get constipated with toxic ideas about a country of their own" (339). On the score of United States involvement in Central America during the first half of the century, Hurston seems almost prophetic. The "giant of the Western World," the United States has had to watch out for the "little Latin brother" who is not particularly selfish but "just too full of rumba" and "must be taught to share with big brother before big brother comes down and kicks his teeth in. A big brother is a lovely thing to have" (340). Hurston cites one further irony when she says that "our principles . . . are not to leave the United States unless we take them ourselves"—a reference to American displeasure with Japan, which in 1942 was "plagiarizing" our "song about keeping a whole hemisphere under your wing" (340–41). It comes as little wonder that an American editor would in the middle of World War II suggest that Hurston omit the international commentary as irrelevant to the autobiography.

"Seeing the World as It Is" might have been written by June Jordan for one of her *Progressive* columns. Hurston's attack on the ironies of American acquisitiveness is the standard fare for contemporary journalists of the left—for *The Nation's* Alexander Cockburn for instance. In a key summary passage, Hurston presents a common socialist critique: "the doctrines of democracy deal with the aspirations of men's souls, but the application deals with things. . . . Desire enough for your own use only, and you are a heathen. Civilized people have things to show to the neighbors" (343). While she refused to depict "the darker races" as "visiting angels, just touristing around here below" (343)— such a view would itself be evidence of abstractionism—her attack on Anglo-Saxon pride and greed, as the following passage indicates, is as unremitting as that of any full-fledged Marxist or socialist critic: "The idea of human slavery is so deeply ground in that the pink-toes can't get it out of their system" (343). Hurston is understandably concerned that readers not view her as someone whose bitterness has gotten out of hand; thus her most "radical" wish is that Franklin Roosevelt, "the blond brother" whose liberalism she questions, leave office by pointing "with pride to the fact that his administration had done away with group-profit at the expense of others. I know well that it has never happened before, but it could happen, couldn't it?" (343)

It could happen, yes, but not as long as the existing capitalist structure remains intact. One of the most engrossing features of "Seeing the World As It Is" is its mixture of sentiments from both the left and the right. The central irony of Hurston's wish is that she concludes this chapter by deliberately distancing herself from the left and its goal of a less class-structured society. As always, her objection is not without its own brand of humor: "If the leaders of the left feel that only violence can right things, I see no need of fingernail warfare. . . . If what they say is true, that there must be this upset, why not make it cosmic? A lot of people would join in for the drama of it, who would not be moved by guile" (346). Hurston objects to the left in general and to communism in particular. In answer to those who have asked why she would not join a "party of protest" (obviously a reference to Richard Wright), Hurston responds by noting that she can "see many good points in, let us say, the Communist Party. Any one would be a liar and a fool to claim that there was no good in it" (344). Hurston also claims, like Hellman and Porter, that she does "not have much of a herd instinct," or, rather, if she "must be connected with the flock," then she would just as soon be the shepherd (345).[8] In brief, Hurston can see no point in a society that would allow for what she calls horizontal rather than vertical movement. When she says that "the able at the bottom always snatch the ladder from under the weak on the top rung" and that this "is the way it should be" (345), she appears to have forgotten her earlier remark about Franklin Roosevelt, his four freedoms, and group profits at the expense of others.

Hurston's real objection to the left is its obsession with class, an objection rooted in her ethics of individualism. If nation and race are unsuitable boundaries for the self, class fares no better—"I found that I had no need of either class or race prejudice, those scourges of humanity" (323). Whatever the inconsistencies in her vision, the fact remains that Hurston defines herself within a system of ethics that transcends nation, class, and—above all else—race. Abandoning the solace of easy generalization, she chooses what she calls "the richer gift of individualism." The essence of her worldview is presented in these lines, which, as she knew, flew in the face of Marxist ideology: "When I have been made to suffer or when I have been made happy by others, I have known that individuals were responsible for that, and not races. All clumps of people turn out to be individuals on close inspection" (323).[9]

Hurston is not alone among southern women writers in making ethics a key component of her self-writing; ethics are central to the selves constructed by each of the women in this study, particularly Hellman, Porter, and Smith. The comparison with Smith is especially revealing and worth pursuing at length. Born in Florida only five years apart and in towns that relied upon the same sources of income (such as turpentine), the two women grew up in houses that became centers of community life. Smith's father was a successful businessman (he ran the turpentine mills) and Hurston's father was both minister and mayor. As Hurston recalls in *Dust Tracks*, her house "was a place where people came. Visiting preachers, Sunday school and B.Y.P.U. workers, and just friends" (26). Both writers record many of the same community rituals; Hurston, in fact, was born during one of the hog-killing seasons that Smith recalls in detail in her memoir, *Memory of a Large Christmas* (1962). The central difference was of course the racial makeup of the two towns. Jasper was traditionally segregated, Eatonville was, as Hurston puts it, an experiment in self-government for African-Americans. This difference is crucial: Smith's formative years in a town that segregated blacks from whites—and the mind from the body—left an impact equal to that of Hurston's childhood development in a supportive community that was not constantly reminded of racial difference.

While each writer had a problematic relationship with at least one parent, and while each received injunctions to be ever mindful of her place, each nonetheless developed an extraordinary sense of self and a deep need for recognition.

Both writers would eventually achieve the recognition they desired, but not before each had taken a journey beyond the protective borders of her childhood world. Keen observation and a shared love of reading had much to do with their ability to recognize the flaws in a culture that could so easily tolerate segregation, sexism, and imperialism, and yet fail to question itself. A significant feature of each writer's career is her need to subvert authority and to demystify what Smith calls the sex-race-religion-economics tangle. This affinity is especially apparent in *Killers of the Dream* and "Seeing the World As It Is," where the two writers clearly establish themselves as debunkers of American as well as southern myths.

The radicalism of their social critique was clearly exceptional for its day. In addition to their denunciations of sexism and colonialism, both writers stop just short of endorsing miscegenation, the ultimate southern taboo. As noted earlier, Smith said that if sexual relationships between the races were not meant to be, it would be physically impossible for members of different races to mate. For all her attempts to celebrate the African-American culture of her native Eatonville—and hence to instill cultural pride in her people—Hurston also understood the need for cultural crossover and ethnic diversity. On the subject of miscegenation, Hurston makes an assessment in *Dust Tracks* that, surprisingly, survived the censor's scissors:

> I have been told that God meant for all the so-called races of the world to stay just as they are, and the people who say that may be right. But it is a well-known fact that no matter where two sets of people come together, there are bound to be some inbetweens. It looks like the command was given to people's heads, because the other parts don't seem to have heard tell. When the next batch is made up, maybe Old Maker will straighten all that out. Maybe the men will be more tangle-footed and the women a whole lot more faster around the feet. That will bring about a great deal more of racial purity, but a somewhat less exciting world. (236)

For all their humor and sarcasm (as well as their delight in toppling idols), both Smith and Hurston stress the illogicality of racial purity; in

Hurston's words, "There will have to be something harder to get across than an ocean to keep East and West from meeting" (236).[10] Sadly, in 1942 Hurston concluded that the "Old Maker" seems to have lost interest in the races altogether: "Perhaps in a moment of discouragement He turned the job over to Adolf Hitler and went on about His business of making beetles" (236).

In 1977 southern journalist Anne Braden wrote, "Most white Southerners who come to understand the great social issues of our world do so through that long, painful, passageway of the struggle with racism. In a society that built its economy, its culture, its very existence on racism, it can be no other way" (51). Braden's journalism, like that of Lillian Smith, substantiates her thesis, though there is no reason to limit her observation to whites. It was their understanding of racism on the home front that kept both Smith and Hurston from supporting early United States involvement in World War II. How, each asked, could the United States fight fascism abroad and tolerate Jim Crow at home? The issue of race would be the decisive factor in the kind of art each produced and in her reputation as a southern woman writer. As intensely as Hurston wished to show that African-Americans were not culturally deprived, Smith consciously set out to expose what she perceived to be positive proof of the Anglo-Saxon's pathological behavior: his deeply rooted need to place himself above others. Perhaps the greatest irony is that Hurston was silenced for her refusal to write protest or social-document fiction that addressed racism and its consequences right up front, while Smith was silenced because this was—at least in part—the kind of literature she chose to produce.

Neither Smith nor Hurston saw much point in rehashing the southern past, and despite the fact that the South remained a segregated culture throughout their lifetimes (both lived to the same age, sixty-nine), each chose to remain, with the exception of fairly brief intervals, in the South. Hurston, it is often noted, is buried in a segregated cemetery; Smith is buried in the garden of her mountain home in north Georgia. Given their similar viewpoints and mutual connections (Edwin Embree and the Rosenwald Foundation, for example), it would be interesting to know to what extent they read one another's work. How did Smith respond to the liberal *Saturday Review*'s decision to honor *Dust Tracks on the Road* with its 1943 Anisfield Wolf Award for the most significant contribution to race relations in the field of creative literature?[11] Hurston's autobiography was not reviewed in *South To-day*. However, Paula Snelling did review *Their Eyes Were Watching God* in 1937, praising Hurston's gifts as a writer but objecting to her novel in much the same terms as did Richard Wright and the leftist press.[12] It may be that Hurston and Smith were of such different temperaments that they would not have looked past their differences (Hurston abhorred Franklin Roosevelt, one of Smith's cultural heroes) in order to see the commonality of their beliefs, in particular their insistence that an absorption with one's racial identity obscures an apprehension of the mystery that constitutes human life—a mystery that each would come to appreciate more fully through the insights of mystical philosophers like Pierre Teilhard de Chardin and Benedictus de Spinoza.

It is her high regard for the mystery of the individual human being that fed each writer's suspicion of the left with its taint of collectivism. Each maintained that a change in the socioeconomic structure would not last without evidence of the society's inner psychological transformation as well. It is on the nature and possibility of change, however, that Hurston and Smith part ways. While Smith remained committed to her belief that men and women could effect sweeping social reform and psychological change—she saw the 1954 Supreme Court desegregation decision as evidence of such change—Hurston was more skeptical than Smith and, indeed, became suspicious even of American liberals. Ironically, it is Hurston who, of all the women in this study, publicly expressed the most conservative and, in the case of her opposition to the 1954 Supreme Court decision, the most reactionary social views. Because *Dust Tracks* appeared eighteen years before her death, one might justifiably question its relevance to the self-image that Hurston projects in some of her subsequent pieces, particularly "What White Publishers Won't Print," which appeared in the *Negro Digest* in 1950, and those pieces that appeared in the *Saturday Evening Post* and the ultraconservative *American Legion Magazine*.

As readers who are knowledgeable about Hurston's life are aware, she was in the fall of 1948 the victim of the sensationalized accusation that she had sodomized a ten-year-old boy. Arrested, released on bail, and finally cleared (she was not even in the country at the time the incident was said to have occurred), Hurston was nonetheless devastated by the charges and especially by the callous reaction of the African-American press. Hemenway cites a letter to Carl Van Vechten in which Hurston reminds him not to forget that this ugly episode of her life did not take place in the South but "in the so-called liberal North [New York]." She then turns her attention to the question of American justice and laments, "This has happened to me, who has always believed in the essential and eventual rightness of my country" (quoted in Hemenway 322). Though Hurston subsequently recovered from the depression revealed in this letter, Hemenway speculates that the morals charge "pushed a woman with growing conservative instincts even further to the right, making her suspicious and paranoid. . . . She was never again so belligerently independent as she had been earlier" (322).

One can accept Hemenway's suggestion that the arrest with its subsequent publicity drove Hurston further to the right—he even notes that at one point she blamed the left for the whole affair—but did Hurston in fact become less independent? Other than a brief review and a short story for the *Post*, her first publication following the morals charge was a searing indictment of the white-dominated publishing industry, in which, once again, she expresses what can only be defined as progressive or liberal sentiments: "I have been amazed by the Anglo-Saxon's lack of curiosity about the internal lives and emotions of Negroes, and for that matter, any non-Anglo-Saxon peoples within our borders, above the class of unskilled labor." Again like Smith, Hurston claims that the Anglo-Saxon's apparent refusal to know more about the darker races has serious consequences for the nation as a whole, for "man like all other animals fears and is repelled by that which he does not understand, and mere difference is apt to connote something malign" (*I Love Myself* 169).

Indirectly, Hurston explains why *Dust Tracks* appeared in an edited form that did not convey all of her initial intentions for the book. Publishers, though they are not a particularly malign group, print chiefly what they believe will bring in a profit. They "cannot afford to be crusaders" unless for some reason the crusade has become a popular one that might increase their sales. For the most part, they look to what she calls the American Museum of Unnatural History with its stockbarrel of unexamined stereotypes and its many fears of what it deems to be the other. To illustrate, Hurston notes that publishers shy away from books about romantic or sexual relationships between members of a minority unless the romance in some way subsumes the racial struggle.

For the sake of the national welfare Hurston urged people to see that "minorities do think, and think about something other than the race problem"; further, she challenged her readers to acknowledge the simple truth that the man who fears difference does so because he believes "if people were made right, they would be just like him" (171).

It is nearly impossible to imagine a conservative literary critic or cultural commentator expressing these views in 1942; yet these remarks also indicate why Hurston dissociated herself from the often race-oriented liberal agenda. An African-American literature that did not consciously work towards improving race relations rarely received the full endorsement of the liberal critic—white or black. In one of her first essays, "How It Feels to be Colored Me" (1928), Hurston wrote that she was "colored" but, she insisted, not "tragically colored." She wanted no part of "the sobbing school of Negrohood who hold that nature somehow has given them a lowdown dirty deal and whose feelings are all hurt about it" (*I Love Myself* 153). Hurston said she had "no separate feeling about being an American citizen and colored," that she was a mere "fragment of the Great Soul that surges within the boundaries. My country, right or wrong" (155).

There is no evidence to suggest that Hurston ever departed from this view; she continued to believe that with self-initiative the African-American could succeed within the American system. Hurston's values are announced at the very beginning of her 1942 profile of Lawrence Silas, a prominent and well-to-do African-American cattleman in central Florida. Silas, she writes, "represents the men who could plan and do, the generations who were willing to undertake the hard job—to accept the challenge of the frontiers. And remember he had one more frontier to conquer than the majority of men in America. He speaks for free enterprise and personal initiative. That is America" ("Lawrence of the River" 18). In 1943, a year later, Hurston wrote a brief piece for the "Clinical Notes" department of the *American Mercury* in which she praised the general tone of a statewide Florida Negro Defense Committee meeting she had attended. "Nobody mentioned slavery, Reconstruction, nor any such matter," she gleefully remarked. "It was a new and strange kind of Negro—without tears of self-pity. It was a sign and symbol of something in the offing" ("Negroes Without Self-Pity" 603).[15]

Just seven years later, however, Hurston was excoriating African-American voters for allegedly selling their votes during the infamous

1950 Florida Democratic senatorial primary between Congressman George Smathers and Senator Claude Pepper. In "I Saw Negro Votes Peddled," she expresses her dismay that the Political Action Committee of the CIO would attempt to shape the course of a southern election, but her real target is not the CIO; it is the African-American whose right to participate in southern primaries had been severely restricted for generations. Aware that "corrupt politicians buy white votes, and that unthinking white voters sell them, and often cheaply," Hurston insisted that the right to vote "ought to be held in higher regard by Negroes than any other citizens of the United States" (55). The pawns of scalawags and carpetbaggers during Reconstruction, and the victims of a series of subsequent disfranchising measures (most notoriously the Grandfather, Property, and Literacy Clauses), African-Americans had been "called upon to pay for what their exploiters had done" (57). Hurston finds it amazing that any self-respecting man or woman of "color" could in 1950 be deceived by those who billed themselves as friends—especially, it might be added, if those friends were from the left.

"What is hard to explain," Robert Hemenway asserts, "is why Zora Hurston would support Smathers over Pepper, or complain about vote-selling and fail to mention that systematic exclusion from the political process made it hard to take voting seriously" (329). Hemenway has a valid point (Hurston did not always see the full implications of her argument), but it is not particularly difficult to see why she, in her brief incarnation as a Democrat, would oppose Pepper, who, in the minds of many southerners, represented the then current "Communist threat"—evidenced in a damning pamphlet distributed throughout the state at the time of the campaign: *The Red Record of Claude Pepper*. It is doubtful, however, that many African-Americans read Hurston's piece. She could place it only in the *American Legion Magazine*, a publication that had little use for Claude Pepper, the Florida congressman who, by the time of his death in the late eighties, would be regarded as a major voice of southern liberalism—an antagonist of corporate greed, institutionalized racism, exploitative wages, and an effectively outspoken advocate of nationalized health care and federal programs for minorities and the elderly.[14]

Actually, Pepper's progressive politics had little to do with Hurston's opposition; in fact, during the year of the Smathers/Pepper primary, she published a laudatory endorsement of Republican Robert A. Taft in his bid for the presidential nomination. Hurston praised Taft's record on measures as favorable to African-Americans as any proposed by Claude Pepper, including "antipoll tax legislation, FEPC, consideration of the civil rights bills, housing and rent programs, discrimination in selecting displaced persons for admission to the United States, withholding Federal education funds wherever racial discrimination was practiced, cloture, attempts to limit debate and break up filibustering, antilynch bills" ("A Negro Voter Sizes Up Taft" 150). Hurston devoted a part of the article on Taft to cleansing the word "liberal" from its devious connotations. The word should mean more than "Pro-Negro," she charges, because in this sense it actually excludes African-Americans. Unlike Eleanor Roosevelt or Henry Wallace, blacks are rarely identified as "liberals, since, naturally, the relaxing of racial lines is something that must come from the other side of the race line" (151). Taft, who called himself a liberal, was the man who could address new meanings of the word; a la Jefferson, Taft represented true liberalism: "As he sees it, 'A liberal is a man who believes in freedom of thought, who is not a worshiper of dogma.' " Above all, Taft was a liberal who was also clearly immune to any connection with the left and its desire for "greater government control and Federal handouts" (151).

By 1950 Hurston no longer made any pretense of seeing some good in the Communist party; rather, she gave into and helped to fuel the growing paranoia that had gripped the nation. "Why the Negro Won't Buy Communism," which appeared in 1951 in the *American Legion Magazine*, is surely, to her readers, Hurston's most regrettable piece of nonfiction. Here she succumbs to the most farfetched myths about the Kremlin and its American connections. "As an inducement to join up," she claims, black "prospective party members were grinningly offered white mates" (56). She then indulges in a rather shameless rewriting of history. "Russia claims a great victory form World War II," she asserts, "when in fact, it was something like Max Schmeling lying flat on the canvas yelling 'Owoooo'—then demanding the championship of the world" (59). In the course of the article, Hurston denounces the Lincoln Brigade, the intervention of the Communists in the Scottsboro Case (she claims they wrested control from the NAACP), and the African-American artists who sold out and subscribed to the party formula of "you can't win, Negro, you can't win" (58). It would be easy to dismiss this article were it not the work of Hurston and if it did not so forcefully address what may be the key issue in any twentieth-century intellectual's political self-definition: his or her relationship to communism. Looking past the claptrap of Hurston's article, one sees that she believes communism is no less racist than capitalism and that her deepest concern is what she deems to be the Communist's perception of the African-American as someone who can be easily used. She seems to have forgotten her earlier antiwar stance when she asks, "Are these commies so blind through the eyes that they have not seen us always in there fighting just like anybody else in a common cause? From the Revolution on down" (59).

Hurston's essays of the early fifties are not likely to be reprinted, even though, as Karla Holloway observes, "Writing the kind of fiction that had given her so much success in her earlier career was perhaps less emotionally fulfilling than her political involvement" (7). Alice Walker included none of this material in *I Love Myself* (1979), which at the time of this writing is the only anthology of both Hurston's fiction and nonfiction. Yet a piece like "Why the Negro Won't Buy Communism" retains more than curiosity value, especially for the Hurston scholar and the twentieth-century cultural historian. Here is Hurston once again refusing to accept a philosophical system that she believes is rooted in pity and collectivism rather than strength and respect for the individual. Here is Hurston arguing that out of nothing more than sheer dialectics have the Soviets created "a permanent lower class" (56), and here—perhaps most disturbingly—is Hurston equating "the average Negro" with "the average American," whose overriding goal is social mobility and material wealth. She quotes what she claims is a remark made to her by "one rich and well-born matron": "We do not employ Americans of any color as domestic help. White or black there are no American servants. They are all millionaires, temporarily out of funds. Instead of being content where they are, they plan to be the boss themselves next year" (56).

As if to prove exactly how confounding Hurston in her later years could be, between 1951 and 1953 she published a series of articles in the *Pittsburgh Courier* which stressed just how far from average the status of the African-American remained. Hurston had become interested in the trial of Ruby McCollum, an African-American and modestly wealthy Florida woman who murdered her white lover, a prominent doctor and state senator, Dr. Clifford LeRoy Adams. McCollum, who had borne the doctor one child, was pregnant by him again when he attempted to end the affair. In an angry and impulsive moment, McCollum shot him. The white judge who presided at her trial in Suwannee County wanted to settle the affair without outside agitation and thus denied Hurston or any other reporter the opportunity to speak with McCollum; at whatever cost to justice he also intended to protect the doctor's image from Ruby's accusations. Hurston was able to interest William Bradford Huie, a prominent liberal and one of her editors at the *American Mercury*, in McCollum's trial, and while none of her *Courier* articles have been reprinted, Huie's *Ruby McCollum: Woman in the Suwannee Jail* (1956) does include a lengthy section by Hurston (pp. 89–101) which represents her reaction to the event and its participants.

"My comprehensive impression of the trial," Hurston writes, "was one of a smothering blanket of silence. . . . It was as if one listened to a debate in which everything which might lead to and justify the resolution had been waived" (89). For Hurston, the whole sordid event "amounted to mass delusion by unanimous agreement" (89); McCollum's alleged motive—an argument over the doctor's bill—had been agreed upon by everybody except McCollum herself. Consequently the trial assumed a nightmarish quality. "It was like a chant," Hurston writes: "The Doctor Bill; the Mad, Mean Nigger Woman. It was dogma. It was a posture, but a posture posed in granite. There was no other circumstance in the case, let alone an extenuating one. This was the story; and the community was sticking to it. The press was requested to take the community's story, not to dig up any 'confusing' material. And the press took it" (92).

Hurston uses the term "community" in its inclusive sense to mean both races, and she is particularly strong in dissecting the mixed nature of the community's self-protective reaction. She explains, for instance, why many African-Americans denounced McCollum for crossing the "color line," for forgetting her place and "messing around with that white man in the first place" (90). Such denunciations revealed a code of behavior at work; they "let you understand that [these men and women] were play-acting in their savage denunciation of Ruby." In a startling passage—coming so closely on the heels of "Why the Negro Won't Buy Communism"—Hurston adds, "The sprig of hyssop was in their hands, and they were sprinkling the blood of the paschal lamb around their doorways so that the Angel of Death would pass over them. This, never you forget, was West Florida" (Huie 91). At last, Hurston's reader might exclaim, a clear acknowledgement of the South beyond Eatonville and evidence that Hurston understood the plight of those African-American southerners who had not been brought up with the security and lack of fear that characterized her own childhood community.

Hurston reveals a side of her sympathy that she had not revealed so openly before. When the McCollum yardman, also the courthouse janitor, "recounted loudly how he prayed for Ruby's execution," Hurston says she could bear this man no resentment: "The story in which the poor triumph over the fortunate must be eternal; and heaven must ever be where the earth's humble become superior to the earth's powerful. So to see Ruby brought low was satisfying to Suwannee County coloreds" (92–93). Hurston does not stop here, however, and she does indict those African-American men at the trial who said they opposed miscegenation while priding themselves on the many skin shades of the black race; and she indicts men—black and white—for a form of sexist colonialism in their relationships with women: "From the cave man to the instant minute, to the victor has gone the spoils, and the primmest spoils are women. We will know that the blessed millennium has arrived when this is no longer so" (95).

As for the other half of the community—the white division—Hurston is equally perceptive. Since he represents the chief problem, Hurston centers her discussion on Judge Adams (no relation to the man Ruby shot). The judge's regional and archaic mannerisms are not the issue for Hurston. Though he yielded his authority to "the local dogma as to motive," she wants to know the answer to a question that Lillian Smith might also have asked: "Was such action on his part native to the judge's spirit, or was he captive of geographical emotion and tradition?" The answer is what she might have expected, which forces her to conclude that what took place "in the courtroom was nothing more than a mask; that the real action existed on the other side of [Mc-Collum's] silence" (59). Though the Supreme Court of Florida eventually overturned the verdict, McCollum spent over twenty years in a mental hospital before she was released in 1976. As Hurston concludes, much to her sorrow, "The community will had been done" (101).

The trial represented a total violation of Hurston's ethics—of her belief in respect for the individual human being without regard to race, sex, nation, or class. In "Why Negroes Won't Buy Communism," Hurston had claimed that the African-American was "merely lawing and jawing for a better adjustment into the [American] framework as is" (58); in her pieces on Ruby McCollum she shows how inadequate the framework can become if the community chooses to assert its will. One wishes that her Red-baiting of the early fifties was evidence of a temporary lapse in Hurston's judgment, but as Larry Neal, one of her earliest critics, observed in the early seventies, Hurston, unlike Richard Wright, "was no political radical. She was, instead, a belligerent individualist who was decidedly unpredictable and perhaps a little inconsistent. At one moment she could sound highly nationalistic. Then at other times she might mouth statements that, in terms of the ongoing struggle for black liberation, were ill-conceived and even reactionary" (161). To Neal's assessment one might add that, while Hurston did in fact denounce the left (she did not join the Republicans solely because they belonged to the party of Mr. Lincoln), she could still, if so motivated, speak with the powerful voice of liberal dissent. Her occasional inconsistency was evident in *Dust Tracks*; it only became more pronounced in the late forties and early fifties.

Zora Neale Hurston has generated a great deal of controversy and disagreement among her reviewers and critics—as much as any other major American writer—and *Dust Tracks On a Road* has remained at the heart of the controversy. One of the book's early reviewers observed, "Always Zora Neale Hurston felt that she was a special, a different sort of person—not in any unpleasantly cocky way, but as almost any one does who has energy and ability and wants to use them" (Sherman 44). Ann L. Rayson, the first critic to give substantial attention to Hurston's autobiography, takes an opposing view: "Imbued with a sense of her own mythic charm, she reveals dreams, visions, and other significations that are meant to cause the reader to mark her off from common humanity" (41). For Rayson, Hurston's self-creation is deliberately messianic in tone; she is the "Melvillian isolato" (42), the "black, female Benjamin Franklin" (43).

With the publication of an expanded *Dust Tracks* in 1984, Henry Louis Gates noted that a number of reconsiderations were in order. While Gates, like most of Hurston's critics, acknowledges with deep appreciation the demanding and complicated work of her biographer, he cannot accept Hemenway's contention that *Dust Tracks* is a book beneath Hurston's talents—a "text diminished by her refusal to provide a second or third dimension to the flat surfaces of her adult images" (43). "Rereading Hurston," Gates counters, "I was struck by how *conscious* her choices were. The explicit and the implicit, the background and the foreground, what she states and what she keeps to herself" (43). Gates shows that Hurston not only censors "all that her readership could draw upon to pigeonhole or define her life as a synecdoche of 'the race problem' " but that she achieves two other feats as well: "she gives us a *writer's* life . . . in a language as 'dazzling' as Mr. Hemenway says it is," and she successfully refuses to reconcile but rather chooses to navigate between "the linguistic rituals of the dominant culture and those of the black vernacular tradition" (43).

Hurston understood the immense complexity of producing her autobiography. In one of her *Pittsburgh Courier* articles on Ruby McCollum, she makes this observation: "The truth is that nobody, not even the closest blood relatives, ever really knows anybody else. The greatest human travail has been in the attempt at self-revelation, but never, since the world began, has any one individual completely succeeded. There is an old saying to the effect that: 'He is a man, so nobody knows him but God' " (quoted in Dance 333). This remark is not cited as an apology for *Dust Tracks*. It is clear that, despite their inherent limitations, Hurston saw the value of those forms of writing that place the self at their center, and it is clear that she worked according to what she believed were her own gifts and limitations—what one might call her own ethics of self-representation. Like the other writers in this study, Hurston's goal was self-definition rather than intimate self-disclosure (though much of what she reveals is of an intimate nature). *Dust Tracks* is full of direct statements about Hurston's Eatonville upbringing, her subsequent travels, her desires and beliefs. Yet as an artist, Hurston knew that she could best reveal her quest for self-knowledge, her contradictions, and her mode of imagining by means of indirection. The title of her autobiography, with its many connotations, is an appropriate clue to the book that follows.[15]

More than her white contemporaries, Hurston deliberately works through disguises, as Gates and others have acknowledged. What may not be acknowledged often enough is Hurston's sense of satire, her love of play, and the many-layered dimensions of her humor, all of which are clearly visible in her autobiography's original conclusion:

> I have no race prejudice of any kind. My kinfolks, and my "skin folks" are dearly loved. My own circumference of everyday life is there. But I see the same virtues and vices everywhere I look. So I give you all my right hand of fellowship and love, and hope for the same from you. In my eyesight, you lose nothing by not looking just like me. I will remember you all in my good thoughts, and ask you kindly to do the same for me. Not only just me. You, who play the zig-zag lightening of power over the world, with the grumbling thunder in your wake, think kindly of those who walk in the dust. And you who walk in humble places, think kindly too, of others. There has been no proof in the world so far that you would be less arrogant if you held the lever of power in your hands. Let us all be kissing-friends. Consider that with tolerance and patience, we godly demons may breed a noble world in a few hundred years or so. Maybe all of us who do not have the good fortune to meet, or meet again, in this world, will meet at a barbecue. (285–86)

Through the folksy disguise, Hurston extends her hand to the white reader while poking fun at his or her sense of superiority. The Eatonville ethnographer turns commonplace assumptions on their heads; from her point of view, the powerful are not always arrogant and the lowly are seldom humble. Ann Rayson may be right to claim that, put any other way, "a comment like this would elicit considerable hostility from friends and foes alike" (39).

At the end of her autobiography, Hurston can enjoin her readers to produce a more noble world, constructed on a more solid ethical foundation, while letting her folksy and deliberately ambiguous images suggest a more likely possibility. Hurston only appears to believe along with Lillian Smith that men and women might one day evolve into a higher, more moral form of being. The close proximity of "kissing friends" (a sometimes pejorative term, often used in a context of sarcasm), "we godly demons," and "barbecue" suggests a more frightening, more sinister scenario: devolution rather than evolution. Shortly after its initial publication, the *New Yorker* carried this snippet: "*Dust Tracks on a Road*, by Zora Neale Hurston. The author of 'Mules and

Men' tells her life story. Warm, witty, imaginative, and down-to-earth by turns, this is a rich and winning book by one of our few genuine, Grade A folk writers. Seems naive here and there, but it probably isn't" (71). In 1942 the *New Yorker* was on to something.

Coda

"For some of us," Sydney Janet Kaplan writes, "feminist criticism originated in a recognition of our love for women writers" (37). Kaplan's experience parallels my own. In an undergraduate survey of southern literature in the midseventies, I was lucky enough to have a professor who did not exclude women writers from his syllabi. In his office one afternoon, I borrowed a book I had not read: *The Mortgaged Heart* (1971), Carson McCullers's posthumous collection of early stories, essays, and poems. Though I found McCullers's apprentice fiction to be of great interest (I had just read her more famous novels), I was most intrigued by her self-reflective pieces, by the ways in which she conceptualized her own work and her own response to the world. Her small body of occasional prose led me to similar writing by her contemporaries (and forerunners) and, eventually, to the present consideration of southern women's self-writing.

Mixed with the pleasure I have taken in the work of southern women is, however, a certain anger, what Kaplan has called "the second initiating impulse" of feminist criticism (53)—an impulse that, again, need not be confined to one gender. It did not take me long to discover that southern women's self-writing, though it encompasses texts as diverse as Ellen Glasgow's *A Certain Measure* (1943) and Lillian Hellman's *An Unfinished Woman* (1969), has not figured prominently in most assessments of southern literature, this despite the prompting of critics, old and new, that we enlarge the southern mansion (the phrase is Lillian Smith's) to make room for more of its inhabitants. The all too frequent omission of women writers from the intellectual history of the Southern Renaissance suggests, as I have indicated, the inability of masculinist critics to accomodate women's texts to paradigms derived almost solely from the texts of men.

My aim in this study has thus been to look carefully at a large body of writing without the usual assumptions about "southernness." What I have tried to say is this: here are several of the South's most distinguished women writers, here are the ways they have defined themselves, here are some of the dotted lines that Eudora Welty referred to when asked if she had read the work of other southern women writers of her generation. Welty was right to play down any "passing about of influences," but she would not, I believe, object to an intertextual study of her work and that of her contemporaries. In their overview of theories of influence and intertextuality, Jay Clayton and Eric Rothstein identify the various advantages of an intertextual approach, including its refusal to subordinate minor to major works and, perhaps most significant, its preference for probing and even "supplementing" a text in order to display not only its implications but also its "implicatedness" (19).

If any one thread is central to an understanding of the self-writing of Lillian Smith, Ellen Glasgow, Eudora Welty, Lillian Hellman, Katherine Anne Porter, and Zora Neale Hurston, it is their shared independence, their need to define themselves as intense individualists. The value that each attached to individualism is embodied most fully in Smith's image of the self and its interior life as that of a pseudopod that must be allowed to grow without constraints. Individualism is at the heart of each writer's refusal to merge her identity with that of others, be it a group of writers in Harlem, Nashville, or Paris. During her stay in Germany, Katherine Anne Porter observed head-on the appalling potential of unexamined group identification; and even Lillian Hellman observed that radicals—intense individualists such as herself—rarely make good revolutionaries. In a mideighties interview, Eudora Welty said that she could not see the logic of "any kind of group existing for its own sake," adding that she "could never have belonged to anything like Bloomsbury. There wasn't any danger! Everything aside—qualifications aside—I just wouldn't have flourished in a group like that, all talking to each other. I'm just interested in people as individuals and caring for individuals so much" (Devlin 26).

Welty was of course expressing the key component of liberalism, which, as Susan Moller Okin observes, "values the individuality that is promoted and preserved by the respect for personal preferences and for the need for privacy" and which "is well aware of the dangers that can result from the imposition of supposed 'community standards'" (40). We have seen the relevance of Okin's definition. In *Scoundrel Time* and *The Never-Ending Wrong*, Lillian Hellman and Katherine Anne Porter affirm their own choices—as well as their own mixed motives—while ardently denouncing those who have, often at the service of a larger community, established themselves as the true enemies of liberal thought, and in *Killers of the Dream*, Lillian Smith exposes the mindless conformity that her childhood South demanded of all but the bravest of southerners, either those who dissented silently or who, like Smith, found the inner resources to lead more daring lives.

Defending liberalism in the late twentieth century requires some courage, and not just because the country has become so alarmingly conservative. Even more significant, as Will Kymlicka writes, is the "commonplace amongst communitarians, socialists and feminists alike that liberalism is to be rejected for its excessive 'individualism' or 'atomism,' for ignoring the manifest ways in which we are 'embedded' or 'situated' in various social roles and communal relationships" (182). Kymlicka takes it upon himself to define and examine "the resources available to liberalism to meet these objections," including its insistence that "we lead our life from the inside" and that we be completely free to dissent (183–84). As Kymlicka makes clear, liberal political morality is no different from the liberal view of the self: "What is central to the liberal view is not that we can *perceive* a self prior to its ends, but that we understand ourselves to be prior to our ends, *in the sense that no end or goal is exempt from possible re-examination*" (190). The view of the southern conservative is, by contrast, that of the communitarian who holds that "we only have confidence in our moral judgments if they are protected socially from the eroding effects of our own individual rational scrutiny" (195). Contending that "a valuable life has to be a life led from the inside" (183), Kymlicka provides the philosophical rationale that undergirds Eudora Welty's insistence—shared by each of the writers in this study—that "all serious daring starts from within."

Still, it has not been my aim to provide a one-dimensional picture of the liberal impulse in southern women's self-writing, for as Susan

Okin correctly observes, "Liberalism's past is deeply rooted in the ideologies that have sustained patriarchy." Particularly, "liberalism has
been constructed around distinctions between the public realm, which
includes politics, and the private, which includes personal and domestic life." Even though these distinctions have evolved with the best of
intentions (to secure freedom and restrain governments), Okin shows
that "in traditional liberal thought the distinction between the public
and the domestic realms rests on the assumption that men inhabit
both, easily moving from one to the other, but that women inhabit only
the realm of family life, where they are properly subordinated to their
husbands" (39). Feminist critics approaching the subject of women's
self-writing have thus demonstrated the means by which traditional
autobiographical theory reinscribes the public-private dichotomy that
has helped to marginalize women's experience.

The key question for Okin and other feminists is "whether and how
we can replace this patriarchal liberalism with a political theory of humanist liberalism" (40), a theory that subverts "the traditional liberal
dichotomy between public and private" and that speaks to the ways in
which "the personal is political" (41). I have attempted to show that
implicit in southern women's self-writing is the challenge that Okin
defines. Given the force of the public-private dichotomy, we can argue
that when a woman writer makes public her inner life, she is—with full
awareness or not—expanding the discourse of liberalism and its engendered ideologies. This holds true whether her aim is to define the deepest sources of her creativity, to trace the tracks that mark the evolution
of her own sense of individualism, to undermine the structures of institutionalized racism, or to denounce the excesses of a conspicuously
illiberal era in our nation's history.

Whatever form it takes, self-definition is an activity that requires
great risks, not the least of which is the problematic relationship between the writer and the reader who must test and then either accept
or reject the authenticity of the self-writer's portrait. The risks are formidable for either gender, but given the nature of patriarchy (in the
South and elsewhere), they seem especially taxing for the woman who,
in Simone de Beauvoir's words, is taught early on to "renounce her
autonomy" and who thus becomes the victim of a vicious circle:
". . . for the less she exercises her freedom to understand, to grasp and
discover the world about her, the [fewer] resources will she find within

herself, the less will she dare to affirm herself as subject" (280). Michael Kreyling uses de Beauvoir's remarks as the basis of a discerning discussion of *One Writer's Beginnings*. De Beauvoir's argument is, I believe, germane to each of the texts I have examined. In each work the writer "exercises her freedom to understand" and to "grasp and discover the world about her." In each case the writer defines the resources that have sustained her sense of identity and that, in the end, have prompted her own daring.

In 1933 Ellen Glasgow proclaimed that "a reasonable doubt is the safety-valve of civilization." The remark comes from one of Glasgow's long out-of-print essays, "What I Believe," written for *The Nation*, one of the country's oldest liberal weeklies. As I reread this piece, along with its longer follow-up, "I Believe," both now reprinted in *Ellen Glasgow's Reasonable Doubts* (1988), I am intrigued by the ways in which Glasgow, in only a few pages, articulates most of the concerns that unite the writers in this study—that is, I am intrigued by the implications of Glasgow's essay as well as the many ways in which it is implicated in the discourse of southern women's self-writing.

Here are some of the tenets of what Glasgow calls her "general theory":

> . . . Leaving the ways and means to specialists, I believe that the private ownership of wealth should be curbed; that our natural resources should not be exploited for individual advantage . . . that our means of distribution should be adjusted to our increasing needs and the hollow cry of "overproduction" banished from a world in which millions are starving; that the two useless extremes of society, the thriftless rich and the thriftless poor, should be mercifully eliminated . . . that the greatest discovery of the mind was neither fire nor electricity but the power to share in another's pain . . . that if man were really civilized, any system ever invented might usher in the millennium. . . . (222)

Her theory is radical in its implications, but like John Dewey, Glasgow was a liberal pragmatist rather than a true revolutionary; hence she thinks it "safer to examine our [existing] structure and make the necessary repairs" and "wiser to profit by the past than to ignore or deny it" (225). Like Lillian Hellman, Katherine Anne Porter, and Zora Neale Hurston, Glasgow would "like to think that a fairer social order might be attained in an orderly way" (222), but she sees that such order is unlikely "so long as the mass of human beings everywhere can find an escape from social injustice and cruelty, not in resisting, but rather in the thrill of inflicting, however vicarious, injustice and cruelty upon others" (223).

As Glasgow turns her attention from economic inequalities to the church and its historical evasions, her critique anticipates that of Lillian Smith. Having "imprisoned its faith in arbitrary doctrines," Glasgow maintains that organized religion "has failed to satisfy the intellectual and spiritual needs of the modern world, in which primitive consecrations and barbaric symbols have lost, for many of us, their earlier significance" (227). Like Smith, Glasgow argues that the greatest need in our time "is not for a multitude of machines, but for a new and higher conception of God" (244). Her skepticism—which she defines as "the only permanent basis of tolerance" (245)—reminds her, however, that "any god of the modern temper" is destined to be an imperfect panacea. Influenced by Charles Darwin at an early age, Glasgow expresses Smith's hope that men and women might ultimately discover more progressive ways of life, but she also observes, along with Hurston, that evolution moves in two directions and that one route is as likely as the other.

At times Glasgow shifts to the past tense, as when she defines her goal as having been the discovery of a philosophy—a personal ethics—and an art that would enable her to apprehend the mysteries she confronted: "What I wanted from life was to live, to feel, and to know as completely as the circumscribed scope of my being allowed" (236). As a woman of letters in the twentieth-century South—a woman "born with a nonconformist mind" during an era in which it was difficult to make even an intellectual rebellion (219)—Glasgow pursued her goals, her search, in a region that has not been traditionally hospitable to the lives of either its artists or its nonconformists. A long-time foe of narrow-minded regionalism, it is only from hindsight that Glasgow can find amusement in a "charming social culture" that "regarded all abstract ideas as dangerously contagious" (238).

After articulating the nature of her various beliefs—after attempting once more to define herself for herself—Glasgow concludes her *Nation* essay with a remark that anticipates her autobiography: "I can see only the vanishing-point in the perspective, where all beliefs disappear and the deepest certainties, if they exist, cannot be comprehended by the inquiring mind alone, but must be apprehended by that inmost reason which we may call the heart" (227). The value Glasgow places on the inner life and its relation to the outer world is another expression of the link between the writers and the self-reflective texts I have discussed—another echo of Eudora Welty's insistence—shall we call it a theory?—that "all serious daring starts from within."

Notes

Chapter 1. SOUTHERN WOMEN OF LETTERS IN THE TWENTIETH CENTURY

1. For example, when she read Robert Fitzgerald's introduction to one of O'Connor's volumes—a section in which Fitzgerald glosses O'Connor's view of the relation between mystery and "manners"—Katherine Anne Porter scrawled the following remark in the margin: "I have been trouping colleges for thirty years, saying there is a mystery that we cannot explore or analyze and it is the heart of the matter, and nobody heard me" (quoted in Gretlund 83).

2. For a more extended analysis of O'Connor and liberalism, see Schaub 116–36.

3. Alan Dawley in *Struggles for Justice: Social Responsibility and the Liberal State* (1991) and Richard Pells in *The Liberal Mind in a Conservative Age: American Intellectuals in the 1940s and 1950s* (1985) provide more complete assessments of twentieth-century American liberalism, its various achievements, tensions, and failings. See also Rosenblum 1–17.

4. With a few significant exceptions—M. E. Bradford, for example—southern conservatives have not been drawn to autobiography and other modes of self-portraiture, and this is true even of the highly literate Agrarian/New Critics. Of this group, only Allen Tate even attempted an autobiography (see Core). This fact is worth noting, though it should not be assumed that southern conservatism necessarily preempts self-analysis. In his Introduction to the collected short stories of Conrad Aiken, Robert Penn Warren suggests that he, like others, has written his deepest self through his fiction: "I have said, or implied, that all or most of the stories (or novels or poems) of a good writer are hewn out of the same block. That big block is, of course, the writer's self—but the self that neither he nor his friends may know much about. (In fact, the real self may be what is created by the hewing)" (ix). Warren's theory is not without merit, yet formal autobiography in the South has nonetheless made its greatest

appeal to the region's liberals. See Lyons 1–17, for a discussion of how self-writing evolved from liberal ideals during the Enlightenment.

5. Myrdal published his book before Malcolm Cowley's *The Portable Faulkner* (1946) renewed interest in Faulkner's writing and subsequently prompted both southern conservatives and liberals to claim the Mississippi writer for their own. On how Faulkner's critical reputation was shaped by both the Agrarian/New Critics and the New York intellectuals, see Lawrence H. Schwartz's *Creating Faulkner's Reputation: The Politics of Modern Literary Criticism* (1988).

6. Under the Freedom of Information-Privacy Acts, I have acquired the FBI files on a number of southern women writers. These files contain no shortage of evidence to suggest that certain powerful people feared the liberal commitments and potential radicalism of not only Lillian Smith and Lillian Hellman (whose file I discuss in Chapter 5) but of others as well.

7. Though one of her most popular essays, "Must the Novelist Crusade?" (*Eye of the Story* 146–58) has forced Welty on a number of occasions to defend herself against the charge that she is indifferent to the South's social and political problems. "What is true," she explains in a typical interview, "is that I don't think of myself as a writer of fiction who seeks to make it a platform for my opinions. I am a very interested citizen and try to keep informed on everything and to vote. But I don't think fiction is the place to air those principles, except for the moral principles of right and wrong—and these I try to let characters show for themselves" (Prenshaw, *Conversations* 226).

8. See, for example, Walter Sullivan's *A Requiem For the Renascence: The State of Fiction in the Modern South* (1976) and M. E. Bradford's *Generations of the Faithful Heart: On the Literature of the South* (1983).

9. Philip Castille and William Osborne use Holman's essay as the Introduction to their anthology, *Southern Literature in Transition: Heritage and Promise* (1983) but follow it with a piece by Cleanth Brooks, "Southern Literature: The Past, History, and the Timeless," which, in effect, does little more than mark the well-known monoliths. "To sum up," Brooks writes, "the southern writers of our century present a culture in which interpersonal relationships are close and important. The family still exists as a normative and stabilizing force. It is culture that is indeed immersed in place and time. Within it, history is vivid and meaningful. Related to the southerner's vivid sense of history and the closeness of his interpersonal relationships is a pervasive religion that undergirds his whole cultural complex" (10). Brooks relies chiefly on works by Warren, Welty, Faulkner, and Percy to illustrate his defining characteristics.

10. King draws particular attention to Woodward's "Why the Southern Renaissance?" (1975) and Simpson's "The Southern Recovery of Memory and History" (1974).

11. Singal's characteristics are a new interest in exploring the depths of the human psyche; an acceptance of the world as "turbulent and unpredictable" in opposition to the Victorian model of "an orderly universe governed by natural law"; a "positive view of conflict, whether personal, social, or political"; a

willingness "to live without certainty, either moral or epistomological"; and a search for reality, "no matter how ugly or distasteful that reality might be" (8).

12. Here is Hobson's rationale for excluding African-Americans from his investigation of the southern "rage to explain": "I limit the study to white Southerners, although agreeing fully with C. Vann Woodward that 'there is no one more quintessentially Southern than the Southern Negro.' I go further and maintain that if any Southern writer possessed, and was entitled to possess, a rage to explain the South, it was the Southern Negro, and I omit black writers—Richard Wright and Ralph Ellison most prominently—only because it would be impossible to do them justice in a work of this scope. The story of their rage to explain is a book in itself" (12–13). Singal's rationale is much the same: "it is true that no black intellectuals appear in my cast of characters. . . . An important study remains to be written on black culture and thought in the modern South, but the task will involve the use of sources quite different from those employed for the present book" (xiv–xv).

13. This statement is intended in the most literal sense. Take, for example, the list of suggested topics for future articles and books that Louis D. Rubin and C. Hugh Holman prepared in 1975. Of the fifty or more suggestions in their "General" category alone, no mention is made of southern writers and questions of gender, though Rubin and Holman do suggest "The southern writer and the minority mentality," "Varieties of southern ambivalence," "Race, class, and party in southern literature" (notice the absence of sex), and "A biography of Carson McCullers," the only southern woman writer to be identified for this distinction. See Rubin and Holman 227–35.

14. See, for example, "Robert Penn Warren: Critic," Louis D. Rubin's analysis and endorsement of Warren's New Critical theory and criticism.

15. Spivey has provided one of the most intriguing assessments of the Agrarians' influence on O'Connor, a writer they clearly favored. He claims, "As a visionary [O'Connor] foresaw much that would happen in the psyches of young people in the latter half of the twentieth century; nevertheless, as a woman of letters following in the footsteps of Caroline Gordon in particular, and of the Agrarians in general, she clung to images of a way of life rapidly dying." Spivey argues that O'Connor's "early attachment to the Agrarians might have hindered her own acceptance of psychic changes going on within herself. The Agrarians were sometimes rigid in their viewpoints. The one thing O'Connor needed above all was less rigidity of viewpoint, less of the logocentrism in herself and her work that she sometimes clung to and yet distrusted" (279).

16. Writing about the book reviews and criticism of Eudora Welty, Ruth M. Vande Kieft notes, "The words *pattern, shape, design, ordering*, come to her more quickly than does *structure*; and *color*, or *atmosphere*, more quickly than does *tone*" ("Looking with Eudora Welty" 239). McCullers seems equally impatient with the formalist approach to art; in "The Vision Shared," she says, "The ingenuities of aesthetics have never been my problems. Flight, in itself, interests me and I am indifferent to salting the bird's tail" (*Mortgaged Heart* 262). McCullers's image of flight can be illuminated by Hélène Cixous who,

in her characteristically poetic manner, uses the image for much the same purpose. Cixous argues that women must not concern themselves with "masculine anxiety and its obsession with how to dominate the way things work—knowing 'how it works' in order to 'make it work.' " For women "the point is not to take possession in order to internalize or manipulate, but rather to dash through and to 'fly,' " for "flying is woman's gesture—flying in language and making it fly" (257–58).

17. While critics never tire of noting McCullers's central theme of loneliness, they rarely anchor their discussions in a larger consideration of her liberal consciousness. In an interview with Ralph McGill, McCullers once said, "All of us seek a time and a way to communicate something of the sense of loneliness and solitude that is in us—the heart is a lonely hunter—but the search of us Southerners is more anguished. There is a special guilt in us, a seeking for something had—and lost. It is a consciousness of guilt not fully knowable, or communicable. Southerners are the more lonely and spiritually estranged, I think, because we have lived so long in an artificial social system that we insisted was natural and right and just—when all along we knew it wasn't." She added, "The fact that we bolstered it with laws and developed a secular liturgy and sacraments for it is evidence of how little we believed our own deceits" (quoted in McGill 217).

18. Domna C. Stanton refers to this tendency as "the age-old, pervasive decoding of all female writing as autobiographical." While pursuing her research on women's autobiographies, Stanton found that " 'autobiography' constituted a positive term when applied to Augustine and Montaigne, Rousseau and Goethe, Henry Adams and Henry Miller, but that it has negative connotations when imposed on women's texts." Further, she discovered that autobiography has been used "to affirm" women's ability to record rather than to "transcend" their personal concerns and has thus "served to devalue their writing." Of particular interest is Stanton's observation that "over the centuries, the anonymous seventeenth-century *Portuguese Letters* had been called autobiographical, spontaneous, natural when ascribed to a woman, but fictive, crafted and aesthetic, when attributed to a man." Stanton clinches her argument by noting that just as George Sand's "fictions had been notoriously branded autobiographical, critical reactions to Colette's work represented a dramatic case of the autobiographical wielded as a weapon to denigrate female texts and exclude them from the canon" (6–7).

19. Fox-Genovese's argument is correct; the problem for some readers is that, judging by her scorn for individualism, Fox-Genovese would appear to be on the side of Tate and the southern traditionalists. See especially Fox-Genovese's recent *Feminism Without Illusions: A Critique of Individualism* (1991).

20. It strikes me as in no way coincidental that each of the writers in this study would at one point or another insist that she was a "writer" or "artist" rather than a "woman writer" or a "woman artist." McCullers in particular felt it necessary to adopt the pose and sometimes even the dress of a man; both she and O'Connor dropped the exclusively feminine part of their names—Lula

and Mary, respectively. While Eudora Welty has claimed that she did not save the *New York Times* book reviews she wrote as Michael Ravenna in 1944 (Prenshaw, *Conversations* 299), one might wonder who suggested that she use a male pseudonym for only those reviews that addressed some aspect of the war. At the time, "Eudora Welty" was a well-known by-line to *Times* readers. Would they have rejected Welty as a commentator on war-related books?

21. This is true of the contemporary scene as well. Women writers in large numbers have been at the heart of what one might regard as a second southern literary resurgence in the 1980s and 1990s. On this subject, see Inge and Linda Tate.

Chapter 2. LILLIAN SMITH: *The Confessional Tract*

1. As Redding S. Sugg, Jr., observes in "Lillian Smith and the Condition of Women," the best way to understand what went on at Laurel Falls Camp is "to recall the plays which the campers and the staff made out of their life together" (158–59). Jo Ann Robinson briefly describes the two camp dramas that have survived—" 'Behind the Drums,' a dramatization of the struggle of black people to free themselves from 'white man's chains, white man's gold, white man's lust,' and 'The Girl,' a portrayal of the female child emerging from a 'large, pale pink egg, lighted from within, the opening covered by layers of pink chiffon' into a long battle against Hates, Fears, Guilts, and Failures." Robinson wisely asks, "Who could guess that these images of black history and female strength were entertained on the ridge of a mountain in north Georgia by little daughters from some of the 'best' white families of the South?" (44–45). See Lillian Smith, "Behind the Drums" (White and Sugg 69–83), and "Growing Plays: The Girl." For an in-depth treatment of Smith's psychological techniques as director of the Laurel Falls Camp, see Gladney.

2. Complete runs of this periodical are rare outside a few large southern universities—Georgia State University in Atlanta, for example, or the University of Georgia in Athens. In *From the Mountain* (1972), Helen White and Redding S. Sugg, Jr., provide a useful history of the magazine—its evolution and cultural significance—as well as a wide selection of its contents.

3. Morton Sosna draws attention to a conversation between two women in Smith's 1959 novel: " 'It is the quality of a relationship that counts,' another woman reassuringly tells one of the guilt-ridden lovers. 'Easy to paste a good label on something spurious and cheap, easy to paste a bad one on something fine and delicate.' Upon hearing these words, Smith's heroine commented: 'When she said this simple, obvious thing it burst on me like a revelation' " (232–33). See Smith's *One Hour* 352–55.

4. *Strange Fruit* sparked a major obscenity trial. Bernard DeVoto provides an interesting legal assessment of the controversy in "The Decision in the *Strange Fruit* Case: The Obscenity Statute in Massachusetts."

5. In their anthology of autobiographical writings by women, Mary Mason and Carol Green use "the idea of the journey" to bring together the work of a

highly diverse group of women writers that includes Julian of Norwich, Anne Bradstreet, Beatrice Webb, H.D., Dorothy Day, and Susan Sontag. According to Mason and Green, the works of these writers illustrate two distinct meanings of the organizing metaphor: "journey as action and movement, implying freedom and the will to choose, and journey as direction, implying a goal beyond the self"—in other words, a journey "that leads not to obliteration but to self-discovery and self-realization" (vii). Mason and Green do not include Smith in their anthology, but her autobiographical writings are further illustration of the metaphor and pattern they describe.

6. The wide variety of definitions illustrates the difficulty of classifying such a work as *Killers of the Dream*, which blends a number of genres. In "Lillian Smith and the Condition of Women," Redding S. Sugg, Jr., calls the book "a highly effective analysis of self-and-milieu" (161). Margaret Jones Bolsterli defines it as a collection of "intensely personal essays" (72). Louise Westling provides one of the most appealing descriptions; she calls the book Smith's "passionate non-fictional testimonial about the evils of racism" ("Lillian Smith as Social Evangelist" 122).

7. Unless otherwise noted, all references are to the 1961 edition.

8. As Susan Tucker observes, "The complex psychology of oppression worked in such a way that black women saw themselves and were seen as stronger than white women. In going into the white home, black domestics saw the problems of white women; they saw particularly another form of oppression in the passivity demanded of white women. They saw specifically that Southern white women, even those in positions of power, attempted to conceal their strength" (95). Tucker offers a probing discussion of the black domestic (the nurse as well as her predecessor the mammy) with attention to both her literary and historical personas.

9. In "Southern Autobiography and the Problem of Race," Melton McLaurin asserts that southern white liberals have rarely betrayed their deepest emotions regarding issues of race. McLaurin's thesis may be accurate, but his analysis of Smith is off the mark. He claims that while Lillian Smith produced what is "in many respects the most radical denunciation of segregation written by a Southerner until after the Civil Rights Revolution of the mid-sixties" (67), even she gives no real insights into her feelings about her relationships with individual blacks, including that of her nurse: "in describing the relationship between the South's black nurses and white children, Smith relies upon a second-person, rather than a first-person narrative, a device that allows her to maintain an emotional distance from her subject" (68). This assessment is inaccurate. As I have shown, Smith provides a first-person account of her Aunt Chloe—a memory charged with emotion—before shifting to the second and third person in order to make her discursive points. McLaurin's chief mistake is to treat *Killers of the Dream* along with autobiographies that focus more exclusively on a writer's personal relationships; he does not appear to accept Smith's book for the kind of document it is.

10. In her Foreword to the first edition of *Killers of the Dream*, Smith iden-

tifies a number of works that have provided her with facts, figures, and quotations, including Gunnar Myrdal's *American Dilemma* (1944), Rupert Vance's *Human Geography of the South* (1932), Howard Odum's *Southern Regions* (1936), and Carey McWilliams's *Brothers Under the Skin* (1947), as well as works that have influenced her thinking about racial relations—Hortense Powdermaker's *After Freedom* (1939) and James Weldon Johnson's *Along This Way* (1933). What Smith stresses, however, is the value of her own observations as a southerner. Since she did not acknowledge the secondary sources in the book's revised edition, one can guess that she no longer felt the need to cite authorities beyond herself.

11. In "Ladies: South by Northwest," sociologists Maxine P. Atkinson and Jacqueline Boles use novels, diaries, memoirs, and historical documents to construct a typology of the lady; they identify twenty "temperamental descriptors that typify this ideal woman: simple, good, passive, delicate, innocent, submissive, mannerly, economical, humble, sacrificing, sympathetic, kind, weak, generous, pious, shallow, nonintellectual, hospitable, rich, and calm" (130). The "defining characteristic," the one that subsumes the others, is "gentility" (128). In their comparison of both modern southern and northwestern women who either aspire to or acknowledge the force of this ideal, Atkinson and Boles have discovered, through intensive surveys, that the contemporary southern woman, unlike her western counterpart, "feels ambivalent, torn between her desire to emulate the true Southern lady and her feelings of personal inadequacy for being unable to do so." This ambivalence does not surprise Atkinson and Boles. "After all," they contend, "the ideal role model did not really exist but was a fiction created to sustain an agrarian economy based on slave labor" (137). See also Atkinson and Boles "The Shaky Pedestal: Southern Ladies Yesterday and Today." In "Myth Against History: The Case of Southern Womanhood," Sara Evans provides a brief but informative historical overview of the white southern woman, with emphasis on the disparity between ideals and reality.

12. A more empirically minded historian than Smith would be less given to assertions based to a large degree on intuitions and personal observation. See Elizabeth Fox-Genovese's *Within the Plantation Household: Black and White Women of the Old South* (1988), 34.

13. Jack Tarver, *Atlanta Constitution*, 27 Oct. 1949: 14. Smith's most hostile reviewers were those closest to home. In addition to Tarver's editorial, the *Constitution* published attacks by Sam F. Lucchese, 20 Nov. 1949: C12, and Ralph McGill, 24 Nov. 1949: B18. "Miss Smith is a prisoner in the monastery of her own mind," McGill charged. "But rarely does she come out of its gates, and then, apparently, seeing only wicked things to send her back to her hair shirt and the pouring of ashes on her head and salt in her own psychiatric wounds." As a native of Atlanta, I was surprised to see that McGill, one of the region's best-known liberals, had participated in the silencing of Lillian Smith.

14. It is also interesting to read Smith's article in conjunction with Eudora

Welty's "Must the Novelist Crusade?" (*Eye of the Story* 146–58), written four years later and in some ways a direct response to Smith's exhortation.

15. See Grigsby for a more detailed treatment of the often-ignored link between the Agrarian movement and racism.

16. One of the most eloquent apologists is Richard Weaver; see, for example, "Agrarianism in Exile." Paul Conkin has provided a reliable history of the Agrarian movement in *The Southern Agrarians* (1988).

17. See Smith's reviews of Henri de Lubac's *Teilhard de Chardin: The Man and His Meaning* and Teilhard's *The Appearance of Man*, both in the *Chicago Tribune Books Today*, 13 Mar. 1966: 1; 28 Nov. 1965: 6.

18. Singal's refusal to treat Smith more extensively may stem from his impression that her insights, bold as they were in the forties, "have about them the ring of the commonplace . . . a certain stilted quality for the present-day reader" (374–75). These are rather curious claims. In the aftermath of the European revolutions of 1989, one can see that racism and sectional egoism are still very much alive. As Daniel Singer has observed, "One of the first 'free' acts of the Bulgarians was to protest against equal rights for Turks, and of the Romanians, to stage a pogrom against Hungarians. Add to this the anti-Semitism without Jews in Poland and with them in Russia, the atavistic hatreds of Azerbaijanis and Armenians, and of various minorities in the Caucasus and Central Asia, and you will recognize that reason still has a tremendous field to conquer" ("Silent Reproach," *The Nation* 4 June 1990: 765).

19. In her biography of McCullers, Virginia Spencer Carr notes that, when *Holiday* commissioned McCullers to write a feature article on Georgia, she intended to use Smith as the "fulcrum" of the piece. McCullers visited Smith and Snelling in November of 1953 in order "to steep herself in North Georgia lore," a visit cut short when she received news that Reeves McCullers, from whom she was then separated, had committed suicide. Like many of McCullers's other projects after 1951, the article never materialized (Carr 404–7).

20. Critics have erred in viewing Smith as a staunch Cold Warrior when, in fact, she wrote one of the first public denunciations of McCarthy, his "ism," and his reckless charges ("A Declaration of Faith in America" 42). In the revised *Killers* (which followed close on *One Hour*, her anti-McCarthy novel), Smith urged people not to succumb to the inquisitorial spirit. A close comparison of the last two chapters of the revised *Killers* with the same chapters from the first edition reveals a softening of Smith's earlier anti-Communist stance. Having seen the dubious results of what is now called liberal anticommunism, Smith appears less willing in 1961 to condone or lay blame on any one group. In 1949 she had included a partisan defense of liberals as the "carriers of the dream"—the only group of men and women who "held on to a belief that man is more important than his institutions" (240). She omitted this passage in the second edition along with her former explanation of why people turn to communism—its promise of a "spuurious" equality in place of "old masks" such as color, race, and religion (242). In the revised edition, Smith still attempts to

dissuade people from embracing a too romantic view of equality (or of communism), but she provides a different rationale, one that reflects her reading of Teilhard de Chardin rather than her distaste for the promises of a socialist state. Men are not equal, she claims; they cannot be equal, "will never be, have never been," and yet "out of these differences, these infinite variations, big and small, comes mankind's chance of evolving into a new being" (246–47).

21. In the same letter, Smith described the reaction of the assembled crowd to her appearance. After getting "a furtive once over by everybody," Smith recalled the following scenario: " 'She's a real lady,' they said to each other and to me, and then they said (to each other and to me) 'she is dressed like Park Avenue. Let's ask her to speak to us tonight.' Just like that. So they asked me" (quoted in Loveland 111–12).

22. The contempt for intellectuals that is nowhere more apparent than in her fiction is a clear indication that O'Connor did not share Smith's belief in human rationality. One of the most intriguing explanations of her attachment to the generallly optimistic Teilhard is given by Frederick Crews, who argues that "the satirically minded O'Connor was anything but a mystic" and that "in embracing Teilhard's pseudoscience, she was doing what she could to neutralize, not exactly a *contemptus mundi*, but a temperamental impatience with what she took to be a virtually universal inanity" (52).

23. Like Smith, Rich was cared for as a child by a black nurse whom she subsequently depicted in much the same way that Smith described her Aunt Chloe. See Rich, *Of Woman Born: Motherhood as Experience and Institution* 253–54. It was, incidentally, a friend of Rich, the Jamaican-born novelist, essayist, and poet Michelle Cliff, who brought together Smith's posthumous collection of essays and letters, *The Winner Names the Age* (1978).

Chapter 3. ELLEN GLASGOW AND EUDORA WELTY: *Writing the Sheltered Life*

1. A brief glance at Conrad Aiken's *Ushant* (1952), Tennessee Williams's *Memoirs* (1975), and Erskine Caldwell's *With All My Might* (1987), to cite autobiographies by three southern men, would serve to substantiate Voss's argument. For a detailed critique of ways in which autobiographical criticism has promoted a conception of self-hood that is male oriented, see Friedman. See also Jelinek, *Tradition* 1–8, and Sidonie Smith 3–19. More general but worthwhile discussions of autobiography that have influenced my thinking are Mazlish, Shapiro, Doherty, and Eakin.

2. Linda Wagner-Martin stands almost alone in seeing *The Woman Within* as one of Glasgow's major achievements. In *Ellen Glasgow: Beyond Convention* (1982), Wagner-Martin states, "Glasgow's characterizations have given flesh to the complexity of the female mind and heart, as she grew herself from being a 'philosophical' novelist whose first book was credited to a male author [Harold Frederic] to a woman writer whose greatest work—*Virginia*, *Barren Ground*, *The Sheltered Life*, *Vein of Iron*, and *The Woman Within*—came from

her own responses to her thoroughly feminine identity" (123). Wagner-Martin's study relies heavily on the Glasgow manuscripts at the University of Virginia.

3. In "Autobiography as De-facement" De Man presents the following question as the basis of his deconstructive argument: "We assume that life *produces* the autobiography as an act produces its consequences, but can we not suggest, with equal justice, that the autobiographical project may itself produce and determine the life and that whatever the writer *does* is in fact governed by the technical demands of self-portraiture and thus determined in all its aspects, by the resources of his medium?" (920). De Man's question is in essence another way of saying that all experience does in the end crumble to literary material.

4. Critics who take MacDonald's position often cite some of James Branch Cabell's typically tongue-in-cheek remarks from *As I Remember It* (1955): "I intend hereinafter to disregard *The Woman Within*. I say merely that it is a book wherein many matters in which I share, or about which I happened to know personally, have been—whether in the behalf of kindliness or of art or of pathos—so very fondly recolored that I distrust the entire book through-out as a factual record. I elect to applaud it rather as a work of genius and as a volume well worthy of its writer" (217–18). Cabell knew Glasgow well but was himself a well-known prevaricator. It is ironic that he would become a major "policing force"—to use De Man's term—regarding the level of her autobiographical facticity. See also Edgar E. MacDonald, "The Glasgow-Cabell Entente."

5. Jelinek makes essentially the same assertion in her earlier *Women's Autobiography: Essays in Criticism* 8–9.

6. Though she would reject convenient Freudian explanations, Glasgow's many unflattering male portraits are rooted to some degree in the unsatisfactory relationship with her father. Certainly few would argue that Francis Thomas Glasgow had much to do with her desire to escape the insidious sentimental tradition in literature; and few would doubt that her attitudes toward religion are caught up in her response to a man who held "little compassion for the inarticulate, and as his Calvinistic faith taught him, the soulless" (14). Glasgow is blunt in voicing her contempt for the God of her fathers and for the Christian symbols and institutionally sanctioned violence that moved such men as her father to pity or wrath. Yet from another perspective, the paternal influence was not especially detrimental to the development of Glasgow's career. Anne Goodwyn Jones draws attention to an interesting biographical sketch in which Marjorie Kaufman highlights a major dimension of this influence: "Ellen Glasgow received more than financial independence from these men [her father and certain paternal relatives]; she had also their business acumen, their competitiveness, their determination to succeed by creating a respectable product which could command recognition and a fair reward." With these qualities Glasgow "was able to shepherd her reputation with the same attention that she gave her novels, and thus in the years before her death to enjoy the honor she had long felt her work deserved" (quoted and discussed in Jones, *Tomorrow* 226–27).

7. "Gerald B—" has been identified variously as a New York aurist, H. Holbrook Curtis (1856–1920); as a New York neurologist, Pearce Bailey (1865–1922); and as a fiction editor with Bobbs-Merrill, Hewitt Hanson Howland (1863–1944). See McDowell 47–48.

8. For an analysis of Glasgow's naturistic vision in terms of women's archetypal experience, see Annis Pratt, "Women and Nature in Modern Fiction," especially 483–86.

9. This need, which should not be dismissed lightly, might best be seen in light of Pamela Rae Matthews's study, " 'Two Women Blended': Ellen Glasgow and Her Fictions." Matthews focuses on one major component of Glasgow's biography—her relationship with Anne Virginia Bennett, the woman who became her long-time companion—in order to explore the many destructive heterosexual relationships as well as the generally submerged homoeroticism of Glasgow's major fiction.

10. For an itemized list of this terrain, see Jelinek, *Women's Autobiography* 10–14.

11. Feminist scholars writing about autobiography have not been inclined to attack one another's arguments in print; there seems to be an understanding that for any differences, they still share the same revisionary goals. Hence it becomes significant when a specific feminist theory or paradigm solicits a primarily negative response. Such is the case with Mason's theory that women define themselves not as autonomous beings but through relationships with others. Neither Domna C. Stanton nor Sidonie Smith mentions Mason by name, but each has serious reservations about her argument, influential though Mason's essay has been. Both question whether Mason's "other" paradigm signals "an essential dynamic of female psychobiography" (Smith 18) or "an acquiescence to the dominant sex through which the female is meant to define and confine the self in our symbolic order" (Stanton 14). Smith takes the questioning one step further: "Or does all autobiographical practice proceed by means of a self/other intersubjectivity and intertextuality?" (19).

Chapter 4. LILLIAN HELLMAN AND KATHERINE ANNE PORTER:
Memoirs from Outside the Shelter

1. Though four of her plays feature southern settings and themes, critics will probably continue to debate the extent to which Hellman is in fact a "southern writer." While she refuses to overplay her southern connections, Hellman has acknowledged their importance. When asked in a 1975 interview if she in fact considered herself a southerner, Hellman responded: "Well, I have no right to, because the New York years now far outweigh the Southern years, but I suppose most Southerners, people who grew up in the South, still consider themselves Southern." Like other writers from the South, Hellman drew attention to her ancestry: "It wasn't simply a question that I was brought up and down from the South. I came from a family, on both sides, who had been Southern-

ers for a great many generations" (Bryer 186). See Holditch for an illuminating discussion of Hellman as a southern writer.

2. Nicola Sacco and Bartolomeo Vanzetti, two Italian immigrants, were put to death on 23 August 1927 for the robbery and murder of a paymaster and a guard outside a shoe factory in Braintree, Massachusetts. The two men were anarchists and apostates, and as such they aroused great fear among New Englanders who were already alarmed by the Red Scare of the early twenties and who, in any event, had no desire to alter the existing power structure. Their trial became the cause célèbre of the late twenties; the many artists and intellectuals who protested on their behalf (including those in Europe like John Galsworthy, H. G. Wells, and Thomas Mann) agreed that it was the political beliefs of the two men, rather than any hard and fast evidence of robbery and murder, that sent them to the electric chair. A generally reliable history of the Sacco-Vanzetti affair is Roberta Strauss Feuerlicht's *Justice Crucified: The Story of Sacco and Vanzetti* (1977), published the same year as Porter's memoir; of interest also is Paul Avrich's *Sacco and Vanzetti: The Anarchist Background* (1991). For a brief but pertinent analysis of the cultural significance of Sacco and Vanzetti, see Hoffman 400–408.

3. Darlene Harbour Unrue provides one of the most satisfying accounts of how Porter's activities in Mexico helped to shape her subsequent development as an artist. See *Truth and Vision in Katherine Anne Porter's Fiction* (1985), especially the first three chapters.

4. I make this assertion even while acknowledging Porter's betrayal of fellow writer Josephine Herbst to the FBI in 1942. On the surface, such an act would appear to be politically motivated or, considering that Porter and Herbst were once good friends, a deed of pure malice. The latter is the view taken by Herbst's biographer, Elinor Langer, who discovered and made public Porter's brief role as a highly inaccurate informant (245–60). In the revised edition of her biography of Porter, Joan Givner argues for a more sympathetic interpretation of events. Givner believes that Herbst's radicalism in the 1930s had much less to do with Porter's betrayal than did the problematic nature of the two writers' friendship. Possibly frightened by a side of herself that she saw in Herbst, Porter may have been "even more repelled and frightened when she discovered that Josie was under investigation, that her rebelliousness and recklessness threatened to make her an outcast and drag Porter down with her." Givner speculates, "Once again, from the distant past the specter of pariahdom came into Porter's consciousness, a legacy of the long battle she had fought against poverty, disease, and suffocating relationships" (8). The event is a dark point in Porter's career, but it is also, Givner asserts, "a powerful illustration of the difficulty of female friendship and loyalty under patriarchy" (10).

5. In addition to Cook and Navasky, see Larry Ceplair and Steven Englund, *The Inquisition in Hollywood: Politics in the Film Community, 1930–1960* (1980). For more general assessments of McCarthyism see Reeves, Fried, and Kutler.

6. Hellman's last book, *Maybe* (1980), is a sustained meditation on the na-

ture of memory, its processes and deceptions. Shortly after the book appeared, she made this candid remark in an interview: "There's only x amount you remember clearly—or you think you remember clearly. By the time you're 50, let us say, you've seen and known so many places there is a great deal you do not clearly remember. I think most people are not willing to see that or admit it if they do see it" (Bryer 277).

7. See Gellhorn, Jackson, and Spender, "Guerre de Plume"; McCracken, " 'Julia' and Other Fictions by Lillian Hellman"; and Johnson, *Intellectuals*, a chapter of which he titles, "Lies, Damned Lies and Lillian Hellman" (288–305). These three studies set out to prove that Hellman was indeed no book-keeper of her own life, but neither offers what is needed most, a psychoanalytical critique that attempts to explain why Hellman might have needed her "fictions." "Guerre de Plume" focuses on Hellman's apocryphal account of experiences she and Gellhorn shared in Spain in 1937; McCracken and Johnson write with a seemingly less personal purpose, wishing to expose Hellman as untrustworthy and therefore unfit to comment on the moral life of her time. For other perspectives see Wagner-Martin, "Lillian Hellman: Autobiography and Truth," Grossman, and Adams, 121–66.

8. Unless otherwise indicated, all references to *Scoundrel Time* are to the edition that appeared in 1976.

9. John Deedy draws attention to one of Porter's mistakes. He notes that Porter's belief in Vanzetti's innocence is based in part on her conclusion that he had a firm alibi: friends and family testified that he had been selling eels throughout the day of Christmas Eve, 1919. "But, of course," Deedy writes, "Miss Porter has confused the attempted Bridgewater robbery of December 24, 1919, with the South Braintree robbery of April 15, 1920. . . . The murders were committed at South Braintree, and although Vanzetti had an alibi for what he was doing that April day of 1920, it wasn't that he was selling Christmas eels" (572).

10. To Nora Ephron, Hellman said that many intellectuals, liberals, and "pretend-radicals"—the people on her side—now regard themselves as having been anti-McCarthy when in fact they were not: "If they say they were anti-McCarthy, what they mean is that they were anti-Joe McCarthy, not what he represented. I don't remember one large figure coming to anybody's aid. . . . Most radicals of the time were comic but the liberals were frightening" (Bryer 134). Actually, Hellman was never really comfortable with liberalism as a term of self-definition, but by the time Ronald Reagan became president of the United States in 1981, she said to another interviewer that she was saddened that "liberalism seems to have passed away from this country . . . though perhaps it's really there somewhere, quietly" (Bryer 284).

11. The response to Hellman's status as a cultural hero will most likely remain mixed, though clearly divided across the ideological boundaries that were drawn in the late forties and early fifties. The reactions so far have ranged from William Buckley's predictable refusal in the *National Review* to concede anything remotely heroic about Hellman's performance before HUAC, to Rob-

ert Sherrill's insistence in *The Nation* that Hellman "performed the necessary legal maneuvers to stay out of jail; which is to say, she was smart enough not to be physically sacrificed for an era that would not have appreciated the gesture in the slightest" (757). Sherrill gives the subject of Hellman's heroism an intriguing twist: "But in another way she was quite heroic. As all children of Adam Smith know, accepting jail for principle is not nearly so great a sacrifice as rejecting money for principle. Hellman did the latter, in spades" (757). On a similar note, Robert Coles said in the *Washington Post Book World* that Hellman was and perhaps still is "a lonely figure—brave precisely because she was afraid, and knew the power and cunning of her accusers." Coles believes that Kierkegaard would "have loved *Scoundrel Time* for its fine, sardonic humor, its unsparing social observation and, not least, the skill of its narration. . . . He longed for companions who would summon personal memory, among other modes of expression, to the task of making concrete and specific ethical analyses—as opposed to cleverly worded abstractions that conceal as much as they tell" (5). Murray Kempton's piece in the *New York Review of Books* is less enthusiastic, but Kempton looks past his reservations and applauds Hellman for her unwillingness to hurt innocent people: "It was enough for Miss Hellman to have done the single great thing of having once and for all defined the issue" (24).

12. Roger Starr notes Porter's reference to what she and other protestors had been told was a law specifying that anyone arrested more than four times could receive a sentence of life imprisonment. Starr clarifies that the statute in question, Baumes Law, applied only in New York and pertained solely to convicted felons whose habitual offenses could in fact lead to life sentences: "The law had nothing to do with Boston in 1927. But it was essential to Miss Porter to believe this nonsense because it helped her, and presumably others, to narrow the gap between themselves and the two victims of a social disaster for which they held their parents or their own class responsible" (96).

13. Gary Wills's Introduction to *Scoundrel Times* came under severe attack, but on the nature of Hellman's radicalism, Wills's remarks are right on target: "One of the unfortunate results of our generally muddled political terminology is a tendency to think of those on what is called the left as points on a continuum moving out from the center. The difference between, say, liberals, socialists, radicals, and Communists is a matter of degree within a continuum." Wills argues, however, that we should not let our political terminology obscure crucial distinctions. "Cold War liberals were ideologues," Wills asserts, "and ideologues meet each other on the same ground, if only to do battle there. Radicals of the Hellman and Hammett sort cannot even find that meeting place" (32). Wills correctly observes that while radicals are concerned with people as individuals, ideologues focus on orthodoxy. Hellman, he writes, has "spent her life creating vivid and individual people on stage; the thought of a McCarthy intent on destroying whole classes and types of people is almost too horrible for her to contemplate" (34).

14. Joan Givner traces Porter's antipathy to politics to her botched effort in

1922 to set up galleries in the United States for a Mexican folk art exhibition that was organized by, among others, Adolpho Best-Maugard and Miguel Covarrubias. Porter did extensive research for her catalog-essay, *Outline of Mexican Popular Arts and Crafts* (1922), a historical survey that set forth the goals of the exhibition—a work that, regrettably, has not been reprinted since its initial appearance. As Givner points out, "The United States government, which did not recognize Obregon's regime, labeled the show 'political propaganda' and refused to let it into the country. It remained on a railroad siding for two months, until it was finally declared a commercial enterprise, duty was paid, and it was sold to a private dealer in Los Angeles. All those who had worked on it were bitter and disillusioned." Givner cites Porter's remark to Enrique Hank Lopez that she was "as bitter as gall that politicians could have been allowed to do so much destruction, so much damage; that international politics, and oil and finance could ruin art" (*A Life* 167). Porter nonetheless aligned herself with various political causes over the years. For example, in response to a 1938 circular letter on Franco and fascism from the League of American Writers, she loudly denounced "the whole principle and practice of dictatorship in any form, by any class and for whatever reason," and she voiced her long-standing opposition "to any nation attempting to impose its own form of government, no matter what it may be, upon any other nation, either by propaganda or by acts of war" (League, *Writers Take Sides* 47). See Bevevino for an interesting analysis of Porter's evolving political views as revealed in selected letters, essays, and fictional works.

15. The phrase appears in Porter's "On a Criticism of Thomas Hardy" (*Collected Essays* 6). See Edward G. Schwartz, "The Way of Dissent: Katherine Anne Porter's Critical Position."

16. See, for example, Rex Reed's 1975 interview with Hellman (Bryer 179–83), and Enrique Hank Lopez, "Six Days in a Boston Jail," in his *Conversations with Katherine Anne Porter* (99–123). Porter's "conversation" with Lopez differs from her memoir in a few particulars. In the interview, she gives more attention, for example, to the clothes she chose for the occasion, and she tells Lopez that she herself took part in the bawdy behavior of the "wake" that followed the executions. In the revised edition of his book on Porter, George Hendrick and Willene Hendrick claim to favor the version that Porter gave to Lopez; of the two personas, the Hendricks prefer Porter the "charmingly loquacious storyteller" to Porter the "jaded and world-weary author" (134).

Chapter 5. ZORA NEALE HURSTON: *The Ethics of Self-Representation*

1. Closer in spirit to Hurston's experiences is Mary Burgher's contention that from Sojourner Truth to Maya Angelou and Angela Davis, African-American women, despite their often great adversity, have used the autobiography to celebrate their lives (see 107, 109–14). For the simple reason that the African-American tradition of self-writing is more varied than one might suspect, Regina Blackburn urges readers to be duly suspicious of theories that too nar-

rowly define the genre (134, 140). See Plant for an in-depth discussion of Hurston and the limitations of contemporary Afro-American autobiographical theory.

2. Hurston's affinity with Whitman is at times striking. Here is a passage from "How It Feels to Be Colored Me," one of her earliest essays: "At certain times I have no race, I am *me*. When I set my hat at a certain angle and saunter down Seventh Avenue, Harlem City, feeling as snooty as the lions in front of the Forty-Second Street Library, for instance. . . . The cosmic Zora emerges. I belong to no race nor time. I am the eternal feminine with its string of beads" (*I Love Myself* 154–155).

3. Hurston's tale seems almost egomaniacal, but as Ellease Southerland observes in response to the maternal grandmother's disapproval of her early "lies," all of Hurston's novels "show that nature did indeed speak to her" (21).

4. Robert Hemenway identifies this lover, who wished to remain anonymous, as a man of West Indian parentage whom Hurston first met in 1931 and whom she tried to part from a number of times before the affair finally ended. Hemenway notes that the prototype of Tea Cake was quite different from his fictional counterpart; he was a college student studying for the ministry and a cast member of Hurston's musical concert *The Great Day*. Admittedly impatient with her career, Hurston's lover was puzzled by her departure for the West Indies. According to Hemenway, "The man she was leaving remembers that outwardly she was calm and that he was left hurt and confused, wondering if she was 'crying on the inside.' She gave him her answer in *Their Eyes Were Watching God*" (231).

5. Gay Wilentz explores the correspondence between Hurst and Hurston, approximately twenty-five letters and postcards written between 1930 and 1949, in the Fanny Hurst Collection in the Harry Ransom Humanities Research Center at the University of Texas at Austin. From the correspondence, Wilentz concludes that, while Hurston often resented that some readers knew her only because she had worked for Hurst, the relationship between the two writers was "free of the more devastating aspects of the benefactor relationship" (27). Like Virginia Burke, however, Wilentz questions the extent to which Hurst ever really understood Hurston's motives as an African-American artist. Wilentz notes the irony of Hurst, a woman embarrassed by her own ethnic background, parading Hurston into hotels where Hurst herself might have been barred had the managers known that she was Jewish. Wilentz further observes that, like Peola in *Imitation of Life*, Hurst, who could also "pass," chose to deny "her own identity" even while "she was unable to comprehend that Hurston, by being herself, broke through barriers of race and sex" (40).

6. As Claudine Raynaud explains, "The advantage of this technique is to bring the reader back to the moment of enunciation and, thus, to restore the immediacy of the utterance, while the controlling presence of the narrator is still felt in the verb tenses and the pronouns" (118). Raynaud cites Norman Page's definition: "Free indirect speech contrives to present dialogue without the abdication of the narrator's role as the story-teller" (118–19).

7. Arna Bontemps takes a less charitable view in an early and still frequently cited review of *Dust Tracks*. Bontemps writes: "Miss Hurston deals very simply with the more serious aspects of Negro life in America—she ignores them. She has done right well by herself in the kind of world she found" (3).

8. Hurston's views of both Richard Wright and communism had been formulated well before the early fifties. In a review of Wright's *Uncle Tom's Children* (1938), a collection of stories, Hurston denounces those pieces in which "the reader sees the picture of the South that the Communists have been passing around of late. A dismal, hopeless section ruled by brutish hatred and nothing else. Mr. Wright's author's solution, is the solution of the PARTY—state responsibility for everything and individual responsibility for nothing, not even feeding one's self. And march!" ("Stories of Conflict" 32).

9. Elizabeth Fox-Genovese provides a somewhat overstated response to the dangers of Hurston's strident individualism: "For Hurston to admit the conditions or causes of her possible victimization is to belittle herself"; in her desire "to transcend the constraints of group identification . . . she comes close to insisting on being a self independent of body" ("My Statue, My Self" 82).

10. Hurston satirizes the notion of racial purity in "Cock Robin, Beale Street," a folktale she first published in the *Southern Literary Messenger*.

11. In their announcement of the award, the editors praised *Dust Tracks* as "an admirable autobiography revealing the flexibility, the sensitiveness, and the emotional color of the Negro race in America." They noted that the award had a "special timeliness" during a period of world war: "Racial relations intertwined with nationalism might almost be said to be the theme of this war and one of the major problems of the peace. . . . Nothing has more sharply emphasized the democratic problem which we inherited from slavery than the pressures of our present crisis and the obvious need of putting our own house in order before we talk too much of Americanism as a cultural and political success" ("1943 Anisfield Awards" 11). Ironically, this assessment echoes Hurston's own sentiments, but ones she had to omit for the book's initial publication.

12. Snelling writes, "Miss Zora Hurston has certain enviable gifts which few people now writing possess to such a degree. Her ability to transcribe intact the dialect and the colorful phrases of the Negro is seldom matched by writers of either race, and she has a flair for seeing the ridiculous and making the most of it in any situation. These talents would be invaluable as secondary attributes of a person who had a great deal to say and used them as aids in giving life and tempo to her story. But the author seems content again to write a book which scarcely rises above local color and tall tale" (163). Snelling's review is a clear indication of the difficulty Hurston posed not only for intellectuals on the left but even for the southern liberal critic who eagerly sought to promote the works of African-American authors.

13. The *American Mercury* editors followed Hurston's prediction with a passage from Walt Whitman's *Democratic Vistas*: "The eager and often inconsiderate appeals of reformers and revolutionists are indispensable to counterbal-

ance the inertness and fossilism making so large a part of human institutions." The "Clinical Notes" department, which contained observations on American prejudices, was one of the most popular sections of the magazine founded by H. L. Mencken and George Jean Nathan in 1924, a monthly periodical devoted to exposing and poking fun at the "fossilism" of the so-called American way of life. Though the magazine eventually wound up as an organ of the American right, when Hurston's pieces appeared in the early-to-midforties, it was still a prominent voice of American liberalism. See also "The 'Pet Negro' System" (May 1943), "High John De Conquer" (Oct. 1943), and "The Rise of the Begging Joints" (Mar. 1945).

14. For an insightful discussion of the Pepper/Smathers primary and its significance in the course of twentieth-century southern liberalism, see Robert Sherrill's chapter on Smathers in *Gothic Politics in the Deep South*, 146–88.

15. Melvin Dixon notes simply that the title defines Hurston's "preference for mobility" (85). Claudine Raynaud sees something more: "The sense of fullness which could be expected from a writer's retracing her journey to success is denied in the book's very title: The temporariness of the traces left on a road, the fleetingness of dust announce the silences and the voluntary omissions" (112). Francois Lionnet also stresses the title's suggestion of life's fleetingness; in writing her own life, Hurston discovers that "the discursive enterprise of self-portraiture is a process of collecting and gathering, of assembling images and metaphors to portray a figural self, always already caught in entropy and in permanent danger of returning to 'dust,' of becoming again 'part and parcel' of the universe" (115).

Works Cited

Aaron, Daniel. *Writers on the Left: Episodes in American Literary Communism.* New York: Harcourt, 1961.

Adams, Timothy Dow. *Telling Lies in Modern American Autobiography.* Chapel Hill: University of North Carolina Press, 1990.

Aiken, Conrad. *Ushant.* New York: Duell, Sloan and Pearce, 1952.

Andrews, William L. "In Search of a Common Identity: The Self and the South in Four Mississippi Autobiographies." *Southern Review* 24 (1988): 47–64.

Atkinson, Maxine P., and Jacqueline Boles. "Ladies: South by Northwest." In *Southern Women*, edited by Caroline Matheny Dillman, 127–40. New York: Hemispheric Publishing Corp., 1989.

———. "The Shaky Pedestal: Southern Ladies Yesterday and Today." *Southern Studies* 24 (1985): 398–406.

Avrich, Paul. *Sacco and Vanzetti: The Anarchist Background.* Princeton: Princeton University Press, 1991.

Benstock, Shari, ed. *The Private Self: Theory and Practice of Women's Autobiographical Writings.* Chapel Hill: University of North Carolina Press, 1988.

Berry, J. Bill, ed. *Located Lives: Place and Idea in Southern Autobiography.* Athens: University of Georgia Press, 1990.

Bevevino, Mary Margaret. "The Metamorphosis of Economic Disillusionment in Katherine Anne Porter's Society." Ph.D. dissertation, Pennsylvania State University, 1985.

Billson, Marcus. "The Memoir: New Perspectives on a Forgotten Genre." *Genre* 10.2 (1977): 259–82.

Blackburn, Regina. "In Search of the Black Female Self: African-American Women's Autobiographies and Ethnicity." In *Women's Autobiography: Essays in Criticism*, edited by Estelle Jelinek, 133–48. Bloomington: Indiana University Press, 1980.

Blackwell, Louise, and Frances Clay. *Lillian Smith.* New York: Twayne, 1971.

Bloom, Harold, ed. *Zora Neale Hurston: Modern Critical Views.* New York: Chelsea, 1986.

Bolsterli, Margaret Jones. "Reflections on Lillian Smith and the Guilts of the Betrayer." *Southern Quarterly* 27.4 (1989): 71–78.

Bontemps, Arna. "From Eatonville, Fla. to Harlem: Zora Hurston Has Always Had What It Takes, and Lots of It." Rev. of *Dust Tracks On a Road,* by Zora Neale Hurston. *New York Herald Tribune Books,* 22 Nov. 1942: 3.

Braden, Anne. "A Second Open Letter to Southern White Women." *Southern Exposure* 4.4 (1977): 50–53.

Bradford, M. E. *Generations of the Faithful Heart: On the Literature of the South.* La Salle, Ill.: Sherwood Sugden & Co., 1983.

Brockway, George P. " 'You Do It Because You Love Somebody.' " *Saturday Review* 22 Oct. 1966: 53–54.

Brookhart, Mary Hughes. "Reviews of *One Writer's Beginnings*: A Preliminary Checklist." *Eudora Welty Newsletter* 8.2 (1984): 1–4.

Bryer, Jackson R., ed. *Conversations with Lillian Hellman.* Jackson: University Press of Mississippi, 1986.

Buck, Pearl S. Rev. of *Killers of the Dream,* by Lillian Smith. *New York Post,* 23 Oct. 1949: n. p.

Buckley, William F., Jr. "*Scoundrel Time*: and Who is the Ugliest of Them All?" Rev. of *Scoundrel Time,* by Lillian Hellman. *National Review* 21 Jan. 1977: 101–6.

Burgher, Mary. "Images of Self and Race in the Autobiographies of Black Women." In *Sturdy Black Bridges: Visions of Black Women in Literature,* edited by Roseann P. Bell, Bettye J. Parker, and Beverly Guy-Sheftall, 107–22. Garden City, N.Y.: Anchor, 1979.

Burke, Virginia M. "Zora Neale Hurston and Fannie Hurst as They Saw Each Other." *CLA Journal* 20.4 (June 1977): 435–47.

Butterfield, Stephen. *Black Autobiography in America.* Amherst: University of Massachusetts Press, 1974.

Cabell, James Branch. *As I Remember It: Some Epilogues in Recollection.* New York: McBride, 1955.

Cahill, Susan, ed. *Women and Fiction: Short Stories by and about Women.* New York: New American Library, 1975.

Caldwell, Erskine. *With All My Might.* Atlanta: Peachtree Press, 1987.

Caperton, Helena L. " 'The Woman Within': The Autobiography of Ellen Glasgow." *Richmond Times-Dispatch,* 31 Oct. 1954: F6.

Carr, Virginia Spencer. *The Lonely Hunter: A Biography of Carson McCullers.* Garden City, N.Y.: Doubleday, 1975.

Cash, W. J. *The Mind of the South.* New York: Knopf, 1941.

Castille, Philip, and William Osborne, eds. *Southern Literature in Transition: Heritage and Promise.* Memphis: Memphis State University Press, 1983.

Ceplair, Larry, and Steven Englund. *The Inquisition in Hollywood: Politics and the Film Community, 1930–1960.* Garden City, N.Y.: Doubleday, 1980.

Chandler, Marilyn R. "Healing the Woman Within: Theraputic Aspects of Ellen Glasgow's Autobiography." In *Located Lives: Place and Idea in Southern Autobiography*, edited by J. Bill Berry, 78–92. Athens: University of Georgia Press, 1990.

Chubb, Thomas Caldecot. "The Retrial of Joan." Rev. of *The Retrial of Joan of Arc*, by Regine Pernod. Foreword by Katherine Anne Porter. *Saturday Review*, 19 Nov. 1955: 50.

Cixous, Hélène. "The Laugh of the Medusa." In *New French Feminisms*, edited by Elaine Marks and Isabella de Courtivron, 245–64. Amherst: University of Massachusetts Press, 1979.

Clayton, Jay, and Eric Rothstein. "Figures in the Corpus: Theories of Influence and Intertextuality." In *Influence and Intertextuality in Literary History*, edited by Jay Clayton and Eric Rothstein, 3–36. Madison: University of Wisconsin Press, 1991.

Coles, Robert. " 'Are You Now or Have You Ever Been . . .' " *Washington Post Book World*, 9 May 1976: 5.

Collins, Patricia Hill. "The Social Construction of Black Feminist Thought." *Signs* 14.4 (1989): 745–73.

Conkin, Paul. *The Southern Agrarians*. Knoxville: University of Tennessee Press, 1988.

Cook, David A. *A History of Narrative Film*. New York: Norton, 1981.

Core, George. "Lives Fugitive and Unwritten." In *Located Lives: Place and Idea in Southern Autobiography*, edited by J. Bill Berry, 52–65. Athens: University of Georgia Press, 1990.

Cowan, Louise. *The Fugitive Group: A Literary History*. Baton Rouge: Louisiana State University Press, 1959.

Cowley, Malcolm, ed. *The Portable Faulkner*. New York: Viking, 1946.

———. "Southways." Rev. of *Strange Fruit*, by Lillian Smith. *New Republic*, 6 Mar. 1944: 320, 322.

Crews, Frederick. "The Power of Flannery O'Connor," *New York Review of Books*, 26 Apr. 1990: 49–55.

Dance, Daryl C. "Zora Neale Hurston." In *American Women Writers: Bibliographical Essays*, edited by Maurice Duke, Jackson R. Bryer, and M. Thomas Inge, 321–51. Westport Conn.: Greenwood Press, 1983.

Daniell, Rosemary. *Fatal Flowers: On Sin, Sex, and Suicide in the Deep South*. New York: Holt, 1980.

Dawley, Alan. *Struggles for Justice: Social Responsibility and the Liberal State*. Cambridge: Harvard University Press, 1991.

De Beauvoir, Simone. *The Second Sex*. 1949. Translated by H. M. Parshley. New York: Vintage, 1989.

Deedy, John. "Sacco and Vanzetti." Rev. of *The Never-Ending Wrong*, by Katherine Anne Porter. *Commonweal*, 2 Sept. 1977: 571–72.

De Man, Paul. "Autobiography as De-facement." *Modern Language Notes: Comparative Literature* 94.5 (1979): 919–30.

Devlin, Albert J. *Welty: A Life in Literature.* Jackson: University Press of Mississippi, 1987.

DeVoto, Bernard. "The Decision in the *Strange Fruit* Case: The Obscenity Statute in Massachusetts." *New England Quarterly* 19 (1946): 147–83.

Dillman, Caroline Matheny. "The Sparsity of Research and Publications on Southern Women: Definitional Complexities, Methodological Problems, and Other Impediments." In *Southern Women,* edited by Caroline Matheny Dillman, 1–18. New York: Hemispheric Publishing Corp., 1989.

Dixon, Melvin. *Ride Out the Wilderness: Geography and Identity in Afro-American Literature.* Urbana: University of Illinois Press, 1987.

Doherty, Thomas P. "American Autobiography and Ideology." In *The American Autobiography: A Collection of Critical Essays,* edited by Albert E. Stone, 95–108. Englewood Cliffs: Printice-Hall, 1981.

Drake, Robert. "Three Southern Ladies." *Flannery O'Connor Bulletin* 9 (1980): 41–48.

Duke, Maurice, Jackson R. Bryer, and M. Thomas Inge, eds. *American Women Writers: Bibliographical Essays.* Westport, Conn.: Greenwood Press, 1983.

Dunbar, Leslie W. " 'A Southerner Confronting the South.' " Rev. of *Lillian Smith: A Southerner Confronting the South,* by Anne C. Loveland. *Virginia Quarterly Review* 64.2 (1988): 202–14.

Eakin, Paul John. *Fictions in Autobiography: Studies in the Art of Self-Invention.* Princeton: Princeton University Press, 1985.

Edel, Leon. "Miss Glasgow's Private World." Rev. of *The Woman Within,* by Ellen Glasgow. *New Republic,* 15 Nov. 1954: 20–21.

Evans, Sara M. "Myth Against History: The Case of Southern Womanhood." In *Myth and Southern History,* edited by Patrick Gerster and Nicholas Cords, 2: 149–54. 2nd ed. 2 vols. Urbana: University of Illinois Press, 1989.

———. *Personal Politics: The Roots of Women's Liberation in the Civil Rights Movement and the New Left.* New York: Knopf, 1979.

Falk, Doris V. *Lillian Hellman.* New York: Ungar, 1978.

Feuerlicht, Roberta Strauss. *Justice Crucified: The Story of Sacco and Vanzetti.* New York: McGraw-Hill, 1977.

Fiedler, Leslie A. "Decency Is Not Enough." Rev. of *One Hour,* by Lillian Smith. *New Republic,* 4 Jan. 1960: 15–16.

———. *Love and Death in the American Novel.* Rev. ed. New York: Stein and Day, 1966.

Fludas, John. Rev. of *The Never-Ending Wrong,* by Katherine Anne Porter. *Saturday Review,* 3 Sept. 1977: 32.

Fox-Genovese, Elizabeth. "Between Individualism and Community: Autobiographies of Southern Women." In *Located Lives: Place and Idea in Southern Autobiography,* edited by J. Bill Berry, 20–38. Athens: University of Georgia Press, 1990.

———. *Feminism Without Illusions: A Critique of Individualism.* Chapel Hill: University of North Carolina Press, 1991.

———. *Within the Plantation Household: Black and White Women of the Old South.* Chapel Hill: University of North Carolina Press, 1988.

———. "My Statue, My Self: Autobiographical Writings of Afro-American Women." In *The Private Self: Theory and Practice of Women's Autobiographical Writings,* edited by Shari Benstock, 63–89. Chapel Hill: University of North Carolina Press, 1988.

Freemantle, Anne. "The Pursuit of Unhappiness." Rev. of *The Woman Within,* by Ellen Glasgow. *Commonweal,* 19 Nov. 1954: 194–95.

Fried, Richard M. *Nightmare in Red: The McCarthy Era in Perspective.* New York: Oxford University Press, 1990.

Friedman, Susan Stanford. "Women's Autobiographical Selves: Theory and Practice." In *The Private Self: Theory and Practice of Women's Autobiographical Writings,* edited by Shari Benstock, 34–62. Chapel Hill: University of North Carolina Press, 1988.

Gates, Henry Louis, Jr. " 'A Negro Way of Saying.' " Rev. of *Dust Tracks on a Road* and *Moses: Man of the Mountain,* by Zora Neale Hurston. *New York Times Book Review,* 21 Apr. 1985: 1, 43, 45.

Gellhorn, Martha, Laura (Riding) Jackson, and Stephen Spender. "Guerre de Plume." *Paris Review* 79 (1981): 280–307.

Givner, Joan, ed. *Katherine Anne Porter: Conversations.* Jackson: University Press of Mississippi, 1987.

———. *Katherine Anne Porter: A Life.* Rev. ed. Athens: University of Georgia Press, 1991.

Gladney, Margaret Rose. "A Chain Reaction of Dreams: Lillian Smith and Laurel Falls Camp." *Journal of American Culture* 5.3 (1982): 50–55.

Glasgow, Ellen. *A Certain Measure: An Interpretation of Prose Fiction.* New York: Harcourt, 1943.

———. *Ellen Glasgow's Reasonable Doubts: A Collection of Her Writings.* Edited by Julius Rowan Raper. Baton Rouge: Louisiana State University Press, 1988.

———. "Feminism: A Definition." *Good Housekeeping* 58 (May 1914): 683.

———. *The Letters of Ellen Glasgow.* Edited by Blair Rouse. New York: Harcourt, 1958.

———. *The Woman Within: An Autobiography.* New York: Harcourt, 1954.

Glazer, Nathan. "An Answer to Lillian Hellman." *Commentary* 61 (June 1976): 36–39.

Godbold, E. Stanly, Jr. *Ellen Glasgow and the Woman Within.* Baton Rouge: Louisiana State University Press, 1972.

Goldfield, David R. *Black, White, and Southern: Race Relations and Southern Culture, 1940 to the Present.* Baton Rouge: Louisiana State University Press, 1990.

Goodman, Susan. "Competing Visions of Freud in the Memoirs of Ellen Glasgow and Edith Wharton." *Colby Quarterly* 25 (1989): 218–26.

Gray, Richard. *The Literature of Memory: Modern Writers of the American South.* Baltimore: Johns Hopkins University Press, 1977.

————. *Writing the South: Ideas of an American Region.* New York: Cambridge University Press, 1986.

Greene, Jack, ed. *Encyclopedia of American Political Thought: Studies of the Principal Movements and Ideas.* 3 vols. New York: Scribner's, 1984.

Gretlund, Jan Nordby, "Flannery O'Connor and Katherine Anne Porter," *Flannery O'Connor Bulletin* 8 (1979): 77–87.

Grigsby, John L. "The Poisonous Snake in the Garden: Racism in the Agrarian Movement." *CLA Journal* 34.1 (1990): 32–43.

Grossman, Anita Susan. "Art versus Truth in Autobiography: The Case of Lillian Hellman." *CLIO* 14.3 (1985): 289–303.

Hartt, Susan L. "Hellman Recalls the 'Scoundrel Time.' " Rev. of *Scoundrel Time*, by Lillian Hellman. *Miami Herald*, 16 May 1976: E7.

Heilbrun, Carolyn G. "Women's Autobiographical Writings: New Forms." *Prose Studies* 8.2 (1985): 14–28.

————. *Writing a Woman's Life.* New York: Norton, 1988.

Hellman, Lillian. *The Collected Plays.* Boston: Little, Brown, 1972.

————. *Maybe.* Boston: Little, Brown, 1980.

————. *Pentimento: A Book of Portraits.* Boston: Little, Brown, 1973.

————. *Scoundrel Time.* Introduction by Gary Wills. Boston: Little, Brown, 1976.

————. *Three.* Boston: Little, Brown, 1979.

————. *An Unfinished Woman: A Memoir.* Boston: Little, Brown, 1969.

Hemenway, Robert E. *Zora Neale Hurston: A Literary Biography.* Urbana: University of Illinois Press, 1977.

Hendrick, Willene, and George Hendrick. *Katherine Anne Porter.* Rev. ed. Boston: Twayne, 1988.

Hobson, Fred. *Tell About the South: The Southern Rage to Explain.* Baton Rouge: Louisiana State University Press, 1983.

Hoffman, Frederick. *The Twenties: American Writing in the Postwar Decade.* Rev. ed. New York: Free Press, 1962.

Holditch, Kenneth W. "Another Part of the Country: Lillian Hellman as Southern Playwright." *Southern Quarterly* 25.3 (1987): 11–35.

Holloway, Karla F. C. *The Character of the Word: The Texts of Zora Neale Hurston.* Westport, Conn.: Greenwood Press, 1987.

Holman, Hugh. "No More Monoliths, Please: Continuities in the Multi-Souths." In *Southern Literature in Transition: Heritage and Promise*, edited by Philip Castille and William Osborne, xiii–xxiv. Memphis: Memphis State University Press, 1983.

Hook, Sidney. "Lillian Hellman's Scoundrel Time." Rev. of *Scoundrel Time*, by Lillian Hellman. *Encounter* 48 (Feb. 1977): 82–91.

Horowitz, Irving L., ed. *The Anarchists.* New York: Dell, 1964.

Howard, Maureen. "Scoundrel Time." Rev. of *Scoundrel Time*, by Lillian Hellman. *New York Times Book Review*, 25 Apr. 1976: 1–2.

————, ed. *Seven American Women Writers of the Twentieth-Century.* Minneapolis: University of Minnesota Press, 1977.

Howarth, William. "Writing Upside Down: Voice and Place in Southern Autobiography." In *Located Lives: Place and Idea in Southern Autobiography*, edited by J. Bill Berry, 3–19. Athens: University of Georgia Press, 1990.

Howe, Irving. "Lillian Hellman and the McCarthy Years." Rev. of *Scoundrel Time*, by Lillian Hellman. *Dissent* 23 (Fall 1976): 378–82.

Hughes, Langston. *The Big Sea*. 1940. New York: Hill and Wang, 1963.

Huie, William Bradford. *Ruby McCollum: Woman in the Suwannee Jail*. New York: Dutton, 1956.

Hurst, Fannie. "Zora Neale Hurston: A Personality Sketch." *Yale University Library Gazette* 35.1 (July 1940): 17–22.

Hurston, Zora Neale. "Cock Robin, Beale Street." *Southern Literary Messenger* 3 (July 1941): 321–3.

———. "Crazy for This Democracy." *Negro Digest* 4 (Dec. 1945): 45–48. Reprinted in *I Love Myself* 165–68.

———. *Dust Tracks on a Road*. 1942. Edited by Robert E. Hemenway. Urbana: University of Illinois Press, 1984.

———. "Fannie Hurst." *Saturday Review of Literature*, 9 Oct. 1937: 15–16.

———. "High John De Conquer." *American Mercury* 57 (Oct. 1943): 450–58.

———. "How It Feels to Be Colored Me." *World Tomorrow* 11 (May 1928): 215–16. Reprinted in *I Love Myself* 152–55.

———. *I Love Myself When I Am Laughing . . . And Then Again When I Am Looking Mean and Impressive: A Zora Neale Hurston Reader*. Edited by Alice Walker. New York: Feminist Press, 1979.

———. "I Saw Negro Votes Peddled." *American Legion Magazine* 49 (Nov. 1950): 12–13, 54–57, 59–60.

———. "The Last Slave Ship." *American Mercury* 58 (Mar. 1944): 351–58.

———. "Lawrence of the River." *Saturday Evening Post*, 5 Sept. 1942: 18, 55–57.

———. "The Life Story of Mrs. Ruby McCollum." *Pittsburgh Courier*, 28 Feb. 1953: 3.

———. "My Most Humiliating Jim Crow Experience." *Negro Digest* 2 (June 1944): 25–26. Reprinted in *I Love Myself* 163–64.

———. "A Negro Voter Sizes Up Taft." *Saturday Evening Post*, 8 Dec. 1951: 29, 150–52.

———. "Negroes Without Self-Pity." *American Mercury* 57 (Oct. 1943): 601–03.

———. "The 'Pet Negro' System." *American Mercury* 56 (May 1943): 450–58. Reprinted in *I Love Myself* 156–62.

———. "The Rise of the Begging Joints." *American Mercury* 60 (Mar. 1945): 288–94.

———. "Stories of Conflict." Rev. of *Uncle Tom's Children*, by Richard Wright. *Saturday Review of Literature*, 2 Apr. 1938: 32.

———. *Their Eyes Were Watching God*. 1937. Urbana: University of Illinois Press, 1978.

————. "What White Publishers Won't Print." *Negro Digest* 8 (Apr. 1940): 85–89. Reprinted in *I Love Myself* 169–73.

————. "Why the Negro Won't Buy Communism." *American Legion Magazine* 50 (June 1951): 14–15, 55–60.

Inge, Tonette Bond, ed. *Southern Women Writers: The New Generation.* Tuscaloosa: University of Alabama Press, 1990.

Jefferson, Margo. "Self Made: Katherine Anne Porter." *Grand Street* 2.4 (1983): 152–71.

Jelinek, Estelle. *The Tradition of Women's Autobiography: From Antiquity to the Present.* Boston: Twayne, 1986.

————, ed. *Women's Autobiography: Essays in Criticism.* Bloomington: Indiana University Press, 1980.

Johnson, Paul. *Intellectuals.* London: Weidenfeld and Nicolson, 1988.

Jones, Anne Goodwyn. "Faulkner's Daughters: Women of the Southern Literary Renaissance." Address to the Organization of American Historians. Los Angeles, 7 April 1984.

————. "Southern Literary Women as Chroniclers of Southern Life." In *Sex, Race, and the Role of Women in the South*, edited by Joanne V. Woodward and Sheila L. Skemp, 75–93. Jackson: University Press of Mississippi, 1983.

————. *Tomorrow Is Another Day: The Woman Writer in the South, 1859–1936.* Baton Rouge: Louisiana State University Press, 1981.

Jordan, June. "On Richard Wright and Zora Neale Hurston: Notes Toward a Balancing of Love and Hatred." *Black World* 23 (Aug. 1974): 4–8.

Kael, Pauline. "A Woman for All Seasons?" Rev. of *Julia.* Directed by Fred Zinnemann. *When the Lights Go Down.* New York: Holt, 1980. 304–10.

Kaplan, Sydney Janet. "Varieties of Feminist Criticism." In *Making a Difference: Feminist Literary Criticism*, edited by Gayle Greene and Coppelia Kahn, 37–58. New York: Methuen, 1985.

Kaufman, Marjorie. "Glasgow, Ellen Anderson." In *Notable American Women, 1607–1950*, edited by Edward T. James, 44–49. Cambridge, Mass.: Belknap, 1971.

Kazin, Alfred. "The Legend of Lillian Hellman." *Esquire* 88 (Aug. 1977): 28–29, 34.

————. "The Lost Rebel." Rev. of *The Woman Within*, by Ellen Glasgow. *New Yorker*, 30 Oct. 1954: 133–35.

Kempton, Murray. "Witnesses." Rev. of *Scoundrel Time*, by Lillian Hellman. *New York Review of Books*, 10 June 1976: 22–25.

Kilson, Marion. "The Transformation of Eatonville's Ethnographer." *Phylon* Second Quarter (Summer 1972): 112–19.

King, Grace. *Memories of a Southern Woman of Letters.* New York: Macmillan, 1932.

King, Richard H. "Politics and Literature: The Southern Case." *Virginia Quarterly Review* 64.2 (1988): 189–201.

————. "The South and Cultural Criticism." *American Literary History* 1.3 (1989): 699–714.

————. *A Southern Renaissance: The Cultural Awakening of the American South. 1930–1955.* New York: Oxford University Press, 1980.

Knowles, A. S. "Six Bronze Petals and Two Red: Carson McCullers in the Forties." In *The Forties: Fiction, Poetry, Drama,* edited by Warren French, 87–98. Deland, Fla.: Everett/Edwards, 1969.

Kramer, Victor A. "Memoirs of Self-Indictment: The Solitude of Tennessee Williams." In *Tennessee Williams: A Tribute,* edited by Jack Thorpe, 663–75. Jackson: University Press of Mississippi, 1977.

Kreyling, Michael. "Southern Literature: Consensus and Dissensus." *American Literature,* 60.1 (1988): 83–95.

————. "Subject and Object in *One Writer's Beginnings.*" In *Welty: A Life in Literature,* edited by Albert J. Devlin, 212–24. Jackson: University Press of Mississippi, 1987.

———"Words into Criticism: Eudora Welty's Essays and Reviews." In *Eudora Welty: Thirteen Essays,* edited by Peggy Whitman Prenshaw, 224–35. Jackson: University Press of Mississippi, 1983.

Kutler, Stanley I. *The American Inquisition: Justice and Injustice in the Cold War.* New York: Hill and Wang, 1982.

Kymlicka, Will. "Liberalism and Communitarianism." *Canadian Journal of Philosophy* 18.2 (1988): 181–204.

Langer, Elinor. *Josephine Herbst.* Boston: Little, Brown, 1984.

Lauter, Paul. "Race and Gender in the Shaping of the American Literary Canon: A Case Study from the Twenties." *Feminist Studies* 9.3 (1983): 335–63.

League of American Writers. *Writers Take Sides: Letters about the War in Spain from 418 American Authors.* New York: League of American Writers, 1938.

Lionnet, Francois. *Autobiographical Voices: Race, Gender, and Self-Portraiture.* Ithaca: Cornell University Press, 1989.

Long, Margaret. "Lillian Smith: A Match for Old Screamer." *The Progressive* 29 (Feb. 1965): 35–38.

Lopez, Enrique Hank. *Conversations with Katherine Anne Porter: Refugee from Indian Creek.* Boston: Little, Brown, 1981.

Loveland, Anne C. *Lillian Smith: A Southerner Confronting the South.* Baton Rouge: Louisiana State University Press, 1987.

Lyons, John O. *The Invention of the Self: The Hinge of Consciousness in the Eighteenth Century.* Carbondale: Southern Illinois University Press, 1978.

McCracken, Samuel. "'Julia' and Other Fictions by Lillian Hellman." *Commentary* 77 (June 1984): 35–43.

McCullers, Carson. *The Mortgaged Heart.* Edited by Margarita G. Smith. Boston: Houghton Mifflin, 1971.

MacDonald, Edgar E. "Ellen Glasgow." In *American Women Writers: Bibliographical Essays,* edited by Maurice Duke, Jackson R. Bryer, and M. Thomas Inge, 168–200. Westport, Conn.: Greenwood Press, 1983.

————. "The Glasgow-Cabell Entente." *American Literature* 41.1 (1969): 76–91.

McDonald, Forrest. "Conservatism." In *Encyclopedia of American Political Thought: Studies of the Principal Movements and Ideas*, edited by Jack Greene, I: 354–66. 3 vols. New York: Scribner's, 1984.

McDowell, Frederick P. W. "Ellen Glasgow." *American Novelists, 1910–1945*. Vol. 9 of *Dictionary of Literary Biography*, 44–65. Detroit: Gale, 1981.

McGill, Ralph. *The South and the Southerner*. Boston: Little, Brown, 1963.

McKay, Nellie. "Race, Gender, and Cultural Context in Zora Neale Hurston's *Dust Tracks on a Road*." In *Life Lines: Theorizing Women's Autobiography*, edited by Bella Brodzki and Celeste Schenck, 175–88. Ithaca: Cornell University Press, 1988.

McLaurin, Melton. "Southern Autobiography and the Problem of Race." In *Looking South: Chapters in the Story of an American Region*, edited by Winfred B. Moore and Joseph F. Tripp, 65–76. Westport, Conn.: Greenwood Press, 1989.

McWilliams, Carey. "Time Is the Scoundrel." *The Nation*, 19 June 1976: 741–42.

Manning, Carol S. "Little Girls and Sidewalks: Glasgow and Welty on Childhood's Promise." *Southern Quarterly* 21 (1983): 67–76.

Marcus, Greil. "Undercover: Remembering the Witch Hunts." Rev. of *Scoundrel Time*, by Lillian Hellman. *Rolling Stone*, 20 May 1976: 97.

Mason, Mary G. "The Other Voice: Autobiographies of Women Writers." In *Autobiography: Essays Theoretical and Critical*, edited by James Olney, 207–35. Princeton: Princeton University Press, 1980.

——, and Carol Hurd Green, eds. *Journeys: Autobiographical Writings by Women*. Boston: G. K. Hall, 1979.

Matthews, Pamela Rae. "'Two Women Blended': Ellen Glasgow and Her Fictions." Ph.D. dissertation, Duke University, 1988.

Mazlish, Bruce. "Autobiography and Psycho-Analysis: Between Truth and Self-Deception." *Encounter* 35 (Oct. 1970): 28–37.

"Meeting Goer." *Time*, 2 June 1952: 74.

Mellard, James. "The Fiction of Social Commitment." In *The History of Southern Literature*, edited by Louis D. Rubin, Jr., et al., 351–55. Baton Rouge: Louisiana State University Press, 1985.

Mencken, H. L. "The Sahara of the Bozart." *Prejudices, Second Series*. New York: Knopf, 1920.

Miller, Kathleen Atkinson. "Out of the Chrysalis: Lillian Smith and the Transformation of the South." Ph.D. dissertation, Emory University, 1984.

Mollnow, Fran. "Lillian Smith's Memory of a Large Life." *Florida Times-Union Sunday Magazine*, 6 Jan. 1963: 6–7.

Myrdal, Gunnar. *An American Dilemma: The Negro Problem and Modern Democracy*. New York: Harper & Row, 1944.

Navasky, Victor S. *Naming Names*. New York: Viking, 1980.

Neal, Larry. "A Profile: Zora Neale Hurston." *Southern Exposure* 1.3–4 (Winter 1974): 160–68.

Newman, Robert P. *The Cold War Romance of Lillian Hellman and John Melby.* Chapel Hill: University of North Carolina Press, 1989.

Nin, Anais. "The Personal Life Deeply Lived." In *A Woman Speaks: The Lectures, Seminars, and Interviews of Anais Nin,* edited by Evelyn J. Hinz, 153–62. Chicago: Swallow Press, 1975.

O'Brien, Michael. *The Idea of the American South, 1920–1941.* Baltimore: Johns Hopkins University Press, 1979.

————. *Rethinking the South: Essays in Intellectual History.* Baltimore: Johns Hopkins University Press, 1988.

O'Connor, Flannery. *The Habit of Being.* Edited by Sally Fitzgerald. New York: Farrar, 1979.

————. *The Presence of Grace and Other Book Reviews.* Compiled by Leo J. Zuber. Edited by Carter W. Martin. Athens: University of Georgia Press, 1983.

Okin, Susan Moller. "Humanist Liberalism." In *Liberalism and the Moral Life,* edited by Nancy L. Rosenblum, 39–53. Cambridge: Harvard University Press, 1989.

Olney, James. "Autobiographical Traditions Black and White." In *Located Lives: Place and Idea in Southern Autobiography,* edited by J. Bill Berry, 66–77. Athens: University of Georgia Press, 1990.

————, ed. *Autobiography: Essays Theoretical and Critical.* Princeton: Princeton University Press, 1980.

Parker, Rozsika, and Griselda Pollock. *Old Mistresses: Women, Art, and Ideology.* New York: Pantheon, 1981.

Pells, Richard. *The Liberal Mind in a Conservative Age: American Intellectuals in the 1940s and 1950s.* New York: Harper, 1985.

Percy, Walker. *Sign-Posts in a Strange Land.* Edited by Patrick Samway. New York: Farrar, 1991.

Phillips, William. "What Happened in the Fifties." *Partisan Review* 43.3 (1976): 337–40.

Plant, Deborah G. "Zora Neale Hurston's *Dust Tracks on a Road*: Black Autobiography in a Different Voice." Ph.D. dissertation, University of Nebraska—Lincoln, 1988.

Porter, Katherine Anne. *The Collected Essays and Occasional Writings of Katherine Anne Porter.* New York: Delacorte Press, 1970.

————. *The Collected Stories of Katherine Anne Porter.* Introduction by Elizabeth Hardwick. 1964. London: Virago, 1985.

————. *The Days Before.* New York: Harcourt, 1952.

————. Foreword. *The Retrial of Joan of Arc,* by Regine Pernoud. Translated by Joseph Cohen. New York: Harcourt, 1955.

————. *Letters of Katherine Anne Porter.* Edited by Isabel Bayley. New York: Atlantic, 1990.

————. *The Never-Ending Wrong.* Boston: Little, Brown, 1977.

————. *Outline of Mexican Popular Arts and Crafts.* Los Angeles: Young and McCallister, 1922.

Pratt, Annis. "Women and Nature in Modern Fiction." *Contemporary Literature* 13.1 (1972): 476–90.

Prenshaw, Peggy Whitman. "The Antiphonies of Eudora Welty's *One Writer's Beginnings* and Elizabeth Bowen's *Pictures and Conversations*." In *Welty: A Life in Literature*, edited by Albert J. Devlin, 225–37. Jackson: University Press of Mississippi, 1987.

———, ed. *Conversations with Eudora Welty*. Jackson: University Press of Mississippi, 1984.

———, ed. *Eudora Welty: Thirteen Essays*. Jackson: University Press of Mississippi, 1983.

Prescott, Orville. "Books of the Times." Rev. of *The Woman Within*, by Ellen Glasgow. *New York Times*, 1 Nov. 1954: 25.

Ransom, John Crowe, et al. *I'll Take My Stand: The South and the Agrarian Tradition*. 1930. Introduction by Louis D. Rubin, Jr. Baton Rouge: Louisiana State University Press, 1977.

Raper, Julius Rowan. *Without Shelter: The Early Career of Ellen Glasgow*. Baton Rouge: Louisiana State University Press, 1971.

Raynaud, Claudine. "Autobiography as a 'Lying' Session: Zora Neale Hurston's *Dust Tracks on a Road*." In *Studies in Black American Literature*, edited by Joe Weixlmann and Huston A. Baker, Jr., 111–38. Vol. III of *Black Feminist Criticism and Critical Theory*. Greenville, Fla: Penkevill, 1988.

Rayson, Ann L. "*Dust Tracks on a Road*: Zora Neale Hurston and the Form of Black Autobiography." *Negro American Literature Forum* 7.2 (Summer 1973): 39–45.

Reeves, Thomas C. *The Life and Times of Joe McCarthy*. New York: Stein and Day, 1982.

Rev. of *Dust Tracks on a Road*, by Zora Neale Hurston. *New Yorker*, 14 Nov. 1942: 71.

Ribblett, David L. "From Cross Creek to Richmond: Marjorie Kinnan Rawlings Researches Ellen Glasgow." *Virginia Cavalcade* 36.1 (1986): 4–15.

Rich, Adrienne. *Blood, Bread, and Poetry: Selected Prose, 1979–1985*. New York: Norton, 1986.

———. *Of Woman Born: Motherhood as Experience and Institution*. New York: Norton, 1976.

Robinson, Jo Ann. "Lillian Smith: Reflections on Race and Sex." *Southern Exposure* 4.4 (1977): 43–48.

Rollyson, Carl E. *Lillian Hellman: Her Legend and Her Legacy*. New York: St. Martin's, 1988.

Rosenblum, Nancy L., ed. *Liberalism and the Moral Life*. Cambridge: Harvard University Press, 1989.

Ross, Dorothy. "Liberalism." In *Encyclopedia of American Political Thought: Studies of the Principal Movements and Ideas*, edited by Jack Greene, II: 750–63. 3 vols. New York: Scribner's, 1984.

Rubin, Louis D., Jr. "Robert Penn Warren: Critic." In *A Southern Renaissance*

Man: Views of Robert Penn Warren, edited by Walter B. Edgar, 19–37. Baton Rouge: Louisiana State University Press, 1984.

——, et al., eds. *The History of Southern Literature*. Baton Rouge: Louisiana State University Press, 1985.

——, and Hugh Holman, eds. *Southern Literary Study: Problems and Possibilities*. Chapel Hill: University of North Carolina Press, 1975.

——, and Robert D. Jacobs, eds. *South: Modern Literature in Its Cultural Setting*. Garden City, N.Y.: Doubleday, 1961.

——, and Robert D. Jacobs, eds. *Southern Renascence: The Literature of the Modern South*. Baltimore: Johns Hopkins University Press, 1953.

Russell, Bertrand. *A History of Western Philosophy*. New York: Simon and Schuster, 1945.

Schaub, Thomas Hill. *American Fiction in the Cold War*. Madison: University of Wisconsin Press, 1991.

Schmidt, Peter. *The Heart of the Story: Eudora Welty's Short Fiction*. Jackson: University Press of Mississippi, 1991.

Schwartz, Edward G. "The Way of Dissent: Katherine Anne Porter's Critical Position." *Western Humanities Review* 8 (1954): 119–30.

Schwartz, Lawrence H. *Creating Faulkner's Reputation: The Politics of Modern Literary Criticism*. Knoxville: University of Tennessee Press, 1988.

Scott, Anne Firor. *The Southern Lady: From Pedestal to Politics, 1830–1930*. Chicago: University of Chicago Press, 1970.

Shapiro, Stephen A. "The Dark Continent of Literature: Autobiography." *Comparative Literature Studies* 5 (1968): 421–52.

Sherman, Beatrice. "Zora Hurston's Story." Rev. of *Dust Tracks on a Road*, by Zora Neale Hurston. *New York Times Book Review*, 29 Nov. 1942: 44.

Sherrill, Robert. *Gothic Politics in the Deep South*. New York: Ballantine, 1968.

——. "Wisdom and Its Price." Rev. of *Scoundrel Time*, by Lillian Hellman. *The Nation*, 19 June 1976: 757–58.

Simpson, Lewis P. "The Southern Recovery of Memory and History." *Sewanee Review* 82.1 (1974): 1–32.

Singal, Daniel Joseph. *The War Within: From Victorian to Modernist Thought in the South, 1919–1945*. Chapel Hill: University of North Carolina Press, 1982.

Smith, Lillian. "Addressed to White Liberals." *New Republic*, 18 Sept. 1944: 331–33.

——. "A Declaration of Faith in America." *New York Times Magazine*, 21 Sept. 1952: 13, 39, 41–42.

——. "Growing Plays: The Girl." *Educational Leadership* 2 (1945): 349–60.

——. *The Journey*. Cleveland: World Publishing Co., 1954.

——. *Killers of the Dream*. New York: Norton, 1949; rev. ed., 1961.

——. *Memory of a Large Christmas*. New York: Norton, 1962.

——. "Novelists Need a Commitment." *Saturday Review* 24 Dec. 1960: 18–19.

——. *Now Is the Time*. New York: Viking, 1955.

————. *One Hour.* New York: Harcourt, 1959.

————. *Our Faces, Our Words.* New York: Norton, 1964.

————. "Pay Day in Georgia." *The Nation,* 1 Feb. 1947: 118–19.

————. "Personal History of *Strange Fruit*: A Statement of Purposes and Intentions." *Saturday Review of Literature* 17 Feb. 1945: 9–10.

————. *Strange Fruit.* New York: Renyal & Hitchcock, 1944.

————. "Why I Wrote 'Killers of the Dream.' " *New York Herald Tribune Weekly Book Review,* 17 July 1949: 2.

————. *The Winner Names the Age: A Collection of Writings by Lillian Smith.* Edited by Michelle Cliff. Preface by Paula Snelling. New York: Norton, 1978.

Smith, Sidonie. *A Poetics of Women's Autobiography: Marginality and the Fictions of Self-Representation.* Bloomington: Indiana University Press, 1987.

Snelling, Paula. "Signposts Along the Way." Rev. of *Their Eyes Were Watching God,* by Zora Neale Hurston. In *From the Mountain: An Anthology of the Magazine Successively Titled "Psuedopodia," the "North Georgia Review," and "South Today,"* edited by Helen White and Redding S. Sugg, Jr., 163–64. Memphis: Memphis State University Press, 1972.

Sosna, Morton. *In Search of the Silent South: Southern Liberals and the Race Issue.* New York: Columbia University Press, 1977.

Southerland, Ellease. "Zora Neale Hurston: The Novelist-Anthropologist's Life/Works." *Black World* 23 (Aug. 1974): 20–30.

Spacks, Patricia Meyer. "Reflecting Women." *Yale Review* 63 (1973): 26–42.

————. "Selves in Hiding." In *Women's Autobiography: Essays in Criticism,* edited by Estelle Jelinek, 112–32. Bloomington: Indiana University Press, 1980.

————. "Women's Stories, Women's Selves." *Hudson Review* 30 (1977): 29–46.

Spivey, Ted. "Flannery O'Connor, the New Critics, and Deconstruction." *Southern Review* 23.2 (1987): 271–80.

Stanton, Domna C., "Autogynography: Is the Subject Different?' In *The Female Autograph,* edited by Domna C. Stanton, 5–22. New York: New York Literary Forum, 1981.

Starr, Roger. "Sacco and Vanzetti." Rev. of *The Never-Ending Wrong,* by Katherine Anne Porter. *Commentary* 64 (Dec. 1977): 95–96.

Sugg, Redding S., Jr. "Lillian Smith and the Condition of Women." *South Atlantic Quarterly* 71 (1972): 155–64.

Sullivan, Margaret. "Lillian Smith: The Public Image and the Personal Vision." *Mad River Review* 2.3 (1967): 3–21.

Sullivan, Walter. *A Requiem for the Renascence: The State of Fiction in the Modern South.* Athens: University of Georgia Press, 1976.

Symons, Julian. "Injustice Department." Rev. of *The Never-Ending Wrong,* by Katherine Anne Porter. *Times Literary Supplement,* 17 Feb. 1978: 198.

Tate, Allen. *Essays of Four Decades.* Chicago: Swallow Press; 1968.

————, ed. *A Southern Vanguard.* New York: Prentice-Hall, 1947.

Tate, Linda. "Southern Women's Fiction, 1980–1990: Traditions and Revisions." Ph.D. dissertation, University of Wisconsin—Madison, 1991.

Teilhard de Chardin, Pierre. *The Phenomenon of Man.* Translated by Bernard Wall. 1955. New York: Harper and Row, 1959.

Trilling, Diana. "Fiction in Review." Rev. of *Strange Fruit,* by Lillian Smith. *The Nation,* 18 Mar. 1944: 342.

————. *We Must March My Darlings: A Critical Decade.* New York: Harcourt, 1977.

Tucker, Susan. "The Black Domestic in the South: Her Legacy as Mother and Mother Surrogate." In *Southern Women,* edited by Caroline Matheny Dillman, 93–102. New York: Hemispheric Publishing Corp., 1989.

Unrue, Darlene Harbour. *Truth and Vision in Katherine Anne Porter's Fiction.* Athens: University of Georgia Press, 1985.

Vande Kieft, Ruth M. "Eudora Welty and the Right to Privacy." *Mississippi Quarterly* 43.4 (1990): 475–84.

————. "Looking with Eudora Welty." In *Eudora Welty: Thirteen Essays,* edited by Peggy Whitman Prenshaw, 236–57. Jackson: University Press of Mississippi, 1985.

Voss, Norine. " 'Saying the Unsayable': An Introduction to Women's Autobiography." In *Gender Studies: New Directions in Feminist Criticism,* edited by Judith Spector, 218–31. Bowling Green, Ohio: Bowling Green Sate University Popular Press, 1986.

Wagner-Martin, Linda W. *Ellen Glasgow: Beyond Convention.* Austin: University of Texas Press, 1982.

————. "Lillian Hellman: Autobiography and Truth." *Southern Review* 19.2 (1983): 275–88.

Walker, Alice, ed. *I Love Myself When I Am Laughing . . . And then Again When I Am Looking Mean and Impressive: A Zora Neale Hurston Reader.* New York: Feminist Press, 1979.

Warren, Robert Penn. Introduction. *The Collected Stories of Conrad Aiken.* New York: Schocken Books, 1982.

Washington, Mary Helen. "Zora Neale Hurston: A Woman Half in Shadow." In *I Love Myself,* edited by Alice Walker, 7–24. New York: Feminist Press, 1979.

Waters, Pat. *Down to Now: Reflections on the Southern Civil Rights Movement.* New York: Pantheon, 1971.

Watson, Ritchie D. "The Ellen Glasgow-Allen Tate Correspondence: Bridging the Southern Literary Generation Gap." *Ellen Glasgow Newsletter* 23 (Oct. 1985): 3–24.

Weaver, Richard. "Agrarianism in Exile." *Sewanee Review* 58 (1950): 586–606.

Weintraub, Judy. "Two Feisty Feminists Filming Hellman's 'Pentimento.' " *New York Times,* 31 Oct. 1976: 17.

Welty, Eudora. *The Eye of the Story: Selected Essays and Reviews.* New York: Random House, 1978.

———. *One Writer's Beginnings.* Cambridge: Harvard University Press, 1984.

———. "Post Mortem." Rev. of *The Never-Ending Wrong*, by Katherine Anne Porter. *New York Times Book Review*, 21 Aug. 1977: 9, 29.

———, et al. "What Stevenson Started." *New Republic*, 5 Jan. 1953: 8–14.

Westling, Louise. "Lillian Smith as Social Evangelist." Rev. of *Lillian Smith: A Southerner Confronting the South*, by Anne C. Loveland. *Southern Literary Journal* 20.2 (1988): 121–23.

———. *Sacred Groves and Ravaged Gardens: The Fiction of Eudora Welty, Carson McCullers, and Flannery O'Connor.* Athens: University of Georgia Press, 1985.

White, Helen, and Redding S. Sugg, Jr., eds. *From the Mountain: An Anthology of the Magazine Successively Titled "Pseudopodia," the "North Georgia Review," and "South Today."* Memphis: Memphis State University Press, 1972.

Wilentz, Gay. "White Patron and Black Artist: The Correspondence of Fannie Hurst and Zora Neale Hurston." *Library Chronicle of the University of Texas* 35 (1968): 21–43.

Williams, Tennessee. *Memoirs.* Garden City, N.Y.: Doubleday, 1975.

Willis, Susan. *Specifying: Black Women Writing the American Experience.* Madison: University of Wisconsin Press, 1987.

Winston, Elizabeth. "The Autobiographer to Her Readers: From Apology to Affirmation." In *Women's Autobiography: Essays in Criticism*, edited by Estelle Jelinek, 93–111. Bloomington: Indiana University Press, 1980.

———. "Women and Autobiography: The Need for a More Inclusive Theory." Ph.D. dissertation, University of Wisconsin—Madison, 1977.

Wolff, Sally. "Eudora Welty's Autobiographical Duet: *The Optimist's Daughter* and *One Writer's Beginnings.*" In *Located Lives: Place and Idea in Southern Autobiography*, edited by J. Bill Berry, 78–92. Athens: University of Georgia Press, 1990.

Woodward, C. Vann. "Why the Southern Renaissance?" *Virginia Quarterly Review* 51.2 (1975): 222–39.

Woolf, Virginia. *The Common Reader.* New York: Harcourt, 1925.

Wright, William. *Lillian Hellman: The Image, the Woman.* New York: Simon and Schuster, 1986.

Young, Thomas Daniel. *The Past in the Present: A Thematic Study of Modern Southern Fiction.* Baton Rouge: Louisiana State University Press, 1981.

Index